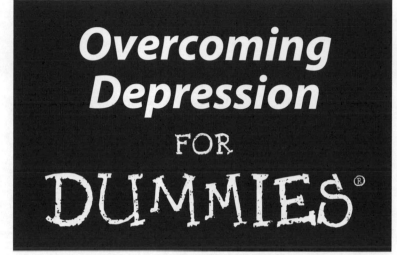

Overcoming
Depression
FOR
DUMMIES®

Overcoming Depression

FOR

DUMMIES®

by Elaine Iljon Foreman, MSc, AFPBSs,
Charles H. Elliott, PhD,
and Laura L. Smith, PhD

Foreword by Professor Mark Williams
Professor of Clinical Psychology, University of Oxford

A John Wiley and Sons, Ltd, Publication

Overcoming Depression For Dummies®

Published by
John Wiley & Sons, Ltd
The Atrium
Southern Gate
Chichester, West Sussex
PO19 8SQ
England

E-mail (for orders and customer service enquires): cs-books@wiley.co.uk
Visit our Home Page on www.wiley.com

For general information on our other products and services, please contact our Customer Care Department within the U.S. at 800-762-2974, outside the U.S. at 317-572-3993, or fax 317-572-4002.

For technical support, please visit www.wiley.com/techsupport.

Wiley also publishes its books in a variety of electronic formats. Some content that appears in print may not be available in electronic books.

British Library Cataloguing in Publication Data: A catalogue record for this book is available from the British Library

ISBN: 978-0-470-69430-5

Printed and bound in Great Britain by TJ International Ltd, Padstow, Cornwall

10 9 8 7 6 5 4 3 2 1

WILEY

About the Authors

Elaine Iljon Foreman M.Sc., AFPBSs. is a Chartered Clinical Psychologist and Associate Fellow of the British Psychological Society. She specialises in the treatment of fear of flying plus other anxiety related problems. Elaine is a Consultant Specialist in Cognitive Behaviour Therapy, accredited with the British Association for Behavioural and Cognitive Psychotherapy, a Fellow of the Institute of Travel and Tourism, and chairs the UKCP Ethics Committee. Her highly specialised Freedom to Flyä Treatment Programme for the fear of flying, and the Freedom from Fear approach for other anxiety-based problems have been developed over thirty years of clinical experience and ongoing research and development of cognitive behaviour therapy. She started research into the treatment of anxiety in 1976 at the Middlesex Hospital Medical School and her continuing interest and success have brought invitations to present her findings in Europe, the Americas, Australia and the Far East. In addition she co-ordinates international research into the field of treatment for fear of flying. Her presentations and workshops are given both nationally and internationally on an ongoing basis to professional and self-help audiences.

Elaine's professional views are regularly sought by TV and radio in recognition of her innovative clinical research into anxieties and phobias, international conference presentations, workshops, and published material in her specialist field. Her most recent publications are *Overcoming Anxiety For Dummies*, co-authored with Charles Elliott and Laura Smith and *Fly Away Fear, A Self-Help Guide to Overcoming Fear of Flying* co-authored with Lucas Van Gerwen, and published by Karnac in May 2008.

Further information on the Freedom to Flyä organisation can be found by visiting www.freedomtofly.biz. The Service Brochure detailing the range of services including workshops and psychological therapy can be obtained by emailing elaine@freedomtofly.biz.

Charles H. Elliott, PhD, is a clinical psychologist and a member of the faculty at the Fielding Graduate Institute. He is a Founding Fellow in the Academy of Cognitive Therapy, an internationally recognized organization that certifies cognitive therapists for treating anxiety, panic attacks, and other emotional disorders. In his private clinical practice, he specialises in the treatment of anxiety and mood disorders. Dr Elliott is the former president of the New Mexico Society of Biofeedback and Behavioral Medicine. He previously served as Director of Mental Health Consultation-Liaison Service at the University of Oklahoma Health Sciences Center. He later was an Associate Professor in the psychiatry department at the University of New Mexico School of Medicine. In addition, he has written many articles and book chapters in the area of cognitive behavior therapies. He has made numerous presentations nationally and internationally on new developments in assessment and therapy of emotional disorders. He is coauthor of *Why Can't I Get What I Want?* (Davies-Black, 1998; A Behavioral Science Book Club Selection), *Why Can't I Be the Parent I Want to Be?* (New Harbinger Publications, 1999), and *Hollow Kids: Recapturing the Soul of a Generation Lost to the Self-Esteem Myth* (Prima, 2001).

Laura L. Smith, PhD, is a clinical psychologist at Presbyterian Behavioral Medicine, Albuquerque, New Mexico. At Presbyterian, she specializes in the assessment and treatment of both adults and children with anxiety and other mood disorders. She is an adjunct faculty member at the Fielding Graduate Institute. Formerly, she was the clinical supervisor for a regional educational cooperative. In addition, she has presented on new developments in cognitive therapy to both national and international audiences. Dr Smith is coauthor of *Hollow Kids* (Prima, 2001) and *Why Can't I Be the Parent I Want to Be?* (New Harbinger Publications, 1999).

Dedication

From Elaine: This book is dedicated to Helga and Nickie Iljon, and to Miriam Skelker, for always being there for me.

From Laura and Charles: We dedicate this book to our family: Alli, Brian, Nathan, Sara, and Trevor. And to our parents: William Thomas Smith (1914–1999), Edna Louise Smith, Joe Bond Elliott, and Suzanne Wieder Elliott.

Acknowledgments

Elaine: So! I lied when I swore I'd never co-author another Dummies book! When the opportunity arose, I jumped at it. My most grateful thanks to the Dummies Team, in particular Simon Bell and Wejdan Ismail

Working with Depression brings to mind elements of the fight of Good against Evil, reminiscent of J.K. Rowling's view. Seeing depression as the loss of hope, she tells how its been her enemy. Depressions revealed as the underlying basis for her depiction of the Dementors, who suck all the joy and hope out of those they attack. Imagine a future in which you will never, ever be happy again. No hope. Emotionally destroyed and dead. An evil time, indeed.

Some very special people in my world have been key players in the fight of Good against Evil – Sharon, Sandy, Zhenya, Graham, Michele, Gill, Jake, Tony, Zenobia, Martin, Corinne, Diz, and Charles. With people like you in the world, Good can only triumph.

Laura and Charles: Okay, we broke our promise and wrote another book. We may have to join Authors Anonymous! We thank our family and friends for putting up with our moans and complaints. We send our heartfelt appreciation to the Rodriquez family, especially Melodie and Adriana, who shared their home and table on holidays so we could write until the last second.

Thanks also to our agents, Ed and Elizabeth Knappman, who have supported our writing. We applaud and appreciate the professionalism of our editors at Wiley Publishing; special thanks to Mike Baker, Norm Crampton, Greg Pearson, Jennifer Bingham, Chrissy Guthrie, Esmeralda St. Clair, and Natasha Graf. Thanks to our technical editors, Cory Newman, PhD, and Howard Berger, MD.

We also appreciate Audrey Hite for taking good care of us. And thanks to Scott Love, computer geek extraordinaire, for designing our Web site and keeping our computers up and running. In addition, we thank Diana Montoya-Boyer for keeping us organized, Tracie Antonuk for her optimistic support of our writing, and Karen Villanueva, our personal publicist.

Finally, we're especially grateful to have been invited into the lives of our many clients over the years. We have profited from what they have taught us about the problems they face. They have provided us with a greater understanding of depression as well as their brave struggle.

Publisher's Acknowledgments

We're proud of this book; please send us your comments through our Dummies online registration form located at www.dummies.com/register/.

Some of the people who helped bring this book to market include the following:

Acquisitions, Editorial, and Media Development

Acquisitions Editor: Wejdan Ismail

Development Editor: Simon Bell

Content Editor: Jo Theedom

Publishing Assistant: Jennifer Prytherch

Developer: Charlie Wilson

Copy Editor: Christine Lea

Technical Editors: Howard Berger, MD,
    Cory Newman, PhD, and
    Dr Daniel McQueen BMedSci MBBS MRCP
    MRCPsych

Publisher: Jason Dunne

Executive Project Editor: Daniel Mersey

Executive Editor: Samantha Spickernell

Cover Photos: Dimitri Vervitsiotis/GettyImages

Cartoons: Ed McLachlan

Composition Services

Project Coordinator: Lynsey Stanford

Layout and Graphics: Reuben W. Davis

Indexer: Ty Koontz

Contents at a Glance

Table of Contents

Foreword

*H*ave you ever had a tune playing over in your mind that you couldn't get rid of? No matter how hard you tried, it kept coming back? Now imagine that what's going round and round in your head is not a tune, but a thought such as: I'm no good, I'm a failure; people would be better off without me. Very soon, you'd feel under attack, exhausted by trying to fight it off. You'd find you couldn't concentrate on anything else. You'd feel guilty and totally defeated, uninterested in life, and unresponsive to your family and friends' attempts to get you to feel better.

If you have felt like this, you'll know the agony of such mental pain. You're not alone. This is depression, and it affects 5 per cent of the population at any one time. It seems to be becoming more common. Fifty years ago, people were most likely to suffer their first major episode of depression in late middle age. Now we find serious depression can strike much earlier: in late teenage and early adulthood. What is more, once a person has been depressed once, there is a risk of the depression returning in the next few months or years, even after a period when it seems to have gone away for good.

What can we do about it? Years ago, it was thought that there were only two approaches to dealing with depression: antidepressant pills, or long-term analytic psychotherapy.But over the last thirty years things have changed.

First, there is a larger range of medication available to choose from, and the pills have become kinder, with fewer side-effects.

Second, there has been a revolution in psychological treatment. Newer, briefer 'talking therapies' such as cognitive and behavioural therapies have been developed. They've been found to be as effective as medication. What's more, the effects of these new psychological treatments last; they prevent you becoming depressed again long after you have stopped coming to therapy.

This book provides a much-needed map to these new ways of approaching depression. Written by experts for everyone, it gives you an excellent guide to the most up-to-date approaches to depression and shows how you can weave your own therapy. Drawing on the latest research, the authors act as trusted guides: with gentleness and good humour, they take us by the hand and explain without preaching, guide without forcing.

This book can be read, but, more importantly, it can also be used.

It offers you a new way to think about yourself, other people and the world around you. It offers many alternatives to fighting endlessly with the thoughts that go round in the head. It offers freedom.

Mark Williams, Professor of Clinical Psychology, University of Oxford.

Author of *The Mindful Way Through Depression*

Introduction

. . . .

World-wide research shows that the number of people suffering from depression is increasing alarmingly. Depression is now so common that one in five people suffer from it at some point in their lives. Yet depression's still stigmatised, with sufferers often afraid to tell families and friends, let alone their employer.

Everyone gets overwhelmed sometimes, but when you descend into depression, the level of misery can feel unprecedented. It can take an inordinate effort to admit to the problem and accept help. But if you choose to admit you have depression and try to combat it, we trust you'll be amazed by the level of support you receive.

Of course, the million-dollar question is 'What can I do about depression?'. Thankfully, this book shows you that the answer is . . . LOADS!

About This Book

We have two primary goals in writing this book. First, we want you to understand the nature of depression. Understanding depression makes the idea of dealing with it less frightening. Second, we present what you're probably most interested in discovering – how to overcome your depression or help someone you care about who has depression.

We leave no stone unturned in our quest to bring you every possible means for battling depression. We draw strategies for defeating depression from the fields of medicine and psychotherapy. We tell you about the newest arsenal of medications that can combat depression. We show you how focusing on your overall health with exercise and nutrition can pay off. Plus, we extract elements from the psychotherapeutic approaches that have stood up to the tests of rigorous research and been verified as highly effective treatments for depression. These approaches include:

- ✔ Behaviour therapy
- ✔ Cognitive therapy
- ✔ Interpersonal and relationship therapy

Then we go one step further. We turn to the new field of positive psychology for ideas on navigating your way from feeling *good* again to feeling *even better*. We want you to make your life more joyful and more meaningful.

Overcoming Depression For Dummies offers you the best advice available based on scientific research. We believe that, if you practise the techniques and strategies we provide in this book, you'll very likely feel better. For many people, this book may be a complete guide for defeating mild to moderate depression. Numerous studies show that self-help often works.

However, depression frequently needs more care and attention than you can receive through self-help. If your depression significantly hinders your ability to work or play, you need to get professional help. No book can completely replace therapy. Start by seeing your family doctor. If you're seeing a therapist or counsellor, you may find that *Overcoming Depression For Dummies* can help augment your therapy. Be sure to discuss that possibility with your therapist. Depression can be conquered; please don't give up.

A Note to Our Depressed Readers

We're keenly aware of the pain and profound despair you may be experiencing. Your sense of humour is probably depleted. With this book, we attempt to lighten a sombre subject with titbits of humour. Some of you may take offence with our attempts or even feel diminished or discounted by this decision. We can understand that reaction. At the same time, your long-term goals need to include rediscovering laughter. Thus, we hope you can try to take our occasional use of wit in the manner we intend it – as another way to help you lift yourself out of the fog of depression.

In addition, we realise that the title *Overcoming Depression For Dummies* may seem offensive to some, especially because when people are depressed, they're prone to make negative, personalised interpretations (see Part II for more information on this topic). However, we assure you that the content of this book is as serious and in-depth as any book on depression. The *For Dummies* format simply enables us to present important material in easily digestible segments. We leave it up to you to determine whether we succeed in doing so.

Conventions Used in This Book

In this book, we avoid the use of professional jargon as much as possible. When we occasionally find it necessary to use a technical term, we pop it in *italics* so that you can easily spot it, and then we clearly define that term. In addition, recognising that there are a number of useful resources available on the Internet, we put web addresses in `monofont`.

We also include numerous stories to illustrate the information and techniques we present. The people you read about aren't real; however, they represent composites of the many wonderful people we've known and worked with over the years. We use an Anecdote icon to indicate where these stories appear in the text.

Finally, if you're reading this book because you want help in defeating your own depression, we recommend that you purchase a notebook. Use that notebook to write out the exercises we present throughout the book. We call these exercises Antidepression Tools and highlight them with an icon. Use your notebook often and reread what you've written from time to time.

Foolish Assumptions

Who'd want to read this book? We assume, perhaps foolishly, that you or someone you care about suffers from depression. We also figure that you want to banish depression from your life. Finally, we imagine that you're curious about a variety of helpful strategies that can fit your lifestyle and personality. If these descriptions strike a chord, then this book is for you.

How This Book Is Organised

We organise *Overcoming Depression For Dummies* into 7 parts and 22 chapters. Here's a little about each part.

Part 1: Discovering Depression and Designing Defences

Chapter 1 explores the costs of depression in economic, social, and emotional terms. We describe what depression looks like in various people. Finally, we provide an overview of the best means for treating depression. In Chapter 2, we cover the difference between the various forms of depression. Furthermore, we explain the difference between grief and depression. Chapter 3 shows you how to find the motivation for taking charge of your own depression. And Chapter 4 tells you how to find and get professional help.

Part II: Seeing Things More Clearly: Cognitive Therapy

More studies support the value of thought therapy (*cognitive therapy*) for the treatment of depression than any other psychotherapy. Part II shows you how certain habitual ways of thinking can be a major contributor to depression. The chapters in this part combine to give you a large toolbox of techniques for changing these dark, distorted thoughts into realistic appraisals of yourself, your world, and your future. You can see that this transformation isn't based on rationalisation or self-deception. Rather, you discover how to subject your thoughts to reasoned scrutiny based on logic and evidence.

Part III: Actively Combating Depression: Behaviour Therapy

When you feel overwhelmed by depression, you likely find yourself disengaging from everyday life. You start doing less and less as you put off tackling even slightly disagreeable tasks. Of greater concern, previously enjoyable activities seem dull, bland, and devoid of pleasure. Part III shows you how to short-circuit 'do-nothingism' and slowly regain confidence and joy. We give you a mental boost to get moving again through exercise and rediscovering healthy pleasures.

Part IV: Adjusting to Changing Relationships

Clinical trials of interpersonal therapy demonstrate the value of addressing the relationship side of depression. Depression has a way of disrupting relationships with friends, family, partners, and other loved ones. And relationship problems can worsen depression. Part IV extracts crucial elements from interpersonal therapy and provides additional ideas for handling relationship difficulties that can increase depression. We cover issues such as communicating in healthy ways and coping with loss and grief.

Part V: Full-Bodied Assault: Biological Therapies to Fight the Physical Foe

Pharmaceutical companies have invested billions of dollars into developing a wide range of antidepressant medications. We review these medications, from the earliest to the most recent, and give you important information regarding their effectiveness and side effects. We also give you some tools for helping make the decision as to whether or not medications make sense for you and your depression. Finally, we explore the role of herbs, supplements, and nutrition in alleviating depression and review a few alternative treatments for depression, such as light therapy.

Part VI: Life After Depression

We have every reason to believe that the information in the first five parts, perhaps in conjunction with professional help, will lift you out of your depression. But what do you do next? Part VI tells you how to deal with possible relapses in the future. We tell you how to reduce the likelihood of such slips and how to deal with them if they do occur. Next, we discuss a new approach called *mindful acceptance* that has recently been found to be very helpful for reducing depression relapse.

We then turn to the field of positive psychology for ideas on how to further enhance your life. We want you to feel better than good again, so we lay out strategies for enhancing your sense of well-being through a sense of purpose and connectedness.

Part VII: The Part of Tens

If you want quick ideas on how to deal with a low mood, you can find them here. Then we show you ten ways to help your kids if they get depressed. We conclude with ten ways to help a friend or partner overcome depression.

Icons Used in This Book

Throughout this book, we use icons in the margins to quickly point out different types of information. Here are the icons you'll see and a few words about what they mean.

Helpful stories and case-studies about people we've known and worked with over the years.

This icon alerts you to an exercise you can use to hammer away at or discover more about your depression.

As the name of this icon implies, we don't want you to forget the information that accompanies it.

This icon emphasises pieces of practical information or bits of insight that you can put to work.

This icon appears when you need to be careful or seek professional help.

This piece of art alerts you to information that you may find interesting, but skipping it won't put you at a disadvantage in the battle against depression.

Where to Go from Here

Most books are written so that you have to start on page one and read straight through. But we wrote *Overcoming Depression For Dummies* so that you can use the detailed Table of Contents to pick and choose what you want to read based on your individual interests. Don't worry too much about reading chapters and parts in any particular order. Read whatever chapters apply to your situation. However, we suggest that you at least skim Part I, because it contains a variety of fascinating facts as well as important ideas for getting started.

In addition, the more severe your depression, the more we urge you to start with Chapter 3 and continue with Part III. These chapters contain a variety of ways for overcoming the powerful inertia that keeps severely depressed people from taking action. After you read those chapters, feel free to continue picking and choosing what you want to read.

Part I
Discovering Depression and Designing Defences

'So your name's 'Joy' — Well, we're off to a good start then.'

In this part . . .

Discover the symptoms of depression and identify whether you or someone you care about may be depressed. We tell you about depression worldwide. And we explain the different forms of depression.

Defeating depression's no walkover. Many obstacles block the path. We identify these blocks and show how you can get past them. In this part, we also provide an overview of the various treatments for depression, and reveal how to obtain the best possible help.

Chapter 1

Understanding and Overcoming Depression

- -

In This Chapter

▶ Looking at depression

▶ Understanding what causes depression

▶ Figuring out the price

▶ Treating depression

▶ Life after depression

- -

Depression can feel like being locked away in a prison. Feeling frightened, alone, miserable, and powerless, you can find yourself withdrawing into a shell. Hope, faith, relationships, work, play, and creative pursuits – the very paths to recovery all seem meaningless and impossible. Like a cruel punishment, depression imprisons the body, mind, and soul.

Though depression may feel isolating and inescapable, we have a set of keys for unlocking the prison door. You may find that the first key you try works, but usually the door is double locked, and opening it needs a combination of keys. We're here to help, and have a pretty impressive bunch of keys for you to try out, taking you from darkness into the light.

In this chapter, we explain the difference between sadness and depression. Next, we show you how to recognise depression across a range of different people. We work out the costs of depression in terms of health, productivity, and relationships and tell you about the treatment options for depression. And finally, we offer you a glimpse of your new life, beyond depression.

Understanding Your Level of Well-Being

But if there was a magic cure for depression, would that be the whole answer? Surprisingly not. Increasingly, we are becoming aware that people who all score zero on a traditional depression rating scale, (i.e. no depression) can nonetheless be in hugely differing emotional states, from just ticking over, to achieving real fulfilment, satisfaction, and happiness. If we see happiness and depression as opposite ends of one continuum, then moods can go beyond depression. We can use just one questionnaire not only to rate presence or absence of depression, but also life satisfaction/well-being. Professor Stephen Joseph and his colleagues developed a very useful self-report questionnaire which builds on this idea to assess the spectrum of well-being, which is shown below. Take a few minutes to complete the questionnaire if you wish to understand your level of well-being.

A number of statements that people have made to describe how they feel are given in Table 1-1. Please read each one and tick the box which best describes how frequently you felt that way in the past seven days, including today. Some statements describe positive feelings and some describe negative feelings. You may have experienced both positive and negative feelings at different times during the past seven days.

Table 1-1	Level of Well-being			
	Never	*Rarely*	*Sometimes*	*Often*
1. I felt dissatisfied with my life.				
2. I felt happy.				
3. I felt cheerless.				
4. I felt pleased with the way I am.				

	Never	Rarely	Sometimes	Often
5. I felt that life was enjoyable.				
6. I felt that life was meaningless.				

To work out your score, use the following scoring key to turn your answers into numbers.

✔ **For items 2, 4, and 5:** Never = 0, rarely = 1, sometimes = 2, often = 3.

✔ **For items 1, 3, and 6:** Never = 3, rarely = 2, sometimes = 1, often = 0.

Now, using the scoring key above, add scores on all 6 items to give a total score, with a possible range of 0 to 18. Most people score between 11 and 13. Higher scores indicate greater happiness. As scores decrease, however, happiness fades into unhappiness, which fades into depression. Research estimates that scores below nine are increasingly indicative of depressive states. If you scored very low on the questionnaire, it is possible that you are suffering from what psychologists call clinical depression. Of course, one short questionnaire can't give us all the answers – that would take a full assessment from a psychologist – but it may be useful in giving you a sense of where you lie on the spectrum of well-being.

Importantly, what this questionnaire shows is that it's not just helping people manage their depression that's important, but also finding ways to increase their happiness.

A key theme throughout this book is that we all can be overwhelmed, and experience depression, if sufficient powerful events occur simultaneously, testing coping skills to the limit – and then beyond. The level of misery, can feel unprecedented. It can take an inordinate effort to admit to the problem and accept help. But if you choose to self-disclose, we trust you'll be amazed by the level of support, and reciprocal revelations.

Feeling Blue, or Depressed?

'For better, for worse; for richer, for poorer; in sickness and in health, 'til death do us part . . .' You may recognise these words from a certain ceremony, dating way back in time. They sum up the inevitability of life's ups and downs, and it's ultimately inescapable end. Even if nothing goes seriously wrong, everyone, sooner or later, is going to die. Expecting to live a life without times of sadness, despair, or grief is unrealistic. But experiencing sorrow makes you truly appreciate life's blessings.

Misfortune and loss can cause sadness and grief, but they don't have to lead to depression. The difference is that sadness and grief lessen in intensity as time passes, while depression often does not (see Chapter 2 for more information about grief and types of depression). Misfortune and loss may feel pretty overwhelming at the time they occur. But time does eventually heal.

Unlike periods of sadness, depression involves deep despair, misery, guilt, and loss of self-esteem. People suffering from depression feel hopeless, helpless, and blame themselves not only for this, but also for just about everything else that goes wrong. Depression disrupts the body's rhythms, often disturbing sleep, appetite, concentration, energy, sexual activity, and enjoyment. The net result is that depression seriously reduces your ability to love, laugh, work, and play.

Depression is a mood disorder making you feel profoundly sad, without joy, despondent, and unable to experience pleasure. Depression appears in a variety of forms, with varying symptoms. We describe these types of depression in Chapter 2, but all of them involve a very low mood or diminished sense of pleasure.

The Many Faces of Depression

Depression can affect anyone regardless of race, social class, or status. Symptoms include deep sadness, loss of energy, loss of interests, low self-esteem, feelings of guilt, and changes in appetite and sleep. These symptoms are experienced by both men and women, young and old. However, the symptoms of a depressed toddler may be different to those of a depressed 80-year-old.

In Chapter 2, we explore the various types of depression. Here, we show you how to identify depression in different people at different life stages.

Young and depressed

Depression can affect children of any age, from preschool through to young adulthood. Experts agree that the rates of depression in young people have gone up enormously. The rates are probably underreported because children aren't usually able to identify that they're suffering from depression, and parents and professionals often fail to recognise the problem. Parents are sometimes reluctant to accept that their children are depressed. Children can often be unaware of their feelings, or not have the words to describe what they are experiencing. They rarely spontaneously tell others what is happening to them. Instead, they may show changes in their behaviour, appetite, and sleep.

Marilyn's mother brings several big bags of fun-sized party treats into school on the morning of her daughter's eighth birthday, and asks the teacher to give them out to the children. The teacher promises to do this and to lead the class in singing 'Happy Birthday' just before break.

At the end of the day, Marilyn's teacher approaches her mother and says, 'I'm worried about Marilyn. We all sang 'Happy Birthday' to her just before break, and all the other children were so excited when I gave out all those lovely chocolate bars. But Marilyn hardly even smiled, and she spent break and lunchtime on her own in the quiet area. In fact, I often see her alone in the playground. She's become much quieter this term and seems less and less interested in the lessons, too. And she doesn't take part the way she used to. Is something the matter?'

When children are depressed, they lose interest in activities that they previously enjoyed. If you ask them if they're sad, they may not be able to put their feelings into words. However, children may show signs of depression, such as low energy or motivation, sleep problems, appetite changes, irritability, low self-esteem, and self-criticism. They may feel unloved, pessimistic, or even hopeless about the future. In fact, depressed children experience more anxiety and physical symptoms than do depressed adults.

Watch children at play for subtle signs of depression. Depressed children may frequently include themes of death or loss into their play. All children's play includes such themes on occasion, but these subjects show up more often in young people who are depressed. You may need to observe children over a period of time because their moods change. They may not seem depressed all the time, (unlike adults with depression). Their moods may go up or down throughout the day. Consult a professional if you have any doubts.

Children, depression, and obesity

The BBC reported in 2008 that one in ten 6-year-olds is obese, and that the total number of obese children has doubled since 1982. On present trends half of all children in England by 2020 are going to be obese. But is this just harmless puppy fat or something more serious? Obese children are more at risk than their thinner counterparts in experiencing depression, low self-esteem, and other mental health conditions. What researchers don't yet know is how the two conditions connect: does depression in children cause obesity, or does obesity cause the depression? Whatever the answer to this question, the findings that depressed children can develop obesity highlights the importance of addressing depression when it occurs. See Chapter 11 for more information on the relationship between food and mood.

Grandparents: Grumpy or depressed?

Some people view old age as inevitably depressing. They assume that the older you get, the greater the deeterioration in quality of life. Of course it's true that the longer you live, the more opportunity you have of experiencing negative as well as positive events. And certain illnesses, aches, pains, and disabilities do become more likely with increasing age, as do losses of family, friends, and social support. Therefore, *some* sadness is to be expected.

Nonetheless, depression is absolutely *not* an inevitable consequence of old age. Most symptoms of depression in the elderly are identical to those in people of all ages. However, the elderly are more likely to focus on the physical, and talk about their aches and pains rather than their feelings of despair. Furthermore, elderly people commonly express regret and remorse about past events in their lives.

Depression interferes with memory. If you notice increased memory problems in Grandpa or Grandma, you likely suspect the worst-case scenario – Alzheimer's disease, otherwise known as dementia. However, these memory problems can often be the result of depression.

And depression in the elderly increases the chances of death. Yet, if you ask elderly people whether they are feeling depressed, they may not recognise their feelings, or may even ridicule the idea. But by denying depression, the older person may not receive the treatment he or she needs.

Elderly men have a particularly high risk of suicide. Men older than 60 are more likely to take their own lives than any other combination of age and gender. If you have any doubts, check out the possibility of depression with a doctor or mental health professional.

Men don't do depression, or do they?

Most studies show that men are half as likely as women to report that they get depressed. Men tend to cover up and hide their depression; they feel far more reluctant to talk about what they see as weaknesses and vulnerabilities than women do. Why?

Many men have been taught that admitting to any form of psychological or emotional problem is unmanly. From early childhood experiences, men get to know how to hide such feelings.

Francis looks forward to retirement from his job as a marketing executive. He can't wait to start travelling and having time for all those hobbies he's wanted to take up for ages. Three months into retirement, his wife of 20 years asks for a divorce. Shocked, yet showing little emotion, Francis makes light of his situation to friends and family, saying, 'Oh well! Life goes on.'

But gradually Francis starts drinking more heavily than usual. He becomes interested in extreme sports. He pushes his abilities to the limit in rock climbing, hang-gliding, and skiing in remote areas. Francis distances himself from family and friends. His normally even temperament turns sour. Yet Francis denies the depression, so obvious to those who know him well.

Rather than admit to disturbing feelings, men commonly turn to drugs or alcohol in an attempt to cope. Some depressed men express anger and irritation rather than sadness. Others report the physical signs of depression, such as lack of energy, body aches, changes in sleep and in appetite, but strongly deny feeling depressed. The cost of not expressing feelings and not getting help may account for the four-fold rate of suicide among depressed men compared to women.

Treating depression in old age

Doctors frequently fail to diagnose depression in the elderly. A report in 2007 concluded that the majority of depressed elderly patients who only see their G.P., and not specialist mental health professionals are likely to go undiagnosed and untreated, with negative mental and physical health consequences. Why? Because the signs of depression are often attributed to the process of normal aging. That's unfortunate, because depression is common – and treatable – in the elderly.

Sometimes antidepressant medications don't work for older people. However, researchers found that interpersonal therapy (see Chapter 4) significantly decreases depression in patients over 60 who previously failed to respond sufficiently to antidepressant medication. There is increasing support for the idea that dealing with personal issues, such as grief, loss, and transitions, may be particularly useful for people in this age group.

Women and depression

Why are women around twice as likely as men to report depression? Biological factors, including those related to reproduction, may play a role. The rates of depression during pregnancy, after childbirth, and before the menopause are higher than at any other times in women's lives. Research on women in 2002 found that women who had given birth had a 27 per cent higher rate of depression or anxiety compared to men. For women who had not given birth, 19 per cent were more likely than men to suffer from anxiety and depression.

Cultural and social factors are likely contribute to women's depression. For example, women are more likely than men to have been sexually or physically abused, and such abuse increases the likelihood of depression. Likewise, risk factors such as low income, stress, and multiple responsibilities like juggling housework, childcare, and a career, occur more frequently in women than men.

Janine gently lays her baby down in the cot. Finally, the little one falls asleep. Exhausted after a tough day at work, Janine desperately longs to go to bed herself. But the washing's piling up, she's got to pay those red bills, and the house is a total tip. Six months ago, her husband changed jobs and became a long-distance lorry driver, and life hasn't been the same since his lengthy absences started. Janine realises her overwhelming fatigue and loss of appetite are quite possibly because she's starting to suffer from depression.

Depression and diversity

Almost everyone has a different experience of depression. Attempting to generalise about depression based on, for example, ethnicity or a cultural group can lead to misperceptions. But risk factors for depression include discrimination, obesity (see the sidebar 'Children, depression, and obesity'), social ostracism, poverty, and major losses such as loss of a job or loved one. And unfortunately, many of these risk factors occur more frequently among minority groups. Being different may take the form of race, culture, physical challenge, or sexual orientation.

As well as these risk factors, many groups face particular obstacles when dealing with depression. For example, some ethnic populations still have limited access to mental health care because of language differences, embarrassment, cultural pressures to deny such problems, and economic pressures. However, the UK government is trying to improve access to resources for minority groups.

Depression and miscarriage

The loss of a baby through miscarriage is a devastating event that often causes depression. The rates of depression are reported as high as 22 to 55 per cent in the year following a miscarriage. And new evidence suggests that depression may play a role in bringing about miscarriages. A recent study published in the scientific journal *Human Reproduction* studied the relationship between depression and miscarriage. A group of women who had previously miscarried were given questionnaires to find out if they had emotional problems. Of the women who then got pregnant, 22 per cent miscarried again. What predicted miscarriage? Depression. So, if you or someone you care about is planning a pregnancy, be sure to get help for any existing depression first.

Getting to the Root of Depression

There are lots of theories about what causes depression. Some experts suggest that depression is caused by imbalances in brain chemistry, while others believe that the chemical imbalances are due to genetics. Others experts are convinced that the cause of depression goes back to childhood. Still others say that depression is a result of negative thinking. There are also those who suggest that depression is caused by impoverished environments and/or cultural experiences. Unwanted patterns of behaviour are also seen as a cause of depression. Finally, some experts have identified relationship problems as the major contributor.

You may well come to the same conclusion as the dodo bird in *Alice in Wonderland* and declare that 'All have won and all must have prizes'. In another sense, nobody deserves a prize. Even though you can find evidence to support each of these views, nobody really knows how these different factors work, which is the most important, which ones influence the others, and how they do so.

In spite of the evidence that scientists don't yet know exactly how the multitude of depression-related factors function and interact, you may come across doctors, psychologists, and psychiatrists who have very strong opinions about what they believe is *the* definitive cause of depression. If you meet a professional who claims there is one single, definitive cause of depression, question that professional's credibility. Most sophisticated experts in the field of depression research know that a single, definitive cause of depression remains elusive and is unlikely to ever be discovered, as depression has many causes.

Yet the field of mental health does have both knowledge and ideas about how depression develops. There is strong evidence supporting the theory that education, thinking, biology, genetics, childhood, and the environment all play important roles in the development, maintenance, and potential treatment of depression. All these factors interact in amazing ways.

For example, a growing body of studies shows that medication alters the physical symptoms of depression such as loss of appetite and energy. And antidepressant medication also improves the negative, pessimistic thinking that accompanies most forms of depression. Perhaps that's not too surprising. (See Chapter 15 for more information about medication.)

Similarly, studies show that psychotherapy alone decreases negative, pessimistic thinking (see Chapters 5, 6, and 7), much like medication does. Some medical practitioners are shocked to find studies showing that certain psychotherapies, even if carried out without antidepressant medication, also alter brain chemistry.

Overall, recent studies on the roots of depression fail to support any theory that puts forward one specific cause of depression. Rather, they support the idea that a variety of physical and psychological factors interact with each other.

TECHNICAL STUFF

The brain's brew

Your brain contains around 100 billion *neurons* (nerve cells), give or take a few. Busy neurons take in information about the state of the world outside and inside the body. These 100 billion nerve cells don't touch each other. They send information back and forth by releasing tiny molecules which the next nerve picks up. This communication process involves chemical messengers, called *neurotransmitters* that move through and between the neurons.

Depressed people do show changes in the balance of brain chemicals. Several theories have been offered to explain the relationship between depression and the chemical messengers. Many researchers believe that neurotransmitters such as norepinephrine,

serotonin, and dopamine play important, interactive roles in mood regulation. Furthermore, these neurotransmitters may interact with other brain chemicals in as yet unknown ways.

What researchers do know is that for some people with depression, the chemical 'soup' may need a different balance of 'spices' or medication. So one person's brain requires a dash of salt (one medication), and for another, pepper (a different medication) may be necessary to lift the depression. But that doesn't necessarily mean that the depression was caused by a lack of pepper or salt, that is, a particular chemical! Experts haven't yet reached agreement on how all this works.

Calculating the Costs of Depression

Depression has always been part of human experience. But some reports suggest the rates are rising (or, at least, the rates of people receiving treatment are rising). No one knows why for sure, but the risk of depression for those born after World War II has mushroomed to the point where the World Health Organization (WHO) estimates that by 2020 depression is going to be the second largest cause of death and disability in the world.

Estimates vary greatly, but today depression appears to occur in 15 to 20 per cent of all people over the course of a lifetime. Furthermore, in any given 12-month period, just under 10 per cent of the population experiences an episode of significant depression. And at this very moment, an estimated 121 million people are suffering from depression throughout the world. That's an awful lot of people.

Guess what? Estimates of depression can only be rough figures. Because many people with depression don't seek help, and many of those with depression don't even realise they're depressed, reliable statistics are almost impossible to find. Whatever the actual figures are, huge numbers of people suffer from depression at some point in their lives. And depression is associated with all kinds of costs.

Adding up the costs of depression

The WHO has created a statistic called the Global Burden of Disease (GBD), listing the economic cost of various diseases worldwide. Depression is now the fifth largest contributor to the GBD. By the year 2020, the WHO predicts that depression is likely to be the second most costly disease.

The financial cost of depression is staggering. Costs have increased sharply and are now estimated to be more than £9 billion a year in the UK. Of this, the direct cost of treatment is an estimated £370 million. The *British Journal of Psychiatry* reported that more than 100 million working days were lost every year due to depression, and in the year 2000, 2,615 deaths were recorded as due to depression.

What are the costs in manpower? Depressed people are off work more often and are less productive when at work. Parents of depressed kids may have to miss work to get their children to therapy appointments. The cost of psychological therapy and medication, even if provided by the NHS, is also part of the total. But remember, treating and easing depression reduces absenteeism, increases productivity, and cuts medical costs.

Personal costs of depression

Economic facts and figures don't begin to describe the human costs of depression. The profound suffering caused by depression affects both the sufferer and the carer. These include:

- The anguish of a family suffering from the loss of a loved one to suicide.
- The excruciating pain experienced by someone with depression.
- The diminished quality of relationships suffered by people with depression and those who care for and about them.
- The loss of purpose and sense of worth suffered by those with depression.
- The loss of joy.

The composer, Berlioz, wrote about his fits of depression:

> *The fit fell upon me with appalling force. I suffered agonies and lay groaning on the ground, stretching out abandoned arms, convulsively tearing up handfuls of grass and wide-eyed innocent daisies, struggling against the crushing sense of absence, against a mortal isolation. Yet such an attack is not to be compared with the tortures that I have known since then in ever-increasing measure.*

Detailing depression's physical toll

Depression's destructive effects go beyond personal and economic costs – depression can damage the body itself. Research provides a constant flow of new information about the intricate relationship between mood and health. Today, we know that depression affects:

- **Your immune system:** Your body has a complex system for warding off infections and diseases. Studies show that depression changes the way the immune system responds to attack. Depression exhausts the immune system and makes people more susceptible to disease.

- **Your skeletal system:** Untreated depression increases your chances of getting osteoporosis, though it's unclear exactly how depression may lead to this problem.

- **Your heart:** The relationship between depression and cardiovascular disease is powerful. Johns Hopkins University studied healthy doctors and found that among those doctors who developed depression, their risk of heart disease increased two-fold. This risk is comparable to the risk posed by smoking. Likewise for those with heart problems, having depression doubled the chance of having another heart attack.

✔ **Your mind:** Although depression can mimic dementia in terms of causing poor memory and concentration, depression also increases the risk for dementia. We're not sure why, but scientists have discovered that an area in the brain thought to govern memory is smaller in those with chronic depression. If left untreated, depression can disrupt and possibly damage connections in your brain and may lead to the degeneration and death of brain cells.

✔ **Your experience of pain:** Depression contributes to the experience of physical pain. Thus, if you have some type of chronic pain, such as arthritis or back pain, depression may increase the amount of pain you feel. Scientists aren't entirely sure how depression and pain interact, but the effect may be due to disruption of neurotransmitters (see Chapter 15 for more information about neurotransmitters) involved in pain perception. Many people with depression fail to realise they're depressed and only complain about a variety of physical symptoms such as pain.

Depression seems to affect everything about the way the whole body functions. For example, altered appetite may lead to obesity, or to under nourishment and serious weight loss. Also, depression is associated with disrupted hormonal levels and various other subtle physiological changes.

Don't get depressed by all these frightening effects that depression can cause! If you're depressed, you can feel better – and we spend the rest of this book helping you to do so. Effective treatments for depression are available and new ones are emerging.

Psychotherapy for your heart

If you have heart disease, depression increases your risk of dying from it. How's that for an opening line? Now, the good news. Psychotherapy can improve your chances of survival. A report suggests that 14 hours of psychotherapy cuts re-hospitalisation rates for cardiac patients by 60 per cent. As well, counselling before medical procedures leads to shorter stays in the hospital following surgery. Unfortunately, only about 12 per cent of hospitals treating heart disease offer psychotherapy to their heart patients. We suspect that if a pill came on to the market that reduced re-hospitalisation rates by 60 per cent, there would be pressure for this to be recognised and available on the NHS. But there's only so much we authors can do: just know that if you have heart disease, don't ignore the importance of your emotions, and do seek help if you notice you are becoming depressed, in relation to your physical condition, or any other area of your life.

Feeling Good Again

Depression is treatable. With good diagnosis and the right help, most people can expect to recover. If you feel a loss of pleasure, reduced energy, a diminished sense of your worth, or unexplained aches and pains, you may be depressed (see Chapter 2 for more information about the symptoms of depression). Please get help (see Chapter 4 for ideas on how to find the right help for you).

Many types of help exist for depression. This book is one of them and falls under the category of self-help. Self-help does work for many people. However, self-directed efforts may not be enough for everyone. In the following sections, we briefly outline the different kinds of help that you may find useful.

You don't have to choose just one option. You may need or want to combine a number of these strategies. For example, many people with depression find the combination of medication and psychotherapy helpful. And using more than one type of psychotherapy, usually completing one type before starting the next, can prove useful as well.

If your depression doesn't start to lift or if you have severe symptoms such as thoughts of suicide, please seek professional help.

Cognitive therapy

Dr Aaron T. Beck developed a system of psychotherapy that he calls cognitive therapy. *Cognitive therapy* is based on the theory that the way you think strongly influences the way you feel. Chapter 4 explains that therapists now often combine cognitive therapy with behaviour therapy (see the following section) in the form of *Cognitive Behavioural Therapy*, or CBT Studies support the value of CBT compared with other approaches to the easing of depression.

Depression causes people to have pessimistic, bleak outlooks, and the cognitive part of CBT helps untangle this distorted thinking. You can find out more about this approach in Part II of this book. We encourage you to have a go. Research shows that CBT even protects you against possible recurrences of depression. Sceptical? Well, where's the harm in trying out CBT?

If you want to know more about CBT, check out *Cognitive Behavioural Therapy For Dummies,* by Rhena Branch and Rob Willson (Wiley).

Overcoming depression

The behavioural part of the CBT approach to the easing of depression has also been shown to bring about effective change. *Behaviour therapy* is based on the theory that altering your behaviour changes your mood. The problem is, when you're depressed, you don't feel like doing much of anything. So, in Part III we help you work out how to take small steps and overcome this block using behaviour-therapy based tools. Also, we tell you how

✔ Exercising can kick-start your battle with depression.

✔ Bringing small pleasures back into your life eases the pain.

✔ Problem-solving strategies can improve coping.

Re-establishing relationships

Depression sometimes follows the ending of a significant relationship, such as the death of a loved one, or getting divorced. But depression can also follow other types of relationship losses – which also change the way you relate to the world. For example, retirement requires you to give up (or lose) one role, that of an employee, and take on another. Major life changes or transitions sometimes lead to depression if you don't have a way of dealing with them. In Chapter 13, we talk about handling loss and transitions.

Depression can also cause problems with important current relationships. In Chapter 14, we suggest various ways of enhancing your relationships. The process of improving your relationships may also lessen your depression.

Finding biological solutions

Perhaps you think the easiest approach to treating depression is found at the chemists or the health food shop. By simply taking the right pill or potion – you're cured! If only it were that simple.

In Chapter 15, we look at the pharmacological therapies. There are quite a few to choose from and we help you sort through the options. We also give you strategies for making the complicated decision of whether antidepressant medication is for you, or whether you'd be better with alternative approaches.

In Chapter 16, we discuss complimentary therapies, bring you information about electroconvulsive therapy (ECT), plus other, less well-known treatments for depression.

Feeling Great

After overcoming your depression, you feel so much better. However, keeping up your improvement is vital. Depression, like the common cold, has a nasty habit of returning. But you can do a lot to minimise or prevent future occurrences – called *episodes* – of depression. We show you how to lessen your chances of becoming depressed again in Chapters 17 and 18. If you become depressed despite these efforts and techniques, we show you how to get on top of your depression again quickly and how to make symptoms more bearable.

So, now you feel better. You feel good. But guess what? You don't have to settle for good. We want you to feel better than good; we want you to feel great – perhaps even better than you've ever felt in your life. That may sound too good to be true. However, in Chapter 19, we suggest ways of adding purpose and meaning to your life. Also, we show you the hidden keys for unlocking your potential for happiness.

Seeing the Sense in Sadness

We begin this book promising relief from depression. However, no therapy, behaviour, or medication can guard against a life free from sadness. And if such a cure existed, we're never going to recommend it.

Because without sadness, what is happiness? In order to recognise and experience great happiness, you must also feel sadness, it is an indispensable part of happiness. Sorrow is the basis of the great plays or emotionally powerful works of art, and of songs that strike a chord in the depths of the soul.

So in writing this book, we wish you a life of happiness that's inevitably woven with moments of pain, so that you know when you are truly happy and living life to the full. Flowers need the sun and the rain, and no life is complete without sadness.

Chapter 2

Detecting Depression

Depression takes many forms, and develops in different ways. Sometimes it deepens slowly but surely, gradually taking over your whole life. At other times depression overwhelms you, giving little, if any, warning. Some people don't realise that they have depression, but others fully recognise the signs. And sometimes depression has no obvious cause, often masquerading as a set of physical complaints including fatigue, sleeplessness, changes in appetite, and even indigestion.

Depression is a disorder of extremes. It can destroy your appetite – or make you insatiably hungry. It can deprive you of sleep – or make you over-whelmingly fatigued, confining you to bed for days at a time. When you are depressed you find yourself pacing to and fro frantically – or frozen with fear. Depression may last for months or years, but it can also lift within a very brief time.

In this chapter, we help you recognise if you or someone you care about is suffering from depression by identifying the effects depression has on individuals. We outline the major types of depression and their symptoms; explore the relationship between illness and depression; discuss when grief crosses the line into depression. We explore the causes of this disorder. And finally, we tell you how you or a loved one can monitor and track your moods if you suspect that you may be battling depression.

Recognising the Damage of Depression

Everyone feels low at times. Financial setbacks, health problems, loss of loved ones, divorce, or failure to meet work targets – events like these can make anyone feel upset or sad for a while. But depression is more than a normal reaction to unpleasant events and losses. Depression is more intense and goes well beyond sadness, affecting both mind and body in disturbing ways.

Depression can affect all areas of your life. There are a several types of depression (see 'Examining the Six Types of Depression', later in this chapter), and they can all affect four main areas of your life. But although depression appears in different forms, they all can disrupt:

- ✔ Thoughts
- ✔ Behaviours
- ✔ Relationships
- ✔ Your body

In the following sections, we consider how depression affects each of these areas of your life.

Dwelling on dark thoughts

When you get depressed, your view of the world changes. The sun shines less brightly, and the sky's covered by dark cloud. Those around you seem cold and distant, and the future looks black. Your mind may focus on recurrent thoughts of worthlessness, self-loathing, and even death. Typically, depressed people experience difficulty in concentrating, remembering, and in making decisions.

For Margaret, depression starts about a year after her divorce. She finds herself thinking that all men can't be trusted. Margaret is attractive, although when she looks in the mirror, she only sees the beginning of wrinkles and an occasional blemish. She decides that even if any good men exist out there, they are going to be repulsed by how awful she looks. She feels tense. Her concentration goes, and she starts to make mistakes at work. Her boss is understanding, but Margaret sees her mistakes as proof of incompetence. Although she believes that she's in a dead-end job, Margaret doesn't see herself as capable of doing anything better. She begins to wonder why she bothers to go into work each day.

Does your mind dwell on negative thoughts? If so, you may be suffering from depression. The following 'Depressive Thoughts Quiz' gives you a sample of typical thoughts that go with depression. Tick each thought that you often have:

❑ Things are getting worse and worse for me.

❑ I think I'm worthless.

❑ No one would miss me if I were dead.

❑ My memory has gone to pieces.

❑ I make too many mistakes.

❑ Overall, I think I'm a failure.

❑ Lately, I find it impossible to make decisions.

❑ I don't look forward much to anything.

❑ I've been feeling down and pretty hopeless over the past month.

❑ The world would be a better place without me.

❑ Basically, I'm extremely pessimistic about things.

❑ I can't think of anything that sounds interesting or enjoyable.

❑ I've found little interest or pleasure in the things I used to do and enjoy.

❑ My life is full of regrets.

❑ Lately, I can't concentrate, and I forget what I've just read.

❑ I don't see my life getting better in the future.

❑ I'm deeply ashamed of myself.

Unlike many of the questionnaires you see in magazines or newspapers, there is no specific score in this one to identify your level of depression. Merely ticking a few items doesn't necessarily mean you're depressed. But the more items you tick, the greater possibility of depression. And if you tick any of the items related to death or suicide, it may well be cause for concern, and a signal to take action.

If you're having suicidal thoughts, you need immediate assessment and treatment. If the thoughts include a plan that you believe you may actually carry out either now, or in the very near future, go to your GP, the local Community Mental Heath Resource Centre, or a hospital Accident and Emergency Department. They have trained staff who can help. If you're not able to get yourself to any of these places, phone 999 for an ambulance.

For more information about depressive thinking and what you can do about it, see Chapters 5 to 8.

Dragging your feet: Depressed behaviour

Not everyone who's depressed behaves in the same way. Some people find themselves speeding up and others find themselves slowing down. While some people can't stay awake, others suffer horribly from lack of sleep.

Douglas drags himself out of bed in the morning. Even after ten hours' sleep, he still feels exhausted, with no energy for anything. He starts being late for work, and frequently takes sick leave. He stops going to the gym, an activity he used to enjoy. He tells himself he'll go back when he finds the energy. His friends ask him what's going on, because lately they hardly see him. He says that he doesn't really know. He's always just so very tired.

Cheryl, on the other hand, has about three and a half hours of sleep a night. She wakes around 3 a.m. with thoughts racing through her mind. When she gets up, she feels a frantic pressure and can't seem to settle to anything. Irritable and bad-tempered, she snaps at her friends and colleagues. Unable to sleep at night, she starts drinking too much. Sometimes she cries for no apparent reason.

Although everyone is different, certain behaviours are typical of depression. Depressed people can feel like they're wading through treacle, or running full speed on a treadmill. Do you feel concerned about your behaviour? The following 'Depressed Behaviour Quiz' can tell you if your behaviour points to a problem. Tick each item that applies to you:

- ❑ I've been having unexplained crying spells.
- ❑ The few times I force myself to go out, I don't have much fun.
- ❑ I can't make myself exercise like I used to.
- ❑ I haven't been going out nearly as much as usual.
- ❑ I've been skipping work quite a bit lately.
- ❑ I can't get myself to do much of anything, even important projects.
- ❑ Lately I've been fidgety and can't sit still.
- ❑ I'm moving at a slower pace than I usually do, for no good reason.
- ❑ I haven't been doing things for fun as I usually do.

All these items are typical of depressed behaviour or, in some cases, a health problem. On a bad day, anyone is likely to tick one or two items. However, the more items you tick, the more likely it is that something's wrong, especially if the problem has been around for more than two weeks.

For more information about depressed behaviour and what you can do about it, see Part III.

Struggling with relationships

Depression affects the way you relate to others. Withdrawal and avoidance are the most common responses to depression. Sometimes depressed people get irritable and critical with the very people they care most about.

Tony trips over a toy left on the living room floor and snaps at his wife Sylvia, 'Can't you get the kids to pick up their damn toys for once?' Hurt and surprised by the attack, Sylvia apologises. Tony fails to acknowledge her apology and turns away. Sylvia quickly picks up the toy and wonders what's happening to her marriage. Tony hardly talks to her any more, other than to complain or tell her off about something trivial. She can't remember the last time they had sex. She worries that he may be having an affair.

Have you or perhaps someone you care about been behaving differently within one or more of your relationships? The following 'Depression and Relationships Quiz' explores some of the ways in which depression affects relationships. Tick the items that describe your situation:

❑ I've been avoiding people more than usual, including friends and family.

❑ I've been having more difficulty than usual talking about my concerns.

❑ I've been unusually irritable with others.

❑ I don't feel like being with anyone.

❑ I feel isolated and alone.

❑ I'm sure that no one cares about or understands me.

❑ I haven't felt like being physically intimate with anyone lately.

❑ I feel like I've been letting down those who are close to me.

❑ I believe that others don't want to be around me.

❑ Lately, I don't seem to care about anyone the way I should.

When you're depressed, you tend to turn away from the very people that may have the most support to offer you. You feel that they don't care about you, or perhaps you can't find any positive feelings for them. You may avoid others or find yourself irritated and snappy.

The more items you ticked in the 'Depression and Relationships Quiz', the more likely it is that depression is affecting your relationships. For more information about how depression can impact upon your relationships and what you can do about it, see Part IV.

Feeling foul: The physical signs of depression

Depression usually shows some physical symptoms. They include changes in appetite, sleep, and energy. However, for some people, the experience of depression *primarily* consists of these physical symptoms and doesn't noticeably affect mood and relationships.

If you experience depression primarily in physical terms you may be unaware of your emotional life. This could be because you were brought up to hide your feelings or your parents told you off for crying or showing other feelings such as excitement or sadness.

When Carl was growing up, his father got angry with him for crying. He said that big boys are tough and that Carl should never show weakness. His father also told him off for getting too excited about Christmas. He said men don't show emotion. Over time, Carl got the knack of keeping his feelings to himself.

After five years of marriage, Carl's wife leaves him; she says that he's an unfeeling and uncaring man. Over the next six months, Carl finds he's lost his appetite, and when he does eat, food just doesn't taste as good as before. His energy drains away. He starts to have headaches and frequent bouts of constipation, and his blood pressure rises.

When he goes to the doctor's surgery, his GP asks, 'Look, Carl, your wife left you just six months ago. Are you sure you aren't depressed?' Carl answers, 'Are you kidding? Depression's something women get! No way can I be depressed!' Nonetheless, after detailed examination, his doctor decides that depression is indeed causing Carl's physical problems. Nothing else fits the pattern.

Are you experiencing certain changes in your body you can't explain? The following 'Depression in the Body Quiz' highlights some of the ways that depression can show itself within your body. You know what to do – tick each item that applies to you.

❑ My blood pressure has risen lately for no obvious reason.

❑ I have no appetite these days.

❑ I haven't been sleeping nearly as well as usual.

❑ My diet is the same, but I'm having frequent constipation for no reason.

❑ I often feel nauseous.

❑ I suffer from loads of aches and pains.

❑ I'm sleeping much more than usual.

❑ I'm always hungry, and for no reason.

❑ My energy has been very low lately.

❑ I've gained (or lost) more than 2 kilograms (about 4.5 pounds), and I can't work out why.

Like the other three quizzes in this chapter, it really doesn't matter exactly how many of the items apply to you. However, be aware that the more items you tick, the greater the chance that you are suffering from depression.

If your depression shows itself in physical symptoms, medication or some other physical remedy is likely to be the best choice for you. See Part V for more information on physical remedies.

The experiences listed in the quizzes may be caused by other health-related problems, not just depression. Therefore, if you're having any worrying physical problems, see your doctor, especially if the symptoms last for more than a week or two.

Examining the Six Types of Depression

In 'Recognising the Damage of Depression', earlier in this chapter, we outline the four broad ways in which all types of depression can affect an individual. In this section, we turn our attention to the six major types of depression to look out for:

✔ Major depressive disorder

✔ Dysthymic disorder

✔ Adjustment disorder with depressed mood

✔ Bipolar disorder

✔ Seasonal affective disorder

✔ Depression related to hormones

There are two classification systems in use for describing mental disorders. We have already mentioned the ICD-10. The other is the American system known as the DSM-IV, or Diagnostic and Statistical Manual, version IV. In the following sections, we describe the six major types of depression and their symptoms based on information in DSM-IV.

Diagnosing clinical depression

Clinical depression is a medical term, and goes beyond the common experience of just feeling sad or low.. To decide whether someone is suffering from a clinical episode of depression, doctors use the diagnostic criteria set out in ICD-10 (the tenth edition of the International Classification of Diseases, published by the World Health Organization). ICD-10 describes and categorises mental disorders to help doctors identify the symptoms necessary to make a diagnosis. It is the classification system normally used by doctors in the U.K.

According to the ICD-10 criteria, a diagnosis of depressive episode means that a person has experienced at least two out of the following three core symptoms for most of the day, nearly every day for a minimum of two weeks:

- **Anhedonia:** Lack of interest or enjoyment in things
- **Fatigue:** Feeling tired or having little energy
- **Low mood:** Feeling low, unhappy, sad or miserable

Recognising the different types of depression can help you work out if you're suffering from depression. But don't go so far as to give yourself a formal diagnosis; that's the job for the professionals.

If you feel that you have significant signs of any of the six types of depression we list, get help. You can start with the advice in this book, but if you don't feel much better within two months, see your doctor or a mental health professional. Seek help even sooner if your depression includes serious thoughts of suicide or hopelessness.

Major depressive disorder: Can't even get out of bed

As with all types of depression, the symptoms of a major depressive disorder occur within the four areas – thought, behaviour, relationships, and the body – described earlier in the chapter in 'Recognising the Damage of Depression'. So what's unique about a major depressive disorder?

Major depressive disorders include a seriously low mood or a notable drop in pleasures and interests lasting for two weeks or more. Sometimes depressed people deny these low feelings and any loss of interest – on purpose, or without being aware of it. However, despite the denial people who know the depressed person well can usually spot the difference.

As well as low mood and lack of pleasure, to qualify as experiencing a major depressive disorder, you usually have a wide variety of other symptoms, such as:

- Clear signs of increased agitation or slowed functioning
- Extreme fatigue
- Inability to concentrate or make decisions
- Intense feelings of guilt and self-blame
- Major changes in sleep patterns
- Repetitive thoughts of suicide
- Striking changes in appetite or weight (an increase or decrease)
- Very low sense of personal worth

With major depressive disorders, these symptoms occur almost every day over a period of at least two weeks or more. Major depressive disorders vary greatly in terms of severity. However, even mild cases of major depressive disorder need treatment.

If you're suffering from an episode of severe major depressive disorder, just how low you feel is difficult for someone who has never had the same experience to imagine. A severe, major episode of depression takes over a person's life and slowly destroys all pleasure. But it does far more than wipe out joy; severe depression can make you feel that you are at the bottom of an unscalable pit of utter, unrelenting despair that stops you from showing and even feeling love. People caught in such a pit of depression lose the ability to care for themselves, others, and even life itself.

If you suffer from such a severe case of depression, there's definitely good reason for hope. Many effective treatments work even with severe depression. So no matter how low and hopeless you feel – do get help. See Chapter 4 for the whole range available.

The daily pain of living begins the moment Edward's alarm wakes him. He spends most of the night tossing and turning. He only falls asleep for what feels like just a few moments, before waking up to another day of despair. He forces himself to get ready for work, but the thought of speaking to others feels overwhelming. He can't face the prospect. He knows that he should at least phone in sick, but can't seem to raise his hand, or find the will to pick up the phone. He realises that he could lose his job, but it doesn't seem to matter. He thinks that he has no future, and that he'll soon be dead, so what does it matter anyway?

Slowly, Edward starts to get dressed, but then at the last moment he changes out of his work clothes, into a track suit, and then goes back to bed. But sleep won't come. His mind fills with thoughts of self-hatred – 'I'm a failure. I'm just useless. There's nothing to live for.' He wrestles with the thought that he should just end it now. Edward suffers from a major depressive disorder.

Major depressive disorders can significantly reduce your ability to function at work or deal with other people. Such disorders deprive you of the very resources you need for recovery. That's why getting help is so important. If you allow the major depressive disorder to continue, it may result in death from suicide. If you or someone you know *even suspects* the presence of a major depressive disorder, you need to seek help promptly. Go to Chapter 4 for information on how to find professional help for depression.

Dysthymic disorder: Chronic, low-level depression

Dysthymic disorder, or *dysthymia*, is similar to major depressive disorder (see the previous section). However, dysthymic disorder is less severe, tends to be chronic, and persists for longer periods of time. With dysthymic disorder, the symptoms occur for at least two years (though often for far longer), with the depressed mood obvious on most days for the majority of each day. However, you only need to display two of the following chronic symptoms, as well as a depressed mood, in order for your condition to qualify as a dysthymic disorder:

- Guilty feelings
- Low sense of personal worth
- Poor concentration
- Problems making decisions
- Thoughts of death or suicide

Compared with major depressive disorder, dysthymic disorder displays fewer physical symptoms such as problems with appetite, weight, sleep, and agitation.

Dysthymic disorder frequently begins in childhood, adolescence, or young adulthood and can easily continue for many years if left untreated. Also, people with dysthymic disorder are at an increased risk of developing a major depressive disorder at some point in their lives.

Major Depression - Understanding psychosis

Psychosis can be one of the serious symptoms of a major depressive disorder. Psychosis is diagnosed when a person is out of touch with reality. People with depression sometimes become so ill that they experience psychotic symptoms:

✔ **Delusions:** These are plainly evident false beliefs, such as thinking the TV is transmitting signals to your brain.

✔ **Hallucinations:** This is when you hear voices or see things that aren't really there.

✔ **Paranoid thinking:** This involves feeling extremely suspicious and distrustful, such as believing that other people are out to get you, or that someone is trying to poison you.

In most cases, depression with psychosis requires hospitalisation.

People with severe depression also may exhibit paranoid or delusional thinking. *Paranoid thinking* involves feeling extremely suspicious and distrustful – such as believing that other people are out to get you or that someone is trying to poison you. *Delusions* range from the slightly odd to bizarre, but they involve obviously false beliefs such as thinking the television is transmitting signals to your brain. The problems of psychosis need professional attention and lie outside of the scope of this book. However, we do detail medications commonly prescribed for these symptoms in Chapter 15.

 Although someone with dysthymic disorder generally isn't as devastatingly despondent as a person with a major depressive disorder, they are frequently lacking in energy and the joy of living. A person suffering from dysthymic disorder isn't always easy to identify, but they are noticeable for being pessimistic, cynical, and grouchy a good deal of the time.

 Caroline doesn't remember ever feeling joy. She's not even sure what the word means. Her parents worked long hours and seemed cold and distant. Caroline studied hard in school. She hoped to win approval and attention for her academic accomplishments. Her parents didn't seem to notice.

Today, Caroline leads a life that's envied by her colleagues. She earns a great salary and is a workaholic within her profession as a mechanical engineer. Yet she senses that she's missing something, feels unsuccessful, and suffers a chronic, uneasy discontent. Caroline has a dysthymic disorder, although *she* wouldn't actually say that she's depressed. She doesn't seek help for her problem because she actually has no idea that life can be different.

 People with dysthymic disorder often see their problems as merely 'just the way they are', and so don't look for treatment. If you suspect that you or someone you care about has dysthymic disorder, get help. You have the right to feel better than you do, and the long-lasting nature of the problem means that it isn't likely to go away on its own. Besides, you certainly don't want to risk developing a major depressive disorder, which is even more debilitating.

Adjustment disorder with depressed mood: Reactive depression

Life's road isn't always easy. You have to expect the rough with the smooth. Most of the time, people handle their problems without extreme emotional upset. At other times, they don't.

Adjustment disorders are reactions to one or more difficult issues, such as marital problems, financial setbacks, conflict with colleagues, and traumatic events including natural disasters. When a stressful event occurs and your reaction lessens your ability to work or participate effectively with others, in combination with symptoms such as a low mood, crying spells, and feelings of worthlessness or hopelessness, you may be experiencing an adjustment disorder with a depressed mood. Adjustment disorder is a much milder problem than a major depressive disorder, but it can still disrupt your life.

Jim is shocked when his boss tells him that he's being made redundant because of restructuring. He starts job hunting but posts in his field are scarce. For the first two weeks, he enjoys catching up on sleep, but soon he starts feeling unusually low. He struggles to open the newspaper to look for work, and stops checking the job websites. Jim begins to feel worthless and loses hope of ever finding a job. His appetite and sleep are still okay, but his confidence plummets. He's surprised when tears stream down his face after receiving another notification that he hasn't made the short list for a job.

Jim isn't suffering from a major depressive disorder. Jim is struggling with what is known as an adjustment disorder with depressed mood.

People suffering from an adjustment disorder with depressed mood quite often don't seek treatment. They assume if they wait long enough, the problem will just go away by itself. However, if you suspect that you or someone you care about has this problem, do get help. Otherwise you may still have difficulties long after the original triggering problem is resolved, and these can become a major problem for you and those around you.

Bipolar disorder: Ups and downs

Bipolar disorder is a mood disorder, just like other forms of depression. However, bipolar disorder is quite different from other types of depression because people with a bipolar disorder can experience episodes of irrational 'highs', called *mania*.

In bipolar disorder, moods fluctuate between extreme highs and lows. This makes the treatment of bipolar disorder different from other types of depression. We want you to be familiar with the symptoms so that you can seek professional help if you experience manic episodes within your depression. Self-help isn't sufficient for the treatment of bipolar disorder.

Although individuals with mania may seem quite cheerful and happy, the people who know them can tell that their good mood is a little too good to be true. During manic episodes, people feel they need less sleep, may show signs of unusual creativity, and have loads more energy and enthusiasm. Sounds pretty good, doesn't it? Who wouldn't want to feel wonderful and totally on top of the world? Well, just hold your horses . . .

The problem with manic episodes related to bipolar disorder is that the 'highs' increase to a level where the person loses touch with reality. During manic episodes, sound judgement goes out the window. People who have bipolar disorder disorder often:

- Engage in risky sexual escapades
- Gamble excessively
- Make foolish business decisions
- Spend too much money, and get into serious debt
- Talk fast and furiously
- Think that they have super-special talents or abilities

Manic episodes can involve mildly unwise decisions and excesses, or reach extremes. People in manic states can cause ruin for themselves or their families. Their behaviour can get so out of control that they may seek hospital treatment and a period of inpatient care. Alternatively, they may be sectioned – detained in hospital under certain sections of the Mental Health Act at the request of the authorities, or their closest relative.

Most people with bipolar disorder also go through cycles of mild to severe depression. They go from feeling great to gruesome, sometimes during the same day. The depression that follows a manic episode can be unexpected and devastating. The contrast from the high to the low is particularly painful. People with untreated bipolar disorder typically feel out of control, hopeless, and helpless. Not surprisingly, the risk of suicide is higher for bipolar disorder than for any of the other type of depression.

Bipolar disorder is generally *chronic* (lasts for a long time), but if you're diagnosed as having bipolar disorder, don't despair. The condition can be successfully managed. Medication and psychotherapy, usually in combination, can ease a lot of the most debilitating symptoms. Research is also finding new treatments and medication.

Emily finishes dressing, grabs her keys, and dashes out the door. She feels so excited that she can hardly wait to share her good news with her friend, Samantha. 'Sam, guess what?' she gushes. 'I've decided I'm going to move to London! I just know I can make it in the theatre. I just have to go! I've handed in my notice and I'm on my way. In fact, I'm leaving today!'

Emily's excitable speech, let alone what she's saying, really worries Samantha. She asks Emily when she decided to move, what she's going to do about the lease on her flat, and does she have a job offer in London? What on earth is she thinking? This is so sudden!

Emily replies that she hasn't been sleeping for the past three days. Her mind has been racing and overflowing with ideas. She has decided that her life is too boring and she needs a change. She says that her boss can go to hell and so can the landlord. She's bought a first-class train ticket using her credit card, and emptied the last £200 from her bank account. She is going to work out what to do when she gets to London. Emily suffers from a bipolar disorder, and is having a manic episode.

Bipolar disorder is a complicated and serious illness. The condition has many subtle variations. If you suspect that you or someone you know has any signs of bipolar disorder, seek professional help at once.

Seasonal affective disorder: Dark depression

Some depressions come and go with the seasons, as regularly as clockwork. People who repeatedly experience depression during autumn or winter may have *seasonal affective disorder* (SAD). They may also experience a few unusual symptoms, such as:

- ✔ A sense of heaviness in the arms and legs
- ✔ Carbohydrate cravings
- ✔ Increased appetite
- ✔ Increased desire for sleep
- ✔ Irritability

Many mental health professionals believe that the reduced amount of sunlight in the winter triggers this form of depression in vulnerable individuals. Support for this theory comes from the fact that this form of depression occurs more frequently among people who live in northern climates where summers are short and winters long and dark. (We discuss evidence concerning treatment of this disorder using bright lights in Chapter 16.)

What does a bear do to get ready for winter? Bears energetically forage for food, get as fat as they can, and then hibernate in a cosy cave. Perhaps it's not a coincidence that people with SAD typically gain weight, crave carbohydrates, have reduced energy, and feel like staying snuggled in bed for the winter.

SAD is increasingly being recognised, and a variety of treatments are available, some with more scientific backing and evidence than others (see Chapter 16 for more detail). Research is also finding new treatments and medication. Taking a walk outside to experience more natural light may be helpful – and certainly can't hurt.

Premenstrual dysphoric disorder and post-natal depression: Horrible hormones?

Occasional, minor premenstrual changes in mood occur in a majority of women. A smaller percentage of women experience significant and disturbing symptoms known as *premenstrual dysphoric disorder* (PDD). PDD is a more extreme form of the more widely known premenstrual syndrome (PMS) or premenstrual tension (PMT).

Although hormones probably play a significant role in PDD, research hasn't yet explained the causes. Women suffering from full-blown PDD experience some of the following symptoms almost every month, during the week before their period. (These same symptoms can also occur – probably because of hormonal fluctuations – in the years leading up to, during, and following menopause.)

- ✔ Anger
- ✔ Anxiety
- ✔ Bloating
- ✔ Fatigue
- ✔ Food cravings
- ✔ Guilt and self-blame
- ✔ Irritability
- ✔ Sadness
- ✔ Tearfulness
- ✔ Withdrawal

Diane drives to the supermarket after work. Impatiently, she pushes her trolley along the aisle, only to find another customer is blocking her way. She feels a rush of annoyance and coughs loudly. The other woman looks up and apologises. Diane quickly overtakes the offending trolley, giving it a shove as she passes.

In the queue, her irritation gets worse. The man in front of her fumbles for his chequebook and discovers he has no cheques left. Then he takes out a handful of change, and after counting it, realises he doesn't have enough. Next, he starts rummaging through his overstuffed wallet for a credit card. Diane finds herself unable to suppress her fury and snaps, 'We don't have all day to queue just waiting for the likes of you! What's the matter with you, anyway?'

The man's face turns bright red and he mutters, 'I'm so sorry, madam.' The cashier mutters under her breath 'That really wasn't necessary. Humiliating him like that! It could happen to anyone.' Suddenly ashamed, Diane breaks into tears and starts sobbing. She feels like she's going crazy. And this isn't the first time Diane has felt this way. In fact, it happens to her almost on a monthly basis.

Postnatal depression is another type of serious mood disorder that's widely thought to be related to hormonal fluctuations, although no one knows for sure how and why the hormones profoundly affect the moods of some women and not others. This depression occurs within days or weeks after giving birth. The symptoms appear quite similar to those of major depressive disorder. (For a complete discussion of these symptoms, see 'Major depressive disorder: Can't even get out of bed', earlier in this chapter.)

Faith had tried unsuccessfully to conceive for the past eight years. She and her husband Sean are overwhelmed with joy when at last the home pregnancy test registers positive. Their cheerful, cosy nursery looks like a picture in a baby magazine, only better, because it's theirs.

Faith and Sean weep with happiness at the sight of their newborn. Faith feels exhausted, but Sean assumes that's normal. He takes charge the first day home so that she can rest. Faith feels the same way the next day, so Sean continues to take over the responsibilities of caring for the baby. Sean becomes alarmed when Faith shows no interest in holding the baby. In fact, she seems irritated by the baby's crying and mentions that maybe she shouldn't have become a mother. At the end of the second week, Faith tells Sean that he can't go back to work because she doesn't think that she can take care of the baby. Faith is suffering from postnatal depression.

Most women feel a bit low shortly after delivery – it's called the 'baby blues'. The down feelings aren't usually severe and they tend to go within two weeks. However, if you begin to feel like Faith in the earlier story, you need to get professional help immediately.

Dangers of Severe Postnatal Depression

Occasionally, women with severe cases of postnatal depression develop psychoses (see the sidebar 'Understanding psychosis' for details of common psychotic symptoms). *Postnatal psychosis* is psychosis that occurs shortly after giving birth. Psychotic beliefs often focus on the baby and can include thinking that the baby is possessed or would be better off in heaven than living here on earth.

The risk of postnatal psychosis increases greatly for any births following an initial diagnosis. In 2007 Richard Talby came home to find his wife and two sons dead. His wife, Susan, had killed the two boys (by suffocation or strangulation), and then hanged herself. Susan suffered postnatal depression following the birth of her youngest son, but had seemed to be doing okay.

As we mention throughout this book, if you suspect that you or some one you know may be suffering from depression, including post-natal depression, do all you can to make sure that you seek professional help.

Linking Drugs, Diseases, and Depression

The interaction of depression with illness and disease can form a vicious cycle. Illness and disease (and related medications) can hasten the onset or intensify the effects of depression. And depression can further complicate the various diseases. Depression can suppress the immune system, release stress hormones, and affect your body and mind's capacity to cope. Depression may increase whatever pain you have and further diminish your crucial resources. In this section, we focus on the role of medication and illness in the development and worsening of depression.

Drugs with depressive side effects

Dealing with an illness is hard enough without having the medication make you feel even worse. Some medication can actually appear to cause depression. Of course, recognising whether it's merely the experience of the illness, or if it's the drug that's causing the depression is difficult. However, in a number of cases, medication does appear to contribute directly to depression.

If you notice inexplicable feelings of sadness shortly after starting a new prescription, tell your doctor. The medication could be causing your feelings, and an alternative treatment that won't affect you in this way may be available. Table 2-1 lists the most common medications that have potential depressive side effects.

Table 2-1	Potentially Depressing Drugs
Medication	*Condition Typically Prescribed For*
Antabuse	Alcohol addiction
Anticonvulsants	Seizures
Barbiturates	Seizures and (rarely) anxiety
Benzodiazepines	Anxiety and insomnia
Beta blockers	High blood pressure and heart problems
Calcium channel blockers	High blood pressure and heart problems
Corticosteroids	Inflammation and chronic lung diseases
Hormones	Birth control and menopausal symptoms
Interferon	Hepatitis and certain cancers
Levodopa, amantadine	Parkinson's disease
Statins	High cholesterol
Zovirax	Herpes or shingles

Depression-inducing illnesses

Chronic illnesses interfere with life. Some chronic illnesses require lifestyle adjustments, frequent GP and hospital appointments, and time off work. These illnesses disrupt relationships, and cause physical pain. Feeling upset by such things is normal. But these problems may trigger depression, especially in vulnerable people.

Also, some illnesses can disrupt the nervous system in ways that cause depression. If you suffer from one of these diseases, talk to your doctor, especially if you find your mood begins to deteriorate. Diseases that are thought to directly influence depression include:

- AIDS
- Asthma
- Cancer
- Chronic fatigue syndrome
- Coronary artery disease and heart attacks
- Diabetes
- Hepatitis

- Lupus
- Multiple sclerosis
- Parkinson's disease
- Stroke
- Ulcerative colitis

Knowing Where Grief Ends and Depression Begins

When you lose someone you love, you're likely to feel pain and sadness. You may experience sleep disturbance and want to withdraw from people. The idea of going out and having a good time probably sounds offensive. Feelings like these can go on for weeks or months. Are these the signs of depression? Yes and no.

Although grieving involves many of the same reactions that are associated with depression, the two aren't the same. Depression almost always includes a diminished sense of personal worth or feelings of excessive guilt. Grief, when not accompanied by depression, doesn't typically involve lowered self-esteem and unreasonable self-blame. Furthermore, the intensity of grief usually diminishes slowly (sometimes excruciatingly slowly) but surely over time. Depression, on the other hand, can sometimes refuse to budge at all.

Mental health professionals don't all agree on how to best deal with grief. Some professionals advocate immediate treatment of any disturbing reactions involving grief; these professionals often advise taking antidepressant medication (see Chapter 15 for more information about antidepressants). Others believe that grief is part of a natural healing process and that is best dealt with by allowing its natural course to unfold.

We tend to agree with this latter group, but if, and only if, the grief isn't complicated by an accompanying depression. (See Chapter 13 where we talk about getting through loss and grief.) Still, the decision is an individual choice. In either case, a grieving person needs to be aware that depression can impose itself on grief. If you're dealing with grief, seek treatment if it goes on too long or includes other serious symptoms of depression.

Monitoring Mood

You may be pretty sure that you or someone you care about has depression. Now what? Keeping track of how your mood changes from day to day is one important step in the recovery process. Why?

- ✔ You may discover patterns (perhaps you get very depressed every Monday).
- ✔ You may discover specific triggers for your depressed moods.
- ✔ You can see how your efforts progress over time.
- ✔ You can quickly decide if you're not making progress, or even if you're getting worse. This suggests that you need to seek help.

We suggest that you keep a 'Mood Diary' (see Table 2-2). You can benefit from tracking your moods and taking notes on relevant incidents, and thoughts. Try it for a few weeks.

Use a rating scale from 1 to 100 to rate your mood each day (or at several regular times throughout the day). A rating of 100 means that you feel ecstatic. You feel on top of the world, perhaps as if you've just won the lottery, or been awarded the Nobel Peace Prize – whatever's really important for you. A rating of 50 means just a normal day. Your mood is fine – neither especially, good, or bad. A rating of 1 is just about the worst day imaginable. Interestingly, we find that most people without depression rate their average mood at around 70, even though we define 50 as middle range.

As well as your mood rating, jot down a few notes about your day. Include anything that may relate to your mood such as:

- ✔ Clashes with friends, colleagues, or your partner
- ✔ Difficult times of the day
- ✔ Falling in love
- ✔ Financial difficulties
- ✔ Loneliness
- ✔ Negative thoughts or daydreams floating through your mind
- ✔ An unexpected promotion
- ✔ Wonderful (or lousy!) weather
- ✔ Work hassles

John suspects that he may have a problem, so he tracks his mood and finds a few interesting patterns. For an example of one week in John's mood diary, look at Table 2-2.

Table 2-2		John's Weekly Mood Diary
Day	**Mood Rating**	**Notes (Events or Thoughts)**
Sunday	20	Not a good day. I just hung around and worried about getting my tax return in for the deadline. And I felt horribly guilty about not finishing off the last bits of the decorating.
Monday	30 (a.m.) 45 (p.m.)	The day started miserably. I got stuck in traffic and was late for work. In the afternoon, things seemed to go more smoothly, though I can't say I felt brilliant.
Tuesday	40	Nothing good, nothing bad today. Just the usual blah blah blah.
Wednesday	30 (a.m.) 40 (p.m.)	I woke up panicking about the new project deadline. I don't know how I'll ever get it done. By the afternoon I'd made a little progress, but I still worry about it.
Thursday	35 (a.m.) 45 (p.m.)	I was thinking about how the days just seem to drag by. I don't look forward to much. To my surprise, in the evening I did enjoy a phone conversation with a friend.
Friday	50	Somehow, by a miracle, I completed the project four hours early. My boss was really impressed with my work – said it was the best yet. But I bet he doesn't think much of the rest of my work.
Saturday	40	Finally got the decorating finished. That felt good, but then I had all this time on my hands and started to worry again.

Coping with grief when a child dies

The loss of a child may be the most profound loss that anyone ever experiences. The grief following a child's death is thought to be more intense, more complicated, and longer lasting than other profound losses. The anguish and loneliness may seem utterly intolerable. Parents may question the value of living. Others who haven't had such a loss may be sympathetic, but they sometimes fail to understand and appreciate the intensity and duration of this type of grief.

We suggest that parents who have lost a child consider contacting a support group such as The Compassionate Friends (www.tcf.org.uk). This group helps bereaved parents and siblings deal with their loss in a supportive environment.

John goes through several weeks of mood diaries. He notices that he usually feels down and miserable on Sunday afternoons. He realises that on Sundays he typically spends time alone and mulls over anticipated difficulties for the next week. He also discovers that mornings aren't exactly the best time of the day, because he worries about the rest of the day. Interestingly, his worries often involve catastrophic predictions (like not meeting deadlines) that rarely come true. Finally, he sees that his mood improves when he tackles projects he's been putting off, like completing the decorating.

You can track your progress whether you're working on your own or with a professional. If you get bogged down, please seek help or discuss the problem with your therapist.

Chapter 3

Breaking Barriers to Change

· ·

In This Chapter

▶ Discovering surprising obstacles to recovery

▶ Finding out what people do to avoid change

▶ Getting round, over, under, or through the obstacles

· ·

In this chapter, we explain why the prospect of change is so intimidating – and the lengths that some people go to avoid facing up to the illness. We show you the reasoning behind the fears that feed procrastination, hopelessness, avoidance, and other self-limiting strategies. And we discuss how certain beliefs, myths, and misconceptions can paralyse your ability to feel better. But most importantly, we show you how to find out which of these problems are blocking your path to progress, and what you can do to overcome them.

Alex has been feeling moderately depressed for the past two years. She reluctantly tried medication for a short time, but didn't like the side effects. She's sure therapy would be an exhausting, long process. She bought a self-help book, but it's sitting on her desk collecting dust. She feels guilty about not reading it, but is convinced no book can possibly help her – no one else can understand her experiences. She sees her situation as hopelessly inescapable.

Alex work as a nurse, and over the years she's seen many depressed patients benefit from self-help, medication, and therapy. Yet Alex still feels stuck and unable to tackle her depression.

Because she's fully aware that effective treatments exist, you may wonder whether Alex actually *wants* to remain depressed. Nothing is further from the truth. Nobody – and we mean nobody – prefers depression to normal moods.

Then why does Alex avoid tackling her depression? She does so for some very common reasons. Indeed, most people with depression are initially slow to start working on overcoming their depression. And when they do tackle it, they frequently slip back into inaction for varying periods of time.

Untying the Knots: Revealing Reasons for Avoidance

At first glance, it may seem strange that you'd avoid searching for a way out if you suffer from depression. Given how horrible being depressed feels, who'd want to stay in this state? But if you do find yourself backpedalling and procrastinating when you think about trying to challenge your depression, it's for good reasons. Fear of change, change-blocking beliefs, and myths commonly underlie failure to take action against depression. You'll discover that reasons for avoidance make far more sense than you may think.

Facing the fear of change

Fear is the key factor underlying inaction and avoidance. We can understand why you may feel both scared and hopeless about working on your depression, and procrastinating about doing anything. But is beating yourself up for avoiding the task of getting your depression under control helpful? Of course not, you're experiencing a normal, human fear of change. This doesn't mean, however, that it's quite okay for your fear to keep you out of the fray on the sidelines, feeling hopeless and avoiding the scariness of change?

In the following sections, we tell you about the two most common types of fear that may be stopping you from taking action.

Fearing more losses

If you have significant depression, you have no doubt experienced profound losses of various types. Such losses may include:

- Belief in positive possibilities
- Relationships
- Security
- Self-esteem
- Status

You understandably fear more loss, and find your mind inevitably overestimating the difficulty of making changes and underestimating your ability to succeed. The fear of hope itself is a big obstacle, because you assume that dashed hopes are far worse than no hope at all. Perhaps you, like many who are depressed, believe that:

- ✔ If you look for friendship, you're likely to be rejected . . . again.
- ✔ If you find a new job, you'll make a mess of it.
- ✔ If you take a chance, you're sure to fail and be humiliated.
- ✔ If you work on your problems, your efforts may be useless.
- ✔ If you dare hope, your hopes are going to be shattered making you feel even worse.

If these beliefs apply to you, it's no wonder that you're avoiding the challenge of change. The fear of additional losses or failures is no trivial matter. It's so easy to decide that not trying at all is better than trying and failing. Your depressed mind tells you that making no attempt at least preserves a small amount of self-esteem. On the other hand, you fear that working hard to improve, and then failing, means that you sink even further into the abyss of the 'ins' wherein dwell incompetence, ineffectiveness, incapability, insufficiency, inferiority, and even – strange as it may sound – *incongruity*.

Avoiding incongruity

The experience of incongruity is another factor that frequently holds back attempts at recovery. That sounds a bit strange, doesn't it? Psychologists have known for decades that people look for consistency in their behaviours and beliefs. When things are congruent, all the pieces fit together as part of a whole, and this simplifies the world. Congruity also makes life feel more predictable.

The preference for congruence can feed the depression. If you're depressed, you're probably discount any positive evidence about you or your world. You may dismiss it, because it contradicts your deep-seated negative view of yourself.

Measuring moods

Two interesting experiments comparing people who did and did not have a low mood have highlighted this. In one experiment, the two groups were shown the same ambiguous picture for a fraction of a section. In the other experiment, both groups were played two simultaneous lists of words, one into their left and one into their right ear.

There was a difference between what the two groups both saw, heard, and remembered. Those with a low mood saw a sad event in the ambiguous picture, and heard and remembered more of the list of negative words. People who had a normal mood did the opposite – seeing celebratory events in the ambiguous picture, and hearing and remembering words from the positive list.

Maintaining stability: Homeostasis

Our bodies try to maintain a consistent, stable state – a process known as homeostasis. When significant fluctuations occur in temperature, hormone levels, fluids, and so on, the body generally tries to reestablish the proper level. Homeostasis may well operate at all levels, from the cellular level to the psychological level, and even interpersonally, in social situations.

The work of Clinical Psychologist Professor Mark Williams and colleagues in Oxford has thrown a very interesting light on these links. Once a person has recovered from an episode of depression, relatively small amounts of negative mood can trigger large numbers of negative thoughts (e.g. 'I am a failure/weak/worthless) along with bodily sensations of weakness, fatigue, or unexplained pain. Both the negative thoughts and the fatigue often seem out of proportion to the situation. People who believed they'd recovered may feel 'back to square one'. Their thinking loops endlessly through such questions as 'What has gone wrong?' 'Why is this happening to me?' 'Where will it all end?' It feels constructive, as if going over such circular, or ruminative thoughts should help them find an answer. But in reality, it all only succeeds in prolonging and deepening the mood disturbance.

Why do people remain vulnerable to relapse? During an episode of depression, negative mood occurs alongside negative thinking and bodily sensations of sluggishness and fatigue. When the episode is past, and the mood has returned to normal, the negative thinking and body sensations tend to disappear as well. However, during the episode an association has been learned, and a link set up, between the various symptoms. This means that when negative mood happens again (for any reason), it will tend to trigger all the other symptoms in proportion to the strength of association. When this happens, the old habits of negative thinking will start up again, negative thinking gets into the same rut, and a full-blown episode of depression may be the result.

The discovery that even when people feel well, the link between negative moods and negative thoughts remains ready to be re-activated is of enormous importance. It means that sustaining recovery from depression depends on learning how to keep mild states of depression from spiralling out of control. This is one of our key aims – to enable you to develop your abilities and skills to do just that. We also believe that you can then start gaining the confidence to believe you will be successful in the future too, based on your new successful experiences.

Although you certainly don't like being depressed, up until now it's probably felt familiar and predictable, while happiness and fulfilment probably sound anything but! Staying stuck in depression's pretty painful, but at least you feel as though you have a little more control, and know what to expect – even it is very little!

We have written this book because we believe wholeheartedly that you can change the state you are in and overcome your depression. Each chapter's packed with techniques and exercises for doing just that.

Identifying change-blocking beliefs

People who are suffering from depression usually have a number of deep-seated beliefs that support and sustain their low mood, and fuel the fears of change. When you're not depressed, the beliefs lurk in the background, and usually don't interfere with your life. But when depression takes hold, the limiting beliefs come to the fore, sabotaging your attempts at recovery.

Change-blocking beliefs are the thoughts and negative expectations you have about yourself and the world that make change seem impossible. Even though you may have first become depressed many years after childhood, these beliefs often stem back to your early years. Exploring the childhood roots of your change-blocking beliefs can help you discover where your beliefs come from, and how these beliefs have more to do with a child's interpretation of events than with everyday reality.

Occasionally, change-blocking beliefs have roots in adulthood. Usually, traumatic events or chronic, repeated occurrences are responsible for these beliefs surfacing in later life. Change-blocking beliefs developed in adulthood can be dealt with in much the same way as the more common, change-blocking beliefs that originate in childhood.

The following sections describe what the most common change-blocking beliefs. We describe each one and give you some tools to deal with them. Then, in the 'Analysing your findings' section, we give you an exercise allowing you to challenge any or all these beliefs if they ever dare try getting in your way.

You may be able to think of additional change-blocking beliefs to the ones we list. For example, in Chapter 7 we discuss the core beliefs that often intensify depression and hinder your attempts to get better. Any of your core beliefs may also be change-blocking beliefs. Carefully review each of the beliefs we list to see if they're making you want to avoid, procrastinate, or see your situation as hopeless. After you've worked on this list, you may also find it useful to review and work on the beliefs in Chapter 7.

Dealing with dependency and inadequacy

Unfortunately, feelings of dependency and inadequacy are very common in people who have depression. If you feel *dependent*, you probably believe that someone other than yourself must cure your depression. And if you think of yourself as *inadequate*, you probably feel incapable of doing anything for yourself.

Believing in your feelings of dependency or inadequacy, you quickly stop taking risks. These change-blocking beliefs make taking risks (like working on your depression and risking failure) seem particularly scary. You feel extremely reluctant, if not totally unable, to independently tackle difficult, challenging tasks.

Dependency and inadequacy beliefs usually accompany such thoughts as:

- ✔ Whatever I try, I make a mess of it.
- ✔ I can't do this without a lot of help.
- ✔ I need help, but no one can help me enough.
- ✔ I don't want to take this risk; I know I'm going to fail and then feel worse than ever.
- ✔ I'm just not strong enough to do this.

The dependency and inadequacy beliefs, and the related thoughts can paralyse you and stop you taking action. And the belief fuels the fear of change because of the assumption that failure is inevitable.

After Donald's father dies when Donald is only 5 years old, his mother becomes increasingly close to him. As a result, she can't bear to see him trying to deal with pain or frustration. If he cries or even whimpers, she rushes to give him comfort. If Donald wants sweets or an ice-cream, she gives them to him – anything to make sure he doesn't get upset. Later, when he's stuck with his homework, she does it for him. Although she has the very best of intentions, she inadvertently fosters the development of Donald's dependency and inadequacy beliefs.

Donald never has the opportunity to find out what his real capabilities are, because his mother always takes over before he has a chance to work through his problems. When Donald is 14, his school tests his IQ and records that he's in the top range. However, his teachers describe him as an underachiever, and Donald believes that he's pretty incompetent, despite the contradiction between his basic belief of inadequacy and his IQ score. Although Donald is in fact very bright, he somehow doesn't see this. Donald's history shows one of the ways in which beliefs of inadequacy and dependency can arise. But not having enough help can also lead to problems: Dependency and/or inadequacy beliefs can also stem from a childhood in which the child gets excessive, harsh criticism, or if parents force their children to be independent at too early a stage. The latter can paradoxically cause the child to feel highly dependent. For example, if parents never provide assistance that's realistically required, their children may give up too easily. A similar result may occur if parents neglect their children, frequently leaving them alone to fend for themselves at too early an age.

If you think that you may have a dependency or inadequacy belief, reflect on your own childhood. Is it possible that:

- ✔ One or more important people harshly criticised you over the years?

- ✔ One or both of your parents stepped in to help you too quickly when you felt frustrated?

- ✔ You rarely got help that you truly needed when you asked for it?

- ✔ Your parents pushed you way too hard?

- ✔ Your parents neglected you and left you alone too often at an early age?

If you answer 'yes' to any of the questions in the previous list, you may now understand the basis of your dependency or inadequacy belief. Do remember that the reasons you reached those conclusions don't mean that you're actually dependent or inadequate! We provide you with some strategies for dealing with these and other dysfunctional beliefs in the 'Analysing your findings' section, later in this chapter (and in Chapter 7 as well).

Uncovering an undeserving outlook

The belief that you're undeserving can also sabotage your attempts to overcome depression. Many people who believe that they're undeserving think that there's something inherently wrong with them. They beat themselves up for the slightest flaw or mistake. They really believe that they don't deserve to feel good or have good things happen to them.

When people feel that they're undeserving, they may put minimal effort into overcoming their depression. They may feel as though depression is what they deserve and can expect out of life during their miserable existence on this planet.

If you frequently have any of the following thoughts, you may believe that you're undeserving:

- ✔ I feel like other people deserve more out of life than I do.

- ✔ I don't expect much out of life.

✔ I think that having needs shows weakness.

✔ I feel guilty when people do things for me.

✔ Bad things only really happen to bad people, so if I'm depressed, I must deserve to be.

✔ I don't deserve to get what I want.

Believing that you deserve less than other people is going to make your depression more difficult to tackle: you may well fear that any happiness will inevitably result in punishment, because happiness is undeserved. You need to root out this belief before making serious attempts at ridding yourself of depression.

You can start working on getting rid of this undeserving outlook by uncovering its roots. People don't feel undeserving without reason. Childhood events often provide the foundation for the undeserving belief. Ask yourself the following questions about your childhood:

✔ Were my parents emotionally unavailable to me?

✔ Did I frequently feel slighted (compared to my brothers or sisters)?

✔ Did one of my parents try to make me feel guilty as a form of punishment?

✔ Was I abused or severely punished?

✔ Were my parents exceptionally unpredictable in the things they punished me for?

If these situations feel familiar, your undeserving belief is probably anchored in childhood. You formed this conclusion about yourself because, as a child, you tried to make sense out of the things that were happening to you. It's natural to decide that you're undeserving if your parents tried to make you feel ashamed and/or failed to express love consistently. Donna's story illustrates one way this undeserving belief can arise.

Donna's mother, Katherine, is what psychologists call a *narcissist*. Katherine thinks far more about her own needs than her child's. When 3-year-old Donna is irritable, Katherine sends her to her bedroom for the rest of the day. Katherine's motivation is to get rid of anything annoying her, rather than to help Donna learn self-control. Katherine deals similarly with Donna's desires. If Donna wants something that will inconvenience her mother, Katherine calls her selfish, greedy, and ungrateful. Donna reaches the conclusion at a young age that she doesn't deserve good things.

In reality, Donna deserves as much out of life as any other child. But she didn't think that she deserved happiness – and she still doesn't today, as an adult, given her upbringing.

Fighting the unfair fight – Just do it!

When people get stuck and avoid working on their depression, they sometimes say, 'It's just not fair! I shouldn't have to work at this! Why did this happen to me?' The belief that depression is unfair and that you ideally shouldn't *have* to work on the problem is understandable.

While we agree that experiencing depression isn't fair, and do wish that you didn't have to put in so much work to do something about it, we are also convinced that:

- ✔ No one truly wants to be depressed.
- ✔ No one deserves to have depression.
- ✔ No one is to blame for having depression.

Depression has many causes (refer to Chapter 1 for more on this topic) including genetics, diseases, childhood experiences, tragedy, abuse, and trauma. You're not to blame for your own depression.

However, as unfortunate and unfair as it may be to have depression, you've got to put effort into overcoming it. No fairy godmother will come along and wave your depression away with a magic wand. Even if you choose medication to help you, you still have to work closely with a trusted GP or psychiatrist, who'll prescribe the medication, monitor possible side effects, and work in partnership with you, rather than 'doing it for you'.

Like other change-blocking beliefs, a preoccupation with unfairness may date back to childhood. Quite commonly, people who focus on unfairness were themselves treated unfairly by their parents when they were children. Exploring the early causes helps you identify some contributors to change-blocking beliefs, laying foundations to develop new, more helpful beliefs.

Rejecting the long-term victim role

Unfortunately, bad things can happen to good people for no reason at all. Negative events potentially may substantially disrupt a person's whole world, including how they view themselves. This disruption usually occurs when:

- ✔ Something really awful happens, such as severe illness or trauma.
- ✔ The negative event was seen as undeserved or unfair.
- ✔ The person feels upset and/or angry about the negative event.

When such undeserved events happen to people, their views about who and what they are change. They can begin believing that they're ill, or are a victim. And beliefs about sickness and victimhood involve an entire set of related self-views and altered behaviours, which we now describe.

People typically shift in both their feelings and behaviours – from independent to dependent, from well to sick, from capable to incapable, from being in control to being helpless, from placid to angry. Such change in beliefs, behaviours, and expectations (that come from perceiving yourself as being in one state, versus its opposite) is normal and natural when traumatic events occur.

In a sense, these new beliefs and behaviours about sickness and victimhood mean that you take on a new role, like an actor in a play. The individual takes on the role of patient or victim, and society, friends, family, and mental health professionals, including doctors, carry out supporting roles as helpers. These helpers have certain expectations for the patient or victim role as well as for their own roles. For example:

- Helpers feel motivated to help.
- Helpers don't see the patient as someone who deserves to be blamed.
- Helpers see themselves as mainly responsible for creating improvement and the patient as a passive recipient of their assistance.
- Certain helpers may be responsible for authorising financial compensation for the victim.
- Helpers believe that it's natural for the patient to feel upset or angry.
- Helpers usually provide sympathy, concern, and support.

The patient and victim roles are legitimate, reasonable, and feel deserved. In a sense, society creates these roles so that people can receive the necessary help when bad things undeservedly happen to them. We suspect that nearly everyone has occupied one or both of these roles at one time or another. So what's the problem? Well, nothing at all if you only take on one of these roles for a short period of time.

Unfortunately, over time, patient and victim roles can easily become permanent, rather than temporary states. As belief in t sickness or victimhood gets established, people focus more and more on the unfairness and awfulness of what's happened to them. They may start feeling furiously angry. The worst part is that, at the same time, they frequently feel helpless to do anything to improve matters.

The best way to decide if a belief in the patient or victim role has taken over your life is to ask yourself the following questions:

✔ Do I frequently think about how unfair life has been to me?

✔ Do I feel angry when I think of what has happened to me?

✔ Do I frequently complain to others about my circumstances?

✔ Do I feel helpless to do anything about my plight?

✔ Do I feel that doing something about my problems undermines the importance of what's happening to me?

If any of the thoughts from the previous list apply to you, it's likely you're entrenched in the victim or patient role. The roles provide no guidance for how to move on. So the problem is...you're stuck.

Here are alternative roles that you may want to consider – the role of the person who's coping and the role of the one who's getting better. People who are coping or improving may have experienced bad (possibly horrible), undeserved, unfair events. But taking on these particular roles means finding a way to dig deep, let go of anger and rage, and focus on what they can do to improve their circumstances. Recovery sometimes takes months or years of hard work, but most people find t the results well worth the effort.

If you find yourself bogged down in these roles, you probably need professional help. See Chapter 4 for guidance on this.

However, even in cases of severe trauma, shifting into a coping mode and working hard towards a better life is your ultimate, though highly challenging achievement. To make this shift, you need to both understand and accept that you deserve peace. But most importantly, you need to appreciate that rediscovering happiness in no way discounts or diminishes the awfulness of what happened to you.

Sometimes people wrestle with the idea that seeking happiness fails to take into account what some one's been through. They may think that a renewed pleasure and zest for life somehow negates previous horrific events. If this type of thinking sounds familiar, you may want to get back on the road to happiness by taking charge, rather than allowing the trauma to subsequently control your life. Try the following techniques:

✔ **Putting it in a vault:** Dr Robert Leahy recommends that you picture in your mind a large bank vault with thick steel doors. Put your mind's videotape of the trauma into the vault and lock it away. The tape stays in the vault, and you can unlock the vault and play the video of the trauma to appreciate the meaning it has for your life anytime you feel a need to do so. However, when you finish viewing the tape, imagine that you lock the trauma away. In this way you can live your life safe in the knowledge that the trauma doesn't need to harm you any further, and it can just stay safely locked in the vault.

✔ **Rewriting the script:** The clinical psychologist Derek Jehu suggests that rather than letting your mind keep replaying the trauma over and over again, you rewrite the script in your brain. First, you acknowledge to yourself that the real events happened, but that replaying the painful events repeatedly in your mind isn't helpful. Then, when the scene starts to play in your mind's eye, you come up with a different, better ending, and switch to visualising that. You tell yourself that neither visual picture is currently happening, - they both exist only in your mind. You discover one scene's so much better to watch than the other, and that you're able to do this without denying the reality of what actually happened.

Analysing your findings

Ridding yourself of change-blocking beliefs isn't the easiest thing in the world to do because, as we say throughout this section, they frequently originated long ago in childhood and adolescence. Reviewing your personal history to understand more about how you acquired these beliefs is a good place to start. This new knowledge can help you to stop blaming yourself for having the beliefs in the first place.

After working out which change-blocking beliefs you have, you can see how these beliefs help and hinder you. A 'Help and Hindrance Analysis' provides you with important ammunition for challenging these beliefs when they get in your way. To do a Help and Hindrance Analysis:

1. **Get a notebook out and make a chart.**

   Draw a line down the middle of your paper. Write down the change-blocking belief that you want to tackle at the top of the page. Then label one column 'Help' and the other 'Hindrance'. See Table 3-1 for a sample analysis.

2. **Write down all the reasons why your change-blocking belief is helpful to you.**

   Perhaps your belief allows you to avoid risks and losses. Maybe others will like you more if you hold on to this belief.

3. **Write down all the reasons why your change-blocking belief gets in your way.**

   Perhaps the belief keeps you from exploring new opportunities ,or prolongs your state of unhappiness.

4. **Review your two lists carefully.**

   Ask yourself whether the advantages or disadvantages seem more compelling. You're likely to find that the disadvantages greatly outweigh the advantages. If so, commit yourself to challenging your change-blocking belief by reading over the Hindrance column often. And see Chapter 7 for more ideas on how to challenge problematic beliefs.

Harry's story shows how he uses the Help and Hindrance technique to his benefit. **Harry** does nothing about his depression for nine months. He hopes his low mood will just go away all by itself, but his depression only deepens. His therapist suggests reading a particular self-help book. After three more months of putting it off, Harry reads a chapter. He discovers he believes he'is undeserving. This prevents him from tackling his depression - he feels that he doesn't deserve happiness. And he's particularly undeserving of pleasure because his depression's meant he's been unproductive as a freelance writer. Although a bit sceptical, Harry does a Help and Hindrance Analysis of his undeserving belief. Table 3-1 shows the results of Harry's analysis.

Table 3-1	Harry's Help and Hindrance Analysis
Belief: Undeserving Outlook	
Help	**Hindrance**
Avoiding pleasure stops me from feeling guilty.	This belief stops me from trying to improve my life.
People won't think I'm self-centred.	I actually feel guilty all the time, whether I have a good time or not.
I'll be satisfied with less.	I always feel unhappy.
I won't be disappointed by hoping for good things.	Thinking I deserve no better is what's keeping me stuck.
If I feel undeserving, maybe it is going to motivate me to be more productive.	Actually, I hate being unproductive, but I think it's my depression that makes me less productive. And if I don't think I deserve better, I'll never be more productive.

Harry concludes that in his analysis, the Help column, which gives supposedly 'good reasons' for why it's worthwhile staying stuck looks almost convincing. Realising this shocks him into deciding he must actively, seriously fight against his undeserving belief each time it tells him to stop doing anything good for himself.

If you use the Help and Hindrance Analysis technique on one or more of your change-blocking beliefs and it doesn't seem to help, don't get too discouraged. We provide many more ways to overcome these and other problematic beliefs in Chapter 7.

Exposing myths: therapy and self-help

Myths and mistaken views about therapy and self-help resources are another major reason why many people avoid seeking help for depression.

We repeatedly hear people discuss therapy and self-help in less than complimentary terms. Of course, rarely do these people go in for therapy or self-help. They avoid such support resources like the plague because they see the process as misguided and useless. If they do begin therapy or self-help, they often avoid taking part fully, and quickly give up because of their misunderstanding about therapy and self-help.

These people buy into the many myths and misconceptions about therapy and self-help. We now discuss the most common myths, and explain why we believe that they're inaccurate:

- **Therapy and self-help are long, complicated processes.** Therapy and self-help do involve some work. However, many studies show that most cases of major depression can be treated successfully with about 20 sessions of the types of therapy we discuss in this book. Other studies have shown that self-help alone can be sufficient toovercome mild to moderate cases of depression, and can be a valuable addition to other types of therapy.

  If you're battling chronic, long-term depression, you may indeed find that you need a longer course of therapy. However, it's likely that you 'll experience a lift in mood within a few months of starting your therapy, and the odds are good that you'll feel that the long-term benefits from continued work are more than worth the effort.

- **Therapy's a get-out – it just comes up with excuses.** People who believe this myth often also believe that they deserve to suffer from depression. If this is one of your beliefs, please read 'Uncovering an undeserving outlook', earlier in this chapter.

  Other people who see therapy as giving you excuses and 'get out' clauses for your problems believe that certain therapies (especially cognitive behavioural therapy; see Part II) simply demand that you see everything as *positive*. But the reality is that these therapies don't ask you to simply see everything as positive. If it's raining, you're not expected to stand at the window saying heartily, 'Oh, what a wonderful day!' Instead, therapy requires you to collect and examine evidence (much like scientists). When you discover evidence that supports a negative aspect about yourself or your world, you work to change what you can and accept what you can't so – 'It's not fair! Why does it always rain on *me*?!' can become 'Now what indoors attraction shall I visit instead of going to the zoo as I'd planned?'

- **Therapy and self-help merely trivialise depression.** Throughout this book, we emphasise that depression is a serious problem – sometimes extremely serious in that suicide poses a significant risk. All good therapists appreciate the seriousness of depression.

On the other hand, we do realise that both self-help and therapy give you techniques that appear fairly straightforward and not particularly complex. These strategies may even feel trivial. After all, you may have battled profound depression for years, and the idea that some simple techniques may help you overcome your depression can feel almost demeaning. Do remember the techniques only seem simple because therapists have worked hard to break down complicated ideas, information, and research findings into easily understood, digestible units.

Sometimes you may feel that a therapist or self-help author is asking you to change too quickly or easily, which can make you feel small, as though your depression is so simply and easily changed. If you're receiving therapy, discuss these feelings with your therapist. If you're attempting to treat yourself with self-help and you feel as though you're being asked to change too quickly, you may benefit from carrying out therapy with a professional as well as using self-help.

✔ **Therapy and self-help ignore the importance of emotions and feelings.** The mental health field appreciates the pain of depression. That's why this field has devoted decades of professional exploration and research to finding ways of easing your depression.

Emotions and feelings are hugely important to therapists. Nevertheless, sometimes therapists ask you to focus more on your thoughts rather than the emotions which those thoughts trigger. So it may feel like your emotions aren't fully appreciated. If you're having therapy, discuss this feeling with your therapist. If you get this reaction while reading a self-help book such as this one, you may want to get help from a therapist who can listen to and appreciate your feelings more completely than an author can from afar.

✔ **Therapy and self-help can't give me what I need.** Well, this statement does have some truth to it. No therapist, or book, can possibly give you *everything* you need.

Try to approach therapy and self-help books with the realisation that your needs can only be partially met. Your best option is to work with a range of different sources including books, therapists, friends and relatives.. And, realistically, can anyone truthfully say they feel 100 per cent fulfilled all of the time? We don't think so!

✔ **Therapy doesn't work.** Hundreds of studies show the effectiveness of the therapies described in this book. While discussing each of these therapies, we also refer to the research behind them. However, not every type of psychotherapy has convincingly demonstrated such effectiveness. If you undertake therapy, we recommend that it's one of the ones we discuss in this book, or alternatively, that you do your homework thoroughly before committing yourself to the therapy.

✔ **I can't change unless I feel totally understood, and no author or therapist can ever understand the complexity and depth of my problems.** It's absolutely true that no author or therapist can ever completely understand every aspect of your depression. Your depression is made up of unique experiences – no one can ever know *exactly* how you feel.

Therapists and authors *do* know a great deal about depression. They listen carefully and are able to fully appreciate the devastating impact of depression. And research shows that therapy works well, despite the therapist not sharing your exact experiences.

✔ **People who go to therapy are weak.** Although this thought effectively prevents many people from seeking help, we fully believe that it's totally baseless. The reality is that seeking help takes a lot of courage because you have to let down your guard and face your vulnerabilities. Who's more courageous – someone who feels compelled to present a false front and avoid exploring any personal vulnerability, or someone who admits to problems and decides to face them head-on? We certainly plump for the latter. It's also worth asking yourself whether waiting until all your teeth have fallen out *before* you go to the dentist is a wise move. Seeking help sooner rather than later is both a good and brave move.

✔ **People just go to therapy to whine and complain.** The majority of people who seek help do have some dissatisfaction with their lives, but the reason they go into therapy is to try to do something about their problems. Therapy has about as much to do with whining and complaining as rapidly flapping your arms has to do with flying.

Breaking Free from Self-Limitations

The earlier sections of this chapter review the many fears that arise when contemplating change , as well as the powerful beliefs and myths that support those fears.

Deciding to deal with depression requires courage, but avoidance results in you sabotaging and limiting yourself. Some people do (or not do!) anything to get away from the fear of working toward recovery.

Self-limitation is anything you do that prevents you from working on your depression and therefore reaching your true potential. You may be self-limiting if:

✔ You find reason after reason for avoiding working on your depression.

✔ You see your situation as hopeless.

✔ You insist that there must be a perfect solution before trying to do anything at all.

✔ You demand to see a guarantee of improvement before you take on the task of changing.

> ✔ You just give up at the very first sign that things aren't working out.
>
> ✔ You repeatedly criticise yourself when you try anything at all, completely demotivating yourself.
>
> ✔ Whenever evidence shows that things are a little better than you thought they'd be, you immediately discount and discard the data.
>
> ✔ You wait for the 'perfect time' for making changes, which never arises.
>
> ✔ You become confused, disoriented, or 'out of it' whenever you try to deal with your problems.
>
> ✔ You repeatedly blame others for your situation, rather than looking at what you can do to solve your problems.

If any of the items in this list apply to you when you are thinking about working on your depression, you're not likely to make any progress until you do something about your self-limitation.

Nearly everyone who has depression at sometime or other tries avoiding dealing with the problem and is also very self-critical. But it's important to catch yourself in the act and then move on again.

The following sections show you how to move on and climb up and out of your depression. We discuss a number of ways of avoiding self-limitation, to start you climbing up that mountain. If one strategy doesn't help particularly, try others.

Avoiding pitfalls

Pitfalls trap the unwary. Problems can increase rapidly and trap you if you can't spot them. You therefore need to to recognise the signs that indicate your depressed mind is setting another trap for you, and pay close attention to your thinking.

Grab a notebook and start a 'Self-Limiting Diary'. Write the days of the week in a column on the left. Then draw up a column on the right headed 'Self-Limiting Strategies'. (See Table 3-2 for a sample diary.) Each day, write down anything you find yourself doing that keeps you stuck in depression and avoiding doing something about it. Looking back at the list of self-limitation strategies in the previous section may help you get started. When you see what you're doing to limit yourself, you're then more likely to be in a position to break out of the self-limiting pattern. Matthew's story shows how this technique works.

Matthew's misery lasts for over a year before he decides to do something about it. He goes to a psychologist who practises cognitive behavioural therapy (CBT). (See Part II for more information about cognitive therapy and Part III for behaviour therapy.) The psychologist quickly identifies that Matthew fears change and consistently sabotages his own recovery efforts. Matthew is late for appointments. His mind wanders when he tries to read self-help materials, he complains about how others treat him, and he insists that his therapist can't do anything to help him.

Matthew's psychologist helps him understand that his behaviour results in him digging an ever deeper hole for himself, stopping him from productively working towards improving matters. It takes some time, but Matthew eventually gets the point. Building on this understanding, his psychologist suggests Matthew keeps a diary of his self-limiting strategies. Table 3-2 shows Matthew's results for the first five days.

Table 3-2	Matthew's Self-Limiting Diary
Day	**Self-Limiting Strategies**
Monday	I stayed in bed for ages and was late for work – again! I lost track of time later in the day and missed half of my therapy appointment, leaving me only 20 minutes to deal with everything. Then I spent ten of those precious minutes telling my psychologist how hopeless I am. *Not very helpful I guess.*
Tuesday	My boss said I'd done a great report. I replied that it wasn't really that good and then pointed out several mistakes. *What good does that do me?*
Wednesday	I got a speeding ticket. Then I told myself I was an idiot for letting that happen. My insurance may increase. Bet I'll probably mess up other things too. I dwelled on the stupid ticket all day long and had an unproductive day at work. *I guess that wasn't too useful.*
Thursday	I met Sheila last week, and she seems to like me. I really want to call her again, but found myself not doing so. Was she just being polite? Maybe she doesn't like me at all? I started thinking I can't stand any more rejection so I put off phoning her, though I'd told her I'd call. *Where will that get me?*

Matthew reviews his diary. He's struck by how many ways he avoids productive work when it comes to dealing with his depression. He fears further loss and rejection, so he avoids taking risks, but this means he's stuck in his depression. Being stuck means he is going to fail in finding a new relationship. When he hears something positive about his work, he refuses to believe his boss and actively disagrees. His self-criticism that follows only lowers his mood still further. And his insistence on his own hopelessness and helplessness just backs him farther into a corner.

Matthew's psychologist helps him understand that he's acting in a self-limiting way for a good reason – he's experiencing the fear of change we review in the 'Facing the fear of change' section, earlier in this chapter. Tracking his self-limitation does seem to help Matthew tackle his problems. As he sees the innumerable ways he avoids efforts to recover, and how he's maintaining his current depressed state, Matthew begins to recognise and avoid the pitfalls of self-limitation. Then, ever so gradually, he stops backing away from change, and starts taking action to resolve his problems.

If you find yourself avoiding and self-limiting, try keeping a self-limiting diary. But don't use your diary as a trigger for self-criticism. Beating yourself up only aggravates self-limitation, by making you feel worse about yourself.

Suspending judgement

If you get stuck in the quicksand of self-limiting thoughts when reading this book or carrying out therapy, try suspending judgement for a while – just let it hang! Experiment with the idea that 'just maybe' therapy can work for you. While you're suspending judgement, work as hard as you can at following the techniques that we describe throughout this book or that your therapist suggests.

Repeating positive, self-affirming statements can help you tackle self-judgement. Therefore, consider repeating one or more of the following statements to yourself on a regular basis:

- ✔ What do I honestly have to lose by trying? I don't have to tell anyone what I've been doing, so no one will even know if my efforts don't work.
- ✔ The only real failure is never trying.
- ✔ Focus on progress, not perfection.
- ✔ When I tell myself off, it really doesn't help. I'm going to try to focus on what I do right more than what I do wrong.
- ✔ Don't judge, just do.

Going slow

You can also limit yourself in a rather surprising way – by working too hard and fast on your depression. Believe it or not, tackling your depression head-on at full speed can cause unexpected problems. Be sure to take it slowly. Going too fast sets you up for unrealistic expectations. Focus on small successes. If you happen to experience a big success, that's great, but savour it a bit and try not to push full speed ahead for a little while.

You're more likely to overcome your depression using a gradual, steady approach rather than going for broke.

Pacing yourself has another advantage – it can help keep you from feeling overwhelmed by the tasks at hand. Some people look at a book such as this one and notice that it contains more than 300 pages plus loads of exercises. They then decide that they can never get through it all. If you think that you may not be able to get through this book, think about the following ideas:

- You don't need to read every single chapter and do every exercise to make significant progress. If a particular exercise doesn't look that relevant to you, don't do it! And certain chapters may not be important for you to read. For example, if you're happy in your relationships, you can skip Chapter 14.

- Looking at the whole picture at once can lead to self-limitation because doing so can feel overwhelming. Focus on one small step at a time. For example, if we'd focused on writing this book as though it had to be finished in just one week, we'd stop writing instantly!

If you have a serious level of depression that includes thoughts of death and hopelessness, or you work on the strategies in this book for six weeks or longer without experiencing any success, please consult a professional for extra help.

Taking two steps forward, and one back

Many people who come to us for help with depression expect to improve, and that's reasonable enough. But all too often they also expect swift, prompt progress that proceeds in a smooth, steady, upward fashion. The only problem with this second expectation is that we have yet to see it happen! Why?

To be honest, we're not entirely sure why, but we do know that most people progress gradually, with many peaks and troughs along the way. It's important not to expect your efforts to materialise as steady change. Change just doesn't progress in that way. Your progress probably looks like Figure 3-1.

As you can see in Figure 3-1, progress includes both peaks and troughs. Like the stick figures in the chart, you're going to go through various stages as you work to overcome your depression:

- **Standing on a peak:** When you occupy this position, you're more likely to form unrealistically positive expectations about how you're progressing. You need to remind yourself that you are likely to experience both ups and downs.

> ✔ **Down in the trough:** At this point, you may be tempted to think that you've never reached such a low ebb before. But the truth is, you may have made progress from where you began, but at these low points, it may be impossible to see the progress you've made. This is especially so if you were on a higher peak earlier. Try to resist making judgements about your progress when you're on an inevitable downturn.

When you're on your way up, you can assess your progress realistically, but you need to resist the temptation to predict too speedy a progression in the future. And when you've taken a dip, try not to then judge how you've been doing overall, because it won't be possible at those times.

We want you to know that the predictable and inescapable downturns in the process of change have an advantage. What? Are we kidding? No, seriously, each dip, though unpleasant, can provide you with useful information about events that trigger your low moods. You can see what to do with such events in Chapters 5 and 6. The key lies in expecting these dips - not beating yourself up for experiencing the inevitable ups and downs inseparable from overcoming depression.

Transforming visions of failure into success

If you're depressed, you've probably written hundreds of failure stories of doom and gloom. O.K., you may not have actually put the words on paper, but we bet your mind's envisaged rejection, failure, wasted efforts, making a mess of things, and humiliation more times than you care to remember. And those images more than likely include rich details of your anticipated lack of skill along with a host of catastrophes that resulted from your expected failure.

Stories about potential failures can cause you to avoid making the effort at improving your depression. Basically, the stories become another form of self-limitation. So, how about considering something different?

Get out your notebook and a pen. Or, if you prefer, sit down in front of your computer. Write a story about how you just may *succeed* at something! Include details about how you're going to approach the challenge, your plans, and the difficulties you anticipate.

Write down how you imagine you're going to overcome those difficulties. Be sure to include any thoughts about your fears, but also include strategies for working your way through the fear. If you have trouble coming up with ideas for getting around the obstacles, ask yourself what someone else may do. Make your story long enough to include the specifics; don't skimp.

Chapter 4

Finding Help for Depression

In This Chapter

▶ Finding the right treatment

▶ Helping yourself with self-help

▶ Getting help through psychological therapy

▶ Discussing medication with a professional

Are you feeling low? It's a fair bet that, because you're reading this book, you or someone you love is being hit by depression. Perhaps you're just a bit down in the dumps, or even feeling like you really are at rock bottom? The good news is that there's a whole range of different types of help available from a number of sources, ranging from bookshops to the therapist's consulting room. The bad news is that the wealth of choice can be bewildering, especially when you find your thinking isn't as clear as you'd like it to be. In this chapter, we untangle confusion by going through your options for getting help and giving you the means to make an informed decision about the huge array of options available.

We give you the necessary information on the three main ways for dealing with depression – self-help, psychological therapy, and medication – so that you can work out what's best for you. And we help you understand the differences between various mental health professionals and identify whether you are well matched with the professional you choose.

Exploring the Self-Help Option

Everyone who's dealing with depression can benefit from self-help. *Self-help* refers to efforts you make on your own, without professional assistance, to deal with your depression. You also have the option of 'guided self-help', where you carry out a lot of the work on your own, but have someone guide you through the various steps. Dozens of studies show the value of self-help for a variety of emotional, behavioural, and medical problems. Some of you may find that self-help alone is all you need. Others may need extra help if self-help alone isn't enough.. However, self-help *can* powerfully boost the effectiveness of psychological therapy and/or medication.

Combining reading self-help with other tried and tested therapies may help to speed up your recovery.

Deciding whether self-help is for you

Before settling on self-help as the one and only way for you to overcome your depression ask yourself the following questions:

- ✔ **Am I having suicidal thoughts?** If the answer is yes, then you do need to see a mental health professional (see the later section 'Discovering who's who in psychological therapies'). The mental health professional is likely to recommend psychological therapy, medication, or a combination of the two, in addition to self-help.

- ✔ **Is my depression seriously interfering with my life in areas such as work, relationships, sleep, appetite, or leisure?** Once again, if the answer is yes, you may be suffering from a major depressive disorder (refer to Chapter 2 for more information on major depressive disorders), which means that you probably need more than just self-help.

If you answer 'no' to both of these questions, self-help may be exactly the right place to start. However, first ask yourself: 'Do I have the desire and motivation to put into practice the advice I receive from self-help sources?' We're not talking about hours of daily study. But for it to work, self-help does require more than just one quick read through of an article or even a book. And you, like many other people, may find that you work better with guidance, reporting back on progress, and having help in understanding and overcoming setbacks.

With depression, it's common to believe that if you do try and tackle it, you're 'bound to fail'. Working with a professional lets you borrow their belief that you *can* change, until you gather together enough evidence to establish your own beliefs. So if you can't confidently answer 'yes' to the question of whether your own motivation is sufficiently robust, talk through your options with a mental health professional.

If you do make the decision to only use self-help, after having considered these points, then great. This book's a pretty good starting point. As well as your self-help book you may want to explore extra self-help resources (see the following section). Work for a while at putting into practice what you discover about yourself, and monitor your progress carefully. You can use the mood monitoring form (the 'Mood Diary') that we outline in Chapter 2 to keep track of your improvement.

If you don't see progress through self-help after two months of effort, start exploring other sorts of help. If at any point you feel discouraged, begin to have suicidal thoughts, or your depression worsens, do seek help from a professional at once. See 'Discovering who's who in psychological therapy', later in this chapter, for more information on mental health professionals.

Reviewing the resources

Choosing the right self-help approach depends on your personal preferences and style. The fact that you're already reading this book suggests that the written word may appeal to you. The following list covers the most common self-help options (more options are listed in the Appendix):

- **Books:** Dozens of books are available for helping you overcome depression. You're probably going to find this is one of the clearest and easiest to follow, but do read through several different self-help books. Even though you may repeatedly see identical suggestions, the repetition helps you remember them. Also, each author has their own way of explaining theories, which can help your understanding. The best books for dealing with depression give you information about treatments that are known to work.

  Books are a fairly inexpensive way of getting help - an obvious advantage. You can find or even order many of the books through your local library or via the Internet. Your GP may also be part of the 'book prescription' scheme, where your doctor helps you choose a book from a list of recommended self-help books and then 'prescribes' it for you. Self-help material also has the advantage of providing a huge amount of information that take a therapist many sessions to cover. And you can refer to the information as often as you need.

  Make sure that the authors of any self-help book that you buy have the right professional qualifications and experience in helping others deal with depression. (We cover the subject of professional qualifications in the 'Discovering who's who in psychological therapy' section, later in this chapter.)

- **Tapes, CDs, videos, and DVDs:** For those who learn best by hearing or seeing, these can be really helpful. As with books, check out the author's qualifications and experience and the effectiveness of the therapy.

- **Self-help groups:** Self-help groups offer support and understanding. People with common problems gather in these groups (meeting up together, or as a 'virtual group' in a 'chat room' via the Internet) to share information and experiences. Members are able to help themselves and each other by sharing their feelings and experiences, and solving problems together. MIND, SANE, and the Depression Alliance are registered mental health charities that offer information concerning the availability of local support groups (See the Appendix for addresses). Often your library has a directory of community resources, as does the Internet.

✔ **Computerised Cognitive Behaviour Therapy (CCBT):** This guided self-help programme 'Beating the Blues' for overcoming depression can help you overcome depression. Healthcare providers make CCBT available via your own computer or at centres.

✔ **Websites:** You can find a huge range of resources relating to depression on the Internet. Putting 'depression resources' into a search engine yielded over one and a quarter million hits! You can take part in recovery programmes (see www.livinglifetothefull.com), check out the NICE guidelines for people with depression (www.nice.org.uk), join chat rooms, download articles, buy products, sign up for computer programmes, and even pay for a therapist offering help by providing advice through email or phone consultations.

We only list tried and tested websites in the Appendix to this book. You need to bear in mind that there is little quality control for what is on offer on the Internet. As well as finding well qualified practitioners who can help you, you'll undoubtedly discover many unqualified, though well-meaning individuals offering you advice, plus outright frauds who also market their products and ideas online.

Confidence tricksters abound on the Internet, offering you all kinds of merchandise that promise prompt relief from depression with little or no effort. Buyer beware! No miracle cures exist for depression.

Many people aren't lucky enough to find the best option to deal with their depression by chance alone. And believing everything you're told also isn't the answer. You are most likely to succeed by carefully evaluating all options for help to find your best choice.

Pursuing Psychological Therapy

Psychological therapy involves working with a therapist using psychological techniques to ease emotional problems. Psychological therapy covers many different approaches, and a wide range of professionals practise these therapies. It can be pretty daunting working out what's likely to be the best source of help for you from this mind-boggling array of options.

But don't start getting depressed about it! In this section, we give you the information you need to find your way through the maze. First, we discuss the types of psychological therapy that have been shown to be effective in treating depression, then tell you how to understand who's who within the mental health professionals, and finally look at finding and working with a therapist.

Uncovering what works: The effective psychological therapies

You may decide you want to read through the thousands of articles available that discuss the effectiveness of psychological therapy for treating depression. However, you'd probably rather not, so we've gone ahead and done some research for you. But new studies are continually being reported, so we do advise you to keep an open mind about the possibility of adding to this list in the future.

The following therapies are proved to be effective and to produce excellent results within a reasonable timeframe:

✔ **Cognitive behavioural therapy (CBT):** CBT is made up of two types of therapy: cognitive and behaviour. *Cognitive therapy* operates on the understanding that the ways in which people think about, perceive, and interpret events plays a central role in how they feel (Part II covers this therapy). *Behaviour therapy* focuses on helping you to change behaviours like finding activities that you positively enjoy and also introducing you to problem solving (Chapters 9 to 12 cover behaviour therapy). Some therapists practise cognitive therapy and behaviour therapy separately, but nowadays most take the combined approach of CBT.

Studies show that changing your way of thinking helps you in overcoming depression. It has also been shown that changing your behaviour can improve the way you feel and ease depression.

For the treatment of depression, no psychological therapy has received as much support as CBT. In fact, the UK Government recently committed £170 million to making CBT treatment available to enable more people to overcome emotional problems (especially depression and anxiety).

Research shows that CBT works equally well as medication for treating depression, and that CBT provides a degree of protection against relapse – something that medication doesn't always do.

Interpersonal therapy (IPT): This type of therapy helps people identify and modify problems in their relationships, both past and present. Like CBT, this approach has also been shown to ease depression about as well as taking medication. Sometimes this method of therapy delves into issues involving loss, grief, and major changes in a person's life, such as retirement or divorce. The IPT approach also includes examining and understanding the relationship between the therapist and client. You can discover how to relate to the therapist in ways that may help you understand what you are doing, and how to improve other relationships. Part IV looks at strategies, such as learning to deal with loss, that are drawn in part from IPT.

Most people aren't aware of how many different types of therapy exist. Here are just a few others: psychoanalysis, client-centered therapy, transactional analysis, Gestalt therapy, hypnosis, eye movement desensitisation reprocessing (popularly referred to as EMDR), and Hakomi therapy.

Indeed the United Kingdom Council for Psychotherapy (UKCP), which accredits Organisations offering training and practice in the various forms of Psychotherapy, has 80 Member Organisations. They divide into 7 main sections. Even the section titles themselves can be confusing to some professionals, let alone to people who do not work in the field!

We will not go into these in any depth, but list them here to give you an idea of the range:

- Analytical psychology – psychoanalytic and psychodynamic
- Cognitive behavioural
- Experimental constructivist
- Family, couple, sexual, and systemic therapies
- Humanistic and integrative psychotherapies
- Hypno-psychotherapy
- Psychotherapeutic counselling

In addition to these 7 Sections, UKCP also covers other Organisations, such as The British Psychological Society(BPS) and the Royal College of Psychiatrists who are what is termed 'Special Members', and the British Association for Counselling and Psychotherapy (BACP).

Although a wide range of therapies have value, some may be more effective than others in overcoming depression. Given that the scientific literature on some types of therapy as applied to depression is quite limited, we suggest that you start with therapies that are proved to be effective for dealing with depression.

Discovering who's who in psychological therapy

Until recently, anyone could call themselves a therapist, psychotherapist, psychological therapist, or counsellor and offer their services to the public irrespective of their training or experience without getting into trouble with the authorities, because these titles weren't regulated. This fact may come as a surprise given the potential for harm to the mental well-being of clients. But the UK Government is now moving to regulate specific professional titles and to specify who has the right to practise psychological therapy.

It's very important to ask about a practitioner's specific training in particular types of psychological therapy, because not all professionals have been trained in the types of psychological therapy that have been found effective for depression (outlined in the preceding section).

In the following list, we review the most common professional titles controlled by professional qualification boards. We also describe the usual training needed to obtain each type of professional qualification. Requirements vary across Europe, but recent legislation has changed so psychologists with European qualifications from outside the UK can practise in the UK, without extensive additional training requirements.

- **Assistant Psychologists (APs):** APs provide a 'helping hand', working closely with clinical psychologists. They may assess clients for various cognitive and behavioural problems, assist in therapeutic/discussion groups, support carers, family members and clients, and provide relevant information to referrers and other professionals. APs are supervised by a clinical psychologist working in the same department or speciality. They have an honours degree in psychology, plus some previous relevant experience such as NHS voluntary or paid work. APs differ in their amount and relevance of previous experience and likewise their level of responsibility, grade, and the specific tasks they carry out in the department.

- **Associate Psychologists:** The training for this new grade, which is between Assistant and Clinical Psychologist, has recently commenced, with the first courses running in Nothumberland from 2005-7.

- **Clinical Psychologists:** Chartered Clinical Psychologists normally complete a Bachelors (first) degree (B.A. or B.Sc.) in Psychology. Usually they undertake further experience, perhaps as a Psychology Assistant, or Graduate Mental Health Worker, or even do the new training for an Associate Psychologist. They then complete a three-year doctoral training degree in Clinical Psychology, which has both academic and clinical components. In addition, they must complete a yearlong internship followed by one or two years of supervised postdoctoral training. The British Association for Behavioural and Cognitive Psychotherapies (BABCP) or the Health Professions Council (HPC) has taken on the role of assessing and checking the maintenance of ongoing continuous development for therapists from both Clinical Psychology and other professions to become registered as accredited CBT therapists.

- **Community Psychiatric Nurses (CPNs) and Community Mental Health Nurses:** These psychiatric nurses work in the community rather than in hospitals. They may be attached to GPs' surgeries, Community Mental Health Teams in Mental Health Resource Centres or Psychiatric Units. They may also visit you in your home. Their role includes offering emotional support and helping you explore ways of living with your problems, anxiety management techniques, and administering psychiatric drugs.

✓ **Counselling Psychologist:** Qualifications in this are by accredited courses, or through an independent route. Training usually lasts three years full-time, or equivalent part-time, at postgraduate level.

✓ **Counsellor:** At present there are no legal minimum qualifications necessary to practise as a counsellor in the UK. The British Association for Counselling and Psychotherapy (BACP; previously the British Association of Counselling) accredits counselling courses and practitioners. BACP-accredited courses are likely to be one year full time, or two-three years part time. At present, BACP doesn't accredit shorter counselling skills courses.

✓ **Gateway mental health worker:** These senior mental health professionals, such as experienced community psychiatric nurses, social workers or psychologists, work with GPs and primary care teams, NHS Direct, and in casualty departments to respond to people who need urgent specialist mental health services. They also help people move smoothly from primary care to specialised services.

✓ **Graduate or primary care mental health worker:** This new role was introduced in the early 2000s. it encompasses various different levels of training and responsibility. Its exact nature and future is still under discussion, especially in light of other developments and legislation.

✓ **Occupational Therapists (OTs):** OTs work for the NHS or social services, and they assess and treat physical and psychiatric conditions. They have a degree in Occupational Therapy, which usually takes three years, and they may also do additional training in psychological therapy, for example, in CBT.

✓ **Psychiatrist:** Psychiatrists first qualify as medical doctors. They then undertake specialist training in Psychiatry, covering the treatment and diagnosis of a range of emotional and psychiatric disorders, including depression. Their training emphasises biological treatments, and allows them to specialise in prescribing medication as well as biological therapies such as electroconvulsive therapy (see Chapters 15 and 16). Psychiatrists also train in psychological therapies including CBT and another form of psychological therapy, psychodynamic psychotherapy, often known as 'psychotherapy'.

✓ **Registered Mental Nurses (RMNs):** RMNs are qualified Nurses who have specialist training in mental health and who have taken a three-year course, usually at a university with some general nursing included. An RMN qualification doesn't make someone a psychotherapist or counsellor, but is a good basis from which to take further training, which is what many nurses now do.

✔ **Social Worker:** Social workers register with the General Social Care Council. They are professionally qualified staff assessing the needs of service users and plan the individual packages of care and support that best help their clients. A Social Worker usually has a first degree in Social Work, but sometimes considerable experience overrides the requirement of a degree.

Finding the right therapist for you

Some people take less time choosing a therapist than they do selecting the best fruit at the supermarket. That's a real shame, because the right therapist can make an enormous difference to both your speed and level of recovery, even allowing you to feel still better than how you were before suffering depression. And in the worst case, the wrong therapist can cost both time, money, and may even actually cause increased emotional distress.

Important issues to consider when you look for a therapist include:

✔ **NHS or private:** Many NHS Clinical Psychology Services have long waiting lists, but there are developments to provide a range of mental health professionals to work directly with GP surgeries and ease the problem of the waiting list. Increasingly the Community Mental Health Teams (CMHTs) don't offer help for the milder forms of depression. GP surgeries can sometimes provide a fixed number of sessions from the practice's counsellor fairly promptly. However, depression that's more severe, while still not qualifying for CMHT criteria, can require longer that the fixed number of sessions available through the GP surgery.

Some people choose to go private, to speed up getting help, or perhaps because they want to see a particular professional or have special concerns about privacy. Private therapy means paying for this yourself, or through private health insurance. If the latter, do ensure your policy covers that particular form of therapy, and therapist for that particular problem. Some insurance companies have lists of preferred provider therapists that they cover, while others allow you to see almost any qualified therapist. Certain ones restrict access to a very narrow choice. A few companies only cover psychological therapies known to be effective, such as the ones in this book.

✔ **Reputation and recommendations:** Therapists can't provide you with the names of satisfied customers, because they're required to respect confidentiality. However, you can find out more about therapists' reputations from other sources. Ask around. Talk to your friends and/or your GP.

Be cautious about advertisements on TV, the Internet, in newspapers magazines and the phone book: they *aren't* especially reliable sources of information about therapists' reputations. Consider checking that the person really is registered with their professional organisation. You can do this by contacting the organisation over the Internet or by phone.

✔ **Availability of appointments:** Therapists vary. Some offer early morning, or evenings, or even weekends, to fit in with your own work commitments, while NHS times are usually but not always 9am to 5pm.

✔ **Training and professional registration:** We discuss the general training requirements for various qualified mental health professionals in the previous section. Remember to ask about training and experience in the therapies that have been shown to work best for depression, such as CBT and IPT (see the earlier section 'Uncovering what works: The effective physiological therapies'.)

Putting time, effort and even money in therapy ultimately pays off in many, sometimes unexpected, ways. For example, studies show that psychological therapy actually cuts visits to the GP, and it also appears to improve both physical and mental health.

Having rapport with your therapist

Most people relate well to their therapist, and make improvements with their depression. They develop what has been called a good 'therapeutic alliance', both working hard and making progress towards a common shared goal. Therapists are generally bright, kind, and skilful. However, therapists and clients sometimes just don't gel.

You may find that you and your therapist just don't have rapport, and feel that your therapist doesn't understand you. Perhaps the therapist closely resembles your ex and every therapy session triggers a flood of painful memories. Or maybe you just don't feel there's a connection between you and your therapist, for no apparent reason.

The quality of the therapeutic relationship (how well you and your therapist relate to each other) has been found to consistently predict therapy outcomes, so it's essential that you feel comfortable. A good relationship is linked to successful therapeutic change.

Here are some questions you may want to ask yourself after you've had a few sessions with your therapist, to help decide the quality of the relationship:

✔ Do I feel like I can tell my therapist just about anything?

✔ Does it seem like my therapist cares about me?

✔ Does my therapist understand me?

✔ Does my therapist seem interested in my problems?

✔ Does my therapist hear what I'm trying to say?

✔ Do I trust my therapist?

✔ Is my therapist non-judgemental and non-critical with me?

✔ Do I feel safe discussing my problems with my therapist?

If you answer any of these questions with a firm 'no', or you answer several of them without a definitive 'yes', discuss your concerns with your therapist. If you feel that you can't discuss these issues with your therapist, ask yourself the reasons for this.

If you find you have good reasons for feeling so unsafe that you can't imagine being open and honest, you probably need to look for another therapist. However, if you have a problem in speaking frankly to your therapist because of shyness or embarrassment, remind yourself that the therapist has been trained to hear your concerns, and that it is both right and necessary that you express them.

How your therapist reacts to your concerns about the quality of your relationship with each other shows whether the relationship can be repaired. Here's how a therapist with good rapport may respond to a client's concerns:

Client: I need to talk to you about something.

Therapist: Sure, what is it?

Client: I've been feeling that I can't be honest with you because I'm afraid you'll be critical.

Therapist: It's very helpful that you're telling me this. Can you help me understand anything about the times when it's felt like I've been critical of you?

Client: Well, last week I told you about my plans to look for another job and you said I shouldn't do it.

Therapist: I guess that sounded to you like criticism, and as if I wasn't supporting you?

Client: Yes, it really did. It felt as if you thought I was stupid.

Therapist: That must have been pretty awful, and I'm sorry you felt like that. But looking at things another way, can you come up with any other reason as to why I might have suggested that PERHAPS (which is what I recall I actually said) it wasn't a good idea to give up your job and try to find something else **at this particular time**?

Client: No. Are you saying there really was another one?

Therapist: Well, yes. I've found that many times, when someone makes major life decisions while they're caught up in a major depression like you are, they often regret it later. I've seen it's just so hard to look at things objectively at times like this. On the other hand, I certainly think we need to explore your unhappiness with your job. And coming to think of it, I probably didn't ask you enough about that. Would you like to tell me more about that now?

That exchange seems to work out pretty well, doesn't it? The therapist listens carefully to the client's concerns, acknowledges having failed to adequately explore the particular issue, and demonstrates an interest in doing so. If your therapist responds to you in this manner, it's likely to be helpful if you stick with the therapy, and the therapist, for a little longer, to see whether the relationship can become more productive.

Sometimes therapists can have their own problems, and they don't respond very well to clients' concerns. Here's an example:

Client: I need to talk to you about something.

Therapist: Sure, what is it?

Client: I've been feeling like I can't be honest with you because I'm afraid you'll be critical.

Therapist: Well, I certainly don't think I've ever criticised you. What on earth's given you that idea?

Client: Well, last week I told you about my plans to look for another job, and you said I shouldn't do it.

Therapist: That's exactly what I said! But it's because you're really in no condition to be looking around for anything else. You're far too depressed to do something like that. And you really thought I was criticising you?

Client: Yes, I did. It felt like you thought I was stupid.

Therapist: But that's ridiculous! You're obviously feeling completely defensive. We need to work on that.

Client: To be honest, I'm just not feeling heard by you.

Therapist: Well, you're wrong. It's absolutely obvious that I'm clearly listening to you.

In this case, the conversation does less than nothing to repair the strained relationship. The therapist reacts defensively and shows no support, empathy, or connection with the client. If your discussions with your therapist often sound like this one, consider going to another professional.

Consulting a Professional about Antidepressants

The decision about whether to take medication to help overcome your depression is a complex one. In Chapter 15, we review in detail the pros and cons of treating your depression with medication. If you do think you may benefit from antidepressants, or are unsure about this, you need to know who to go and see.

Prescribing professionals

Medically qualified doctors prescribe antidepressant medications. GPs and Psychiatrists prescribe these more frequently than other specialist doctors.

✔ **GPs:** Most people go to their GP as the first port of call when they have what they think might be a medical, emotional, or a mental health problem. Your GP may then refer you to a specialist in a particular area, depending on what they think is likely to be the problem. Talking to your GP about symptoms of depression can be a very good way to start your treatment. GPs are responsible for more than 60 per cent of the prescriptions given for emotional disorders.

If you have told your GP about your depression and she doesn't offer any help, follow up, or onward referral, you may want to consider changing your GP. Remember, you do have the right, as well as the need, to access effective help.

✔ **Psychiatrists:** Psychiatrists receive more extensive training in the biological treatments of depression than any other prescribing group of professionals (see 'Discovering who's who in psychological therapy' earlier in this chapter, for more information.) Psychiatrists regularly see patients with depression and other emotional disorders and have a lot of experience with the tricky side effects and drug interaction issues involved with antidepressant medication.

Professionals who don't prescribe

The majority of mental health professionals aren't licensed to prescribe antidepressant or any other medication, although they may have received some training and education about the use and effects of drugs.,. They include counsellors, physiologists, social workers, occupational therapists, psychotherapists and nurses (see the earlier 'Discovering who's who in psychological therapy' for details of these professionals).

Pharmacists aren't allowed to give you prescription drugs without a doctor's prescription. However, pharmacists can advise you on the purchase of over-the-counter medications and complementary therapies (see Chapter 16), if you have a mild, uncomplicated form of depression (refer to Chapter 2 for more information about the different types of depression).

If you decide to take medication and also receive psychological therapy from another therapist, encourage your therapist to talk to the health care professional who is prescribing your medication. Good communication ensures that both professionals work together and head in the same direction, and that there is nothing conflicting in your treatment that may possibly harm your therapeutic progress.

Part II
Seeing Things More Clearly: Cognitive Therapy

'His last owner was a chronic depressive.'

In this part . . .

Cognitive therapy is the most widely researched approach to the treatment of depression. This research has consistently shown that cognitive therapy alleviates depression as well as, or better than, any other strategy in this book. For most of you who are battling depression, cognitive therapy will be one of your main weapons.

In the chapters that follow, we give you an understanding of the connections between depression and habitual ways of thinking. You can discover how depression distorts thinking. We also provide you with the tools to smooth ruffled thinking. Digging deeper, you can unearth the core beliefs that may be fertilising your depressive thinking. We provide ways to deal with troublesome beliefs. Finally, depression often interferes with memory, so we show you what you can do to manage this problem.

Chapter 5

Uncovering Underlying Thought Processes

Have you ever been caught in a traffic jam? Horrible, right? Some people respond to traffic snarl ups by thumping on the steering wheel and muttering choice obscenities. Others turn up the radio and relax to soothing music. What's the difference? The angry people have angry thoughts: 'I just hate getting stuck in traffic. People today just don't know how to drive! I can't stand being late!' Those who are more laid back have thoughts like, 'No sense in getting upset by things I can't control. I'll get there when I get there. Actually, it's quite nice to get the chance to listen to music.'

The way you think about or interpret events greatly affects the way you feel about them. In this chapter, we discuss the relationship between events and the thoughts and feelings that follow them. We also show you how to keep track of your thoughts and feelings, making you aware of how they influence your life. Then we look at how misperceptions, misjudgements, blame, and negative feelings distort thinking, feeding and deepening depression. And finally, we give you the tools and for dealing with those disturbing distortions to your thinking.

Thinking about Cognitive Therapy

Cognitive therapy, and the later development of cognitive behavioural therapy, are by far the most widely researched psychological treatments for depression. Studies repeatedly show that cognitive therapy lifts depression and reduces relapse.

Cognitive therapy is one of the psychological therapies. All psychological therapies involve working on your own, or with a therapist using psychological techniques to reduce emotional problems. Cognitive therapy primarily uses techniques designed to change your way of thinking, making you feel better.

A major idea underpinning cognitive therapy is the interconnected nature of feelings (which we also refer to as emotions) and thoughts. Thoughts strongly influence feelings, and vice versa. Both play an important role in the development and maintenance of depression.

But the story doesn't end there. Physical factors can also play a role in depression. Factors such as fatigue, illness, and changes in blood chemistry can lower your mood, which, in turn, prepares the ground for the development of depressing thoughts.

For example, Colin tosses and turns through a third night. He's not sure what's causing his recent bout of insomnia, but every time he feels he's about to fall asleep, another part of his body itches, or his position becomes uncomfortable. Colin's day begins with a long rush-hour drive; irritability overtakes his usual calm acceptance. His tiredness worsens his growing worry. He starts to think, 'What's wrong with me? I'm not going to be able to get through another day. I feel awful. I can't focus. I'm going to lose my job.'

Colin's thoughts have begun to spiral downwards. Why? Too many consecutive nights of poor sleep bring on fatigue and accompanying negative thoughts. One good night of sleep just may allow Colin to return to normal. Or not. Sometimes, a physical event can start a train of negative thoughts and feelings that may then hang around for quite a while.

No one knows how to determine which of the three ingredients (feelings, thoughts, or physical factors) triggers depression for any particular person. But the good news is that you can interrupt the cycle of depression in various ways, using cognitive therapy, no matter what started the downward spiral. The goal of cognitive therapy is to help you be fully aware of your negative thinking when it occurs, and then to actively reframe those thoughts into more realistic terms. After you've done so over a period of time, your depression is likely to lift.

Research shows that cognitive therapy can be as effective as medication in treating depression. And, surprising as it may seem, like medication, cognitive therapy too has positive effects on brain chemistry, which is one of the physical ingredients of depression. But therapy doesn't have to be an either/or proposition. Deciding whether one, two or all of the therapy options of medication, cognitive therapy, and behaviour therapy (see Part III for information on behaviour therapy) are right for you is complicated. We discuss the issue of combining medication with psychological therapy in more detail in Chapter 15.

Monitoring Thoughts and Feelings, and Relating Them to Life Events

A core element of cognitive therapy (see the preceding section 'Thinking about Cognitive Therapy') involves increasing your awareness of the links between thoughts, feelings, and events in your life. In this section, we show you how to become aware of your feelings about events and to examine the thoughts that go with them.

Some people genuinely are hardly aware of their feelings. Others have difficulty detecting their thoughts. We help you to recognise and identify feelings, and we explain how to work out what you're thinking. You may think that you already know what your feelings and thoughts are, but they aren't always that obvious. After you've got the hang of clearly identifying feelings and thoughts, you can then see the links between your thoughts, feelings, and the events that lead to them, plus keep track of them using a 'Thought Catcher'.

And once you see how events, thoughts, and feelings interconnect, you can then analyse your thoughts to spot the typical distortions that depression inevitably causes. We show you how in the 'Unearthing Distortions in Thinking' section, later in this chapter.

Feeling comfortably numb

Believe it or not, experiencing a full-blown severe depression but remaining unaware of your sad feelings is actually possible. People sometimes try to suppress, deny, and/or avoid unpleasant feelings. They try to feel better by cutting themselves off from their emotions so that they feel comfortably numb. This strategy makes a certain degree of sense, but the problem is that you can't successfully block out all feeling. Denying and/or suppressing feelings doesn't work, and in the long run, only makes things worse.

Trying to squash your feelings down inside you is like putting a lid on a pressure cooker, and then adding extra weights. To your horror the lid then blows off, and all the contents overflow. Research shows that *denial* and *repression* (conscious or unconscious attempts to avoid thinking about uncomfortable emotions and thoughts) are linked to poor emotional health, whereas expressing feelings improves both your physical and mental health.

When people find that denial and repression don't get rid of unpleasant feelings, they sometimes turn to other strategies, such as immersing themselves in their work, binge eating or even abusing drugs and/or alcohol. (Be warned by the old adage: I tried to drown my sorrows, but they just learned to swim!) Unfortunately, avoiding unpleasant and unwanted feelings by trying to distract yourself through excessive work or by taking drugs or excessive eating and drinking only gives fleeting, temporary relief. In the end, these solutions worsen your difficulties, and you dig yourself deeper into depression's hole. And remember what they say – when you find yourself in a hole, stop digging!

Many people (with and without depression) find it difficult to be aware of their feelings. But even if you often don't know what you're feeling, or others say that you're out of touch with your feelings, you can change all this.

If you start concentrating on your bodily sensations, we think you're likely to find the words to describe what you're feeling. It may take you a little time, but paying attention to what your body's telling you helps you in identifying your feelings, and enables you to move on to the next stage.. This is when you link your feelings to your thoughts, which then prepares you for the important Thought Catcher exercise we describe in the 'Designing your Thought Catcher' section, later in this chapter. You can start becoming aware of your bodily sensations by paying attention to the following:

- ✔ Muscle tension

- ✔ Your breathing (Is it fast, slow, deep, or shallow?)

- ✔ A sense of heaviness in your chest

- ✔ Dizziness

- ✔ Posture (Are you relaxed, rigid, or stiff?)

- ✔ Nausea

- ✔ Feeling that your throat is constricted

- ✔ Discomfort of any type

Put aside five minutes a day to actively focus on all of your bodily sensations. Try to think of words which describe the feelings, and which capture your complete physical and mental state. A few suggestions to start you off might be:

Afraid	Low
Anxious	Melancholic
Apprehensive	Miserable
Despondent	Morose
Disturbed	Nervous
Embarrassed	Obsessed
Frustrated	Sad
Guilty	Shaky

Heavy	Sombre
Inadequate	Tense
Insecure	Worried

Some people are fully aware of just how low and distressed they feel. But though they *feel* all the emotions, if anyone asked them about what they're *thinking* in response to events, they may say, 'Absolutely nothing. My mind's a blank. I just feel terrible.' If this describes you, read the next section.

Exposing underlying thoughts

When first coming across cognitive therapy, some people say with total conviction, 'But I never have any negative thoughts!' If this is your reaction, we believe you and know that you may not hear specific words and sentences running through your mind as do many people. However, when we say 'negative thoughts', we're referring to thoughts in a broader sense. Consider thoughts as your *interpretations* or *perceptions* of the important events in your life. They're the way you see or understand what's happening. Thoughts are the *meanings* you consciously or unconsciously assign to what's going on around you.

 You may not be aware of an actual conversation going on in your head when something happens to you, but people do look for the meaning of events they experience. If you feel a sudden rush of feelings, try asking what event immediately preceded the feelings and then think about your perception or interpretation of the event.

For example, if someone says to you, 'You look amazing,' you may not be aware of any particular thoughts. But ask yourself how you interpreted that event. Did you hear the message as a positive statement about your clothes, or that you look in pretty good shape? Alternatively, was the comment sarcastic, meaning that your outfit is totally wrong for you, or that you sure have gained weight? Or perhaps you heard the statement and thought that the person was merely trying to be polite. Those interpretations are part of your thoughts, and they all result in different feelings about the comment.

You may find these questions useful for helping you identify your thoughts about events:

- ✔ What meaning does the event have for you in your life?
- ✔ What worries you about the event?
- ✔ What implications does it have for your future?
- ✔ What do you think the event may mean about you?
- ✔ What went through your mind as you noticed the event?

Designing your Thought Catcher

You can use the Thought Catcher when you experience troubling feelings. It can help you follow through and understand the connections between your thoughts, feelings, and the events that trigger them. Also, the Thought Catcher can help you become more aware of the types of events that bother you and prepare you to confront and overcome any problematic thoughts.

Start a new page in your notebook, and divide it into three columns. In each column, fill in the following information (see Table 5-1 for a sample):

✔ **Feelings:** Use this first column to write down negative feelings (not thoughts) and rate them on a 1 (very mild) to 100 (extremely severe) scale. People often notice their feelings before anything else, even though thoughts have usually preceded the feelings, so focus first on what you're feeling. Sometimes you notice yourself experiencing more than one feeling. Record all the unpleasant feelings - they are the key to what depression is all about.

✔ **Events:** Use the second column to write down the event that preceded or triggered the feeling. Such events are usually things that happen to a person, but sometimes they involve a daydream or image that floats into the mind. If you notice the event before you become aware of the feeling, feel free to fill out the event first. But events do precede feelings. So if you become aware of any feelings, stop and ask yourself what happened just before. Only occasionally is the feeling going to emerge more than half an hour after the event. In most cases, the feeling arises almost immediately.

When writing down the event, try to be as specific as possible: Include where you were, who was there, and what happened.

✔ **Negative Automatic Thoughts (NATS):** Use the third column to record the thoughts or interpretations you have about the event – , your understanding of what happened. These thoughts generally occur automatically without careful, conscious reflection, and are usually negative in some way, which is why they are called Negative Automatic Thoughts. Be sure to take time and reflect on the whole range of reactions and interpretations you have.

Sometimes you'll have slightly different thoughts relating to different feelings, but which all stem from the same event. Look at the thoughts you have that relate to each feeling. For example, if you recently got promoted and your new boss asks you to immediately complete and deliver the report you've been painstakingly working on, you may have feelings of both anxiety and despair. The anxiety-related thoughts may centre on concerns of being told off if you don't finish on time, and despair-related thoughts may focus on the belief that you're overwhelmingly inadequate to handle the new promotion.

Polar bears and negative thoughts

When you hear that negative thinking increases negative emotions, you might think there's a really simple answer – just stop thinking negatively! In other words, just banish any negative thoughts from your mind the moment you detect them. You're cured! If only it were that simple . . .

Back in 1863, Dostoevsky wrote: 'Try to pose for yourself this task: not to think of a polar bear, and you will see that the cursed thing will come to mind every minute.' And now psychologists carry out research looking at attempts to do just that – to suppress thoughts of white bears, amongst other subjects.

Daniel Wegner of Harvard University reviewed 20 years of research on thought suppression.

His conclusion was that overall, suppressing unwanted thoughts doesn't work. Even worse, attempting to do so assures that you're going to end up experiencing the very thoughts you were trying to avoid in the first place, and to a greater extent than if you hadn't tried to suppress them at all.

You may think that cognitive therapy recommends thought suppression, because one of its goals is to help you think in less distorted, negative ways. But we urge you not to attempt to wipe out negative thoughts by attempting to suppress them. Instead, figure out how to use the skills we provide you with for developing new thinking habits – we believe you're going to find it's worth the effort.

Here's an example of how the Thought Catcher works. Gita is a software engineer. She's a bit of a perfectionist, which adds further stress to her already highly demanding job. When one of the computer programs she's working on repeatedly crashes, Gita too crashes. She can't sleep; she can't eat; and thoughts of suicide enter her mind. Gita confides her despair to a close friend who strongly urges her to see a therapist. Gita protests at first, but her friend insists.

Her therapist suggests that Gita constructs a Thought Catcher, allowing her to catch her thoughts whenever she finds herself feeling down. Take a look at Table 5-1 to see what Gita comes up with.

Table 5-1	**Gita's Thought Catcher**	
Feelings (0 to 100)	*Events*	*Negative Automatic Thoughts (or Interpretations)*
Despair (80)	The computer programme(?) EIF I'm working on crashed again.	My boss is going to find out that I don't know what I'm doing and fire me.
Helplessness (95)		
		I'm never going to be able to solve this.

You can see how Gita's thoughts contribute to her low feelings and overall depression. We suggest you fill out a Thought Catcher for about a week. Try to catch in your net at least one or two problematic events each day. After finishing this task, you're ready to tackle the thoughts that lead to your depression.

Unearthing Distortions in Thinking

Cognitive therapy uses the well-established idea that certain thoughts you have in response to events lead to depressed feelings (see the previous section 'Monitoring Thoughts and Feelings, and Relating Them to Life Events'). Now we show you that those thoughts are almost always distorted. By *distorted*, we mean that these thoughts don't accurately reflect, predict, or describe events. In this section, we help you analyse your thoughts in order to identify these distortions. In doing so, you can start clearing your vision and see your world in more accurate terms.

By asking you to examine your thoughts and to look for various types of distortions, we are *not* trying to get you to rationalise away everything bad that happens to you. The goal of cognitive therapy is to show you how to identify, reflect upon, and weigh up your distorted thoughts in order to later rework them in such a way that they match reality (see Chapter 6 for information on developing accurate, replacement thoughts). When reality is really awful, we don't expect or want you to deny that fact. Rather, we want you to cope when events turn out contrary to your hopes.

You may find it helpful to know that people with depression aren't the only ones to have distorted thinking. Every person has, at times, significantly distorted thoughts. Depression merely makes these distortions more frequent and intense. Even those who aren't especially depressed can probably benefit from using our strategies for reducing such distortions. And if you're depressed, discovering new ways of thinking may lead to a far happier life.

If you find yourself objecting to the content of this chapter because what we say sounds oversimplified, or even seems to undervalue the importance of your feelings, please read (or reread) Chapter 3, which talks about common barriers to change, as well as uncovering many of the myths about therapy. The depressed mind may well resist hearing some of the information that follows. If you're depressed, do nonetheless have a go at reading this material, and please take your time before forming conclusions.

We group the various types of thought distortions into four main categories. In the following sections, we discuss each of these types of distortions and show you how they can shape your perceptions of reality as easily as a child can turn a harmless shadow into a wardrobe monster.

Following misleading misperceptions

Distorting reality involves twisting reality in ways that make events look as bleak as you feel. The human mind distorts incoming information in an endless variety of ways. And the depressed mind blows up these distortions to the point that misperceptions masquerade as reality, yet manage only to convey a muddled mass of misinformation. In this section we discuss the most common types of reality distortions. We then use a Thought Catcher (see 'Designing your Thought Catcher', earlier in this chapter) to show you examples of how these distortions join up to deepen depression. Understanding how these distortions operate can start the process of more accurate thinking.

The mind's seven misleading misperceptions

Everyone distorts reality from time to time. Depressed people just do it more often and to a greater depth, and they find the distortions more credible. In the following list, we review common ways in which your mind can distort reality. See if you can recognise any of the following tricks your mind has tried to play on you.

- ✔ **Maximising and minimising:** Your mind uses this distortion to *catastrophise*, or magnify, the importance or 'awfulness' of unpleasant events. This distortion of maximising is also known as *catastrophising*. In a similar fashion, the mind minimises the value and importance of anything positive about yourself, your world, or your future.

- ✔ **Filtering:** The depressed mind typically focuses on any dismal, dark data while screening out more positive information. The not-too-surprising result? Both the world, and even you, appear miserable and hopeless.

- ✔ **Seeing in black and white, all-or-nothing terms:** This distortion puts everything – you, other people, and even events – into stark terms, with no shades of grey. Thus, a single poor performance is taken to mean complete and utter inadequacy. The problem with polarised thinking is that it sets you up for inevitably experiencing a sense of total failure, disappointment, and self-criticism. All-or-none thinking imposes standards that absolutely no one can ever achieve.

- ✔ **Dismissing evidence:** This distortion looks at evidence that may contradict the mind's negative thoughts and dismisses that evidence as not allowable and/or completely irrelevant. For example, suppose you have the thought that you're a failure. Then your boss says that you've earned a promotion for your performance. Your mind may quickly decide that the promotion was both undeserved and meaningless, and that your failure runs much deeper than mere job performance. This misperception is rather like being accused of a crime, and then having the judge throw out as irrelevant every single piece of evidence that proves your innocence. Bet you can guess the verdict. In this case, it's your own mind that throws out the evidence and determines the verdict.

- **Discarding positives:** Similar to dismissing evidence, minimising the positive is a distortion the mind uses to trivialise successes, good outcomes, and positive personal attributes and achievements. So if you're successful in your audition for the lead in a play, you decide that this has to be because the drama group is so desperate and of such a poor standard that they welcome with open arms anyone with minimal talent!

- **Overgeneralising:** This involves looking at a single, unpleasant occurrence and deciding it represents the way things are, and are always going to be. Thus, if you drop your fork on the floor, your mind tells you that you're a clumsy clot who's *always* dropping things. Words like *always* and *never* are tip-offs to this reality distortion.

- **Mind-reading:** Mind-reading occurs whenever you assume, often with unshakable conviction, that you *know* what others are thinking, without checking it out. Thus, someone may not ask out a new acquaintance because, 'I just know she wouldn't go out with someone like me.'

Adding reality distortions to your Thought Catcher

A good way of discovering if your thoughts about events that are happening to you are distorted is to add a fourth column to your Thought Catcher (see the 'Designing your Thought Catcher' section, earlier in the chapter). Label that column 'Reality Distortions' (see Table 5-2 for an example). Examine your thoughts about events carefully and ask yourself which reality distortions apply. You may be surprised to see how often your thoughts lead you astray.

Brandon's story illustrates how reality distortions influence his thoughts and intensify his negative feelings. Brandon works as a supervisor for the local borough transport department. He arrives home from work one day to find a note from his wife saying that she's gone, and has taken the kids with her. The note says that she's had enough of his long work hours, and she plans to find happiness with someone else. Brandon's grief (go to Chapters 2 and 13 for more information about grief) fails to lift, and he slowly sinks into a deep depression over the following year. At this point, Brandon's manager refers him to Occupational Health, who refer him to see a psychologist for help, given his evident distress and the impact this is having on his work.

Brandon's psychologist quickly diagnoses a major depressive disorder (refer to Chapter 2 for more information about major depressive disorders) and decides that cognitive therapy can help. First, as part of this therapy, the psychologist discusses the types of reality distortions that the mind often uses (see the previous section 'The mind's seven misleading misperceptions'). Brandon isn't convinced that he distorts anything in his life, but he agrees to explore the possibility.

Next, the psychologist helps Brandon design his Thought Catcher, so that he can see how he looks at events. Brandon then adds a fourth column to see if he's distorting his reality. Table 5-2 shows what Brandon discovered, somewhat to his surprise, after filling out his Thought Catcher for a few days.

Table 5-2	Brandon's Thought Catcher		
Feelings (0 to 100)	*Events*	*Negative Automatic Thoughts (or Interpretations)*	*Reality Distortions*
Fear (75) Despair (80)	The bus drivers say they are going on strike. The drivers' representative said if it weren't for me, they would have done this long ago.	I'm going to lose my job if the strike lasts more than a couple of weeks, and then I'm likely lose my home. I can't imagine anyone else employing me. I've got minimal formal qualifications, so I'm never going to find another job. I bet the drivers' rep is lying; he probably thinks the strike is my fault for not keeping the drivers happier.	Maximising Overgeneralising Mind-reading Discarding positives Filtering
Upset (78)	My cheque bounced.	I'm making a mess of everything lately. My credit rating's at risk: I'm never going to be able to take out a loan when I need one.	Overgeneralising Enlarging Black and white
Apprehensive (35)	I got an excellent annual performance review.	My manager is just trying to butter me up. He wants me to do longer hours, and I just can't. Next time, I'll probably get a lousy review, unless I agree.	Dismissing evidence Discarding positives Mind-reading

Do you see in Table 5-2 how consistently Brandon's depressed mind distorts his thoughts or interpretations of the things that happen to him? Time and again, his mind maximises the meaning of negative events and also puts them into black and white terms. Even positive events are filtered out or dismissed. Is it any wonder that he ends up feeling fear, despair, sadness, and apprehension?

Notice that Brandon's reaction to the first event contains five types of reality distortions. For example, when he says he 'is going to ' lose his job and his home, and that no one is ever going to employ him again, he's engaging in negative automatic thinking without reflecting on the true probabilities. He's *maximising* with the unquestioned assumption that the strike is likely to continue to the point that he's going to lose both his job and home. He's *overgeneralising* when he decides that if he loses his current job, he's never going to find another. How does the fact that a person loses one job mean that they're **never** going to get another? He's *mind-reading* as well as *discarding positives* when he concludes that the representative is lying to him. Also, he's *filtering* out the positive message from the representative and focusing on imagined negative catastrophes.

Perhaps you're wondering if, just possibly, Brandon's thoughts are *not* actually distortions of reality. For example, perhaps he really is going to lose his job, and maybe the drivers' representative does believe that it's all Brandon's fault for not keeping the drivers happy. Possible? Yes. Of course. However, you can spot that Brandon is more likely to be distorting reality because he doesn't use qualifiers, such as 'possibly', 'maybe', or 'perhaps'. He also doesn't consider other factors, such as how likely it is that his negative assumptions are reality, versus other possible outcomes.

Have a go on a fresh page in your notebook. Divide the page into four columns and as many rows as you need. Start identifying your feelings and see whether you can connect them to the events in your life and the interpretations you make of those events. Then look very closely at those thoughts. Find out if your mind is distorting the meanings of the various daily events.

If you find it easy to spot these reality distortions, you're one step ahead of the game. You're probably going to start noticing doubt creeping into the certainty of your depressed mind's negative automatic thoughts and interpretation of events. It's not a big leap to go from seeing that those interpretations may contain distortions to realising that an alternative, less depressing view of the world may actually be more valid, and may make you feel better. That's the purpose of looking for distortions in thoughts – doing so starts to shake the hold that your depressed mind has on your thinking. (We show you many other ways to actively identify and modify distortions in your thoughts in Chapter 6.)

Table 5-3 contains three more examples of events and sample thoughts (or interpretations), plus the feelings about these events. It also has space for you to think about possible reality distortions embedded in those thoughts. See if you can work out which distortions apply. After you fill in the reality distortions column, have a look at the correct answers provided.

Table 5-3	Practise Finding Reality Distortions		
Feelings (0 to 100)	*Events*	*Negative Automatic Thoughts (or Interpretations)*	*Reality Distortions*
Anger (55) Sadness (70)	You arrive home an hour late from work and your husband says, 'Darling, I was worried about you. What happened?'	He's just paranoid that I'm having an affair. He's always so suspicious! Maybe he wants me to have an affair, so that he has grounds for divorce. After all, with my depression, I haven't been such a great wife lately.	
Anxiety (50)	You're a co-author of *Overcoming Depression For Dummies,* and your project editor tells you that he really likes the first submission and reminds you the next section is due in two weeks. But you're running late.	I'm never going to get this in on time. And if I don't get my part finished, my co-authors will be furious. The editor's bound to get fed up. We might even lose the contract. It won't matter if they liked the first part if the second section's a few days late.	
Despair (65)	You ask someone out for a date. She tells you, 'Sorry, I'm busy that night. Perhaps some other time?'	Obviously, she thinks I'm a loser. She's just being polite when she says 'perhaps some other time.' I'm never going to find someone to go out with. What's wrong with me?	

Now, here are the distortions described in Table 5-3:

- **Event 1, arriving late:** Maximising, overgeneralising, mind-reading, filtering

- **Event 2, late submission of work:** Maximising, filtering, discarding positives, overgeneralising, mind-reading

- **Event 3, turned down for a date:** Maximising, mind-reading, filtering, overgeneralising, black and white

Making misjudgements

The depressed mind acquires a nasty habit of making harsh, critical judgements about almost anything you do, thus deepening depression with each fault-finding episode. We can't remember the last time we worked with a seriously depressed client who didn't display harsh self-criticism. The self-critical judgements then means many people feel guilty for being whatever it is they've just called themselves. Thus, the fact that guilt is an important symptom of major depression is no coincidence. Even people who have little or no depression often judge themselves more negatively than needed. But those with depression sometimes walk around as though they have a scarlet 'G' for *guilty* tattooed on their foreheads.

The 'making misjudgements' type of thought distortion comes in three forms:

- Musts, oughts, and shoulds

- Unfair comparisons

- Self-labels

Like the reality distortions we mention in the earlier section 'Misleading misperceptions', all three of these distortions occur instantly, automatically, and without careful consideration of reality. In the following sections you can find detailed information on each type of misjudgement, and how it leads to unpleasant feelings. When you become aware of how frequently you use 'shoulds', unfair comparisons, and self-labels, you're likely to use them less often – and feel better as a result.

Examining musts, oughts, and shoulds

One of the founding fathers of cognitive therapy, psychologist Dr Albert Ellis (1913–2007), invented the the term 'musturbation'. When we *musturbate* we mentally beat ourselves up with loads of 'musts', 'oughts' and 'shoulds' bringing intense pressure on ourselves to perform. It's as if you're *forcing* yourself to do the tasks. The problem with this is that when you, or others, try to exert force and pressure for something to happen, then, as is written in the Laws of Physics – the opposite happens. One of the key Laws of Physics is that every action has an equal and opposite reaction. And so you end up sabotaging yourself in two ways – first, you don't do the tasks that are really for your own good. Second, you beat yourself up for not doing them.

Inappropriate must, ought, or should statements are guaranteed routes to guilt. These irrational statements imply you're expected to be perfect, all-knowing, and all-powerful – which, of course, you aren't. If you think that people don't use these words a great deal, try really listening to what others say. Tune in and notice whenever you hear any of these words. Some people use them continually. The problem's not only that the depressed mind use these three words frequently, but it takes them very seriously indeed.

What's so awful about *musts, oughts,* and *shoulds?* Nothing really, if you only mean *must* in the sense of *I would like to,* and *ought* as in it would be good if I could, and *should* in the sense of conveying an expectation of what's to come, such as, *The package should arrive today.* But when you use the words in a threatening way and then judge how you are behaving the words can result in high levels of self-criticism.

Start tracking your 'musturbations' today. See if you can use other terms such as 'I'd rather,' 'I want to,' 'it would be better if,' and 'I'd like to.' See the following examples for ideas:

>   **Must statement:** I *must* get down to those Dummies exercises.
>
>   **Alternative statement:** It would be good if I schedule in a time to do the exercises later today.
>
>   **Ought statement:** I *ought to* visit my grandmother.
>
>   **Alternative statement:** It would be a good deed to visit my grandmother.
>
>   **Should statement:** I *should* have done a better job on that project.
>
>   **Alternative statement:** I *would like to have done* a better job on that project.

Another approach to 'shoulds' is to ask yourself where you've seen it written that you *should or shouldn't* do this or that. Is the rule one you've made up for yourself? And if so, is it written somewhere in stone? If not, think about rewriting the rule. Finally, ask yourself if 'should-ing on yourself' (from a great height) helps you or just makes you feel bad. Keep in mind, as we note earlier in this section, that guilt and shame do little to motivate positive behaviour, especially when used to excess.

Conjuring unfair comparisons

Comparing yourself to others in unfair or inappropriate ways is a pretty good way of making yourself really depressed! Many people make such comparisons with alarming frequency and without much thought. Their feelings of personal worth slowly disintegrate each time they put themselves down and compare themselves negatively with someone else. Do any of these sound familiar to you?

- You have a friend who's more successful financially than you are. Therefore, you decide that you're a failure.

- You're a student, and you receive an A– for an exam, but you belittle your performance because a few others got an A Star grade.

- You don't go out on as many dates as a few of your friends, so you decide that you're undesirable.

- You're a teenager who isn't as popular as some of your friends, so you assume that you're a total reject.

- You're a successful writer of self-help books, but a friend of yours writes a *Sunday Times* bestseller, so you decide that your writing isn't worth the paper it's written on.

- You're overweight, and you have friends who are positive stick insects, so you decide that you're a fat pig with no self-control.

- Your neighbour buys a new 60-inch plasma TV, so you think of yourself as inadequate and deprived because you can't afford one.

This list contains great ways of beating yourself up! But you may wonder how such comparisons distort reality. After all, in each case, one or more people are in a different place to you on the ladder of 'success' for a given action or personal quality. But the distortion doesn't lie in noticing that some are doing better than you. That fact is true and absolutely fine, as far as it goes. The problem arises from the self-destructive conclusion that if you don't equal or surpass others, you, *as a consequence*, amount to nothing. The issue is similar to all-or-nothing, black and white thinking we discuss earlier in this chapter in the section 'The mind's seven misleading misperceptions'.

Further distortion occurs when these comparisons focus on one single factor that the other person has, which you don't have. The comparison zooms in on that one isolated issue, and ignores the bigger picture. For example:

- The highly successful friend also happens to overwork himself to the point that he feels miserable and utterly shattered.

- Your extremely slim friends don't have your level of energy, and one has some pretty serious health problems linked to an eating disorder.

- The neighbour with the new, expensive TV happens to have huge credit card debts.

If you focus on a single issue, you can always find someone you know who has more, or is doing better than you. For example, we, the authors, have no doubt that none of us has a sole quality, trait, success, or achievement that someone else couldn't improve upon. Whether we look at our intelligence, personality, writing, appearance, income, or any accomplishments, certainly we'd have no trouble finding others in the world who rank higher. If we compare ourselves on each quality, we can quickly dig ourselves into a black hole by turning these comparisons into personal failure.

When you find you're comparing yourself to others, try doing the following:

- ✔ Tell yourself that focusing on single issues where others do better is a waste of time and only saps any remaining feelings of self-worth. Instead, look at ways of appreciating both your strengths and weaknesses.

- ✔ Don't just compare yourself to the top. Look at the whole picture. How do you rate against the middle, or even the bottom of a normal distribution?

- ✔ Allow yourself to accept average, normal, and even less-than-average qualities as part of your self-perception. All people have certain qualities that lie in each range.

If you struggling with the preceding suggestions, we suggest that you read about the destructive influence of certain core beliefs in Chapter 7. The *perfectionist belief*, which we discuss in that chapter, may lie behind your difficulty. Work on the idea that 'good enough' IS good enough!

Giving yourself loathsome labels

The final distorted method for making misjudgements involves finding a particularly obnoxious label to apply to yourself, such as *disgusting*, *pathetic*, *idiot*, *pig*, *clod*, *misfit*, *freak*, *oaf*, *twit*, and so on. And don't make the mistake of thinking these labels have no consequence. The old adage 'Sticks and stones may break my bones, but words can never hurt me' sounds great, but it isn't true. People frequently do use words that hurt themselves, and others. What do you say to yourself when you stumble, trip, or drop something? Do you call yourself an idiot, or a clumsy clod? Labels like these eat away at your sense of self-worth. And low self-worth is a symptom of depression (refer to Chapter 2 for more information about symptoms of depression). In the following example, Aaron uses many negative self-labels and feels rather horrid as a result.

Aaron works as a DJ at a popular radio station. People readily recognise him and he's in demand for gigs. But Aaron doesn't feel particularly notable, special, or accomplished. He's a lifelong perfectionist who tells himself off for every mistake. A single mispronunciation, and he calls himself a fool. If he inadvertently says something that a few listeners find offensive, he thinks he's a total idiot.

Labels like imposter, *freak*, *monster*, *a nobody*, and *fool* regularly run through Aaron's mind. His self-worth is so low that he believes his audience is only temporarily fooled; and that in the not-so-distant future they're all going to go off him. Thus, he turns down a higher paid job a big city because he's absolutely positive that the more sophisticated city listeners will see right through him and know what a fraud he really is.

If you're a bit like Aaron, start noting down your self-labels. See how often you apply them to yourself in response to mistakes, failures, and even quirks. We call this tool the 'Label Substitution Strategy'. In your notebook, write down the event in one column and the label you attach to yourself in the next column. Then in the third column try substituting an alternative phrase. By doing so, you can start to see yourself more realistically and stop the pain that's brought on by negative self-labels. See Table 5-4 for examples of replacing your labels.

Table 5-4	Label Substitution Strategy	
Event	*Label*	*Label Substitution Thought*
You've put on a few pounds.	I'm a *pig!*	Okay, I gained a few pounds. So what? I can always do something about it if I choose.
You were involved in a car accident.	I'm a *lousy driver.*	Well, it actually was my fault. I guess I'm going to have to try and concentrate more. Statistics do say this happens to most people at one time or another in their lives.
You didn't get the hoped for promotion.	I'm a complete and utter *failure.*	Although I didn't get the promotion, I've had plenty of other success. I guess I have to find out how to take the good with the bad.
You got turned down for a date.	I'm not in the least bit fit or attractive. I'm a waste of space.	So one person said 'no'. How does this make me a freak? If I'm going to succeed in the long run, I've got to expect some rejections.

Self-labels may run through your mind so often that you can't possibly catch them all. If so, don't worry. Just write down the ones that particularly grab your attention and see if you can substitute other thoughts. If you find this exercise difficult, you may want to read Chapter 6 and return to this exercise at a later date.

Assigning blame to the wrong source

Another type of thought distortion involves blaming the wrong source(s) for your problems. This distortion can take one of two forms:

- Most often, people with depression *personalise* problems – they blame themselves entirely for their current plight.

- Alternatively, some people place blame for all their problems on others, thereby disowning any responsibility for making changes in their lives.

Try examining all the possible causes of your particular problem and dividing the responsibility in a reasonable, fair manner. You can only do work on the part of the problem that you own – the part that you're actually responsible for.

Rosemary tells her psychologist that her son is having big problems with his behaviour at school. Rosemary's conclusion? She's a *bad mother*, full stop. As well as using a global self-label (see the earlier section 'Giving yourself loathsome labels'), Rosemary personalises the entire problem. She believes that her poor parenting totally causes her son's behaviour.

The psychologist asks Rosemary to list all the possible causes for her son's misbehaviour. With some thought, she realises that Lionel's father has a lot to do with how Lionel is behaving, and also that the school is failing to set limits for Lionel. Also, her son is hanging out with the wrong crowd at school.

Then Rosemary's psychologist asks her to consider what overall proportion of the problem she may have responsibility for, and to think of any specific things she's done within her son's upbringing. Rosemary discovers she can divide up the responsibility for her son's behaviour , so only some of it is attributed to her, whole other parts are re-attributed to others. Her task is to take action on the bits that she attributes to herself. The psychologist asks her to think about what she can do with the part of the problem which she owns, and for which she's responsible. We call this 'Responsibility Re-allocation and Action'.

Responsibility re-allocation and action enables you to avoid immersing yourself in guilt and self-blame. It allows you to take responsibility for *your* part of the problem, and you do what you can with it. If it involves something that's over and done with, then you can recognise that no action is needed or possible. But you can try to let go of the guilt, because feeling guilty will lead you nowhere.

To put it into practice, turn to a new sheet of paper in your notebook and draw columns for listing all the contributors to your problem, the percentage of the problem that's truly your responsibility, your role in the development of your problem, and any specific actions you can now take to reduce your problem. When you complete this exercise, you're likely to understand that you're not totally responsible for your problem and you can hopefully forgive yourself more easily. And you can develop ideas for what you can do about your problem for the future.

Table 5-5 shows what Rosemary comes up with after doing this task.

Table 5-5   Rosemary's Responsibility Reallocation and Action

Problem: Lionel's Behaviour

Contributors	Percentage I Own	My Specific Role	Specific Actions I Can Take
Peers, school, father, myself (mother), biology and genetics, neighbour-hood, TV, wider culture, random events, Lionel himself (he is 15 years old after all)	Realistically, I think I own about 20 per cent of Lionel's problem. His father is far too critical, which I reckon is a serious contribution. But 20 per cent, I have to own.	I overcompensated for the strictness of his father by being way too soft. As a result, I let Lionel get away with far too much.	1. We can go to family therapy and work out the differences in our parenting styles.

2. I can read, 'Why Can't I Be the Parent I Want to Be?' by Laura Smith and Charles Elliott.

3. I can start setting firm limits with Lionel. |

Getting enslaved by emotions and fooled by feelings

Most people with depression have endless negative thoughts about events. The mind then uses the accompanying emotions as cues or evidence for supporting the truth of those thoughts. The reasoning goes something like this:

✔ I've done something wrong. I feel guilty. Because I *feel* guilty, I decide that I must have done something wrong.

✔ There's something the matter with me. I *feel* ashamed, so there must be something peculiar about me.

✔ I'm hopeless. Because I *feel* so horribly hopeless, I must be a really hopeless case.

✔ I can't do anything if I don't feel like doing it, and if I'm just not in the mood!

The problem is that feelings all too often occur in response to distorted views of events. So the very feeling that you're using as a way of proving your thought probably arose in connection with a negative or distorted thought in the first place.

Feelings are *not* facts.

If everyone suffering from depression relied on following their feelings, few are ever going to improve even with therapy. If you're depressed, you most likely don't feel like putting energy into doing anything about it, because you have so little energy to start with. And if you listen uncritically to feelings of hopelessness (refer to Chapter 3), you're probably going to conclude that you have no reason to improve your lot.

Don't get us wrong; feelings and emotions are important. Positive feelings give you information about what you like and don't like. Negative emotions can alert you to danger and help you in recognising that something isn't right in your life. Feelings are what make us human. We value and respect feelings. Much of the intention of this book is to help you find ways of feeling better.

However, we suggest that you resist using feelings as though they're facts. Dr David Burns, a psychiatrist, calls the temptation to view feelings as facts, 'emotional reasoning'. He also notes that a common example of such flawed reasoning is to determine your personal worth based on feelings. Thus, if you *feel* awful, you decide that you must *be* awful. But what if you feel really wonderful? Does that actually mean that you *are* wonderful, or merely that you're feeling pretty darn good.

Start exploring your use of emotional reasoning. Become aware of times when your mind tells you to avoid doing something merely because you don't *feel* like it. Ask yourself if you've felt that way in the past, but successfully pushed through the feeling anyway. Did you end up feeling better when you pushed through, or when you gave into the feeling?

Also, take a look at Chapter 6 for information on how to answer back to distorted thoughts and the feelings they cause. As you see how many ways these distortions lead to unpleasant feelings, you're likely to understand that feelings sure don't equal facts.

Don't think that we're saying all negative feelings are wrong, and all positive feelings are right, and to be blown up at every opportunity. If that's the case you may easily find yourself eating loads of fattening foods and consuming drugs and alcohol in copious quantities, simply because they feel good! What we mean is that if you allow yourself to be ruled and dominated by feelings, your vision of reality and of yourself can be blocked out.

Chapter 6

Dispersing the Dark Clouds of Depressive Thinking

....

In This Chapter

▶ Tracking events, thoughts, and feelings

▶ Dealing with your thinking

▶ Weighing the evidence

▶ Designing alternative thoughts

▶ Investigating your thought repair toolkit

....

*Y*ou need skills to defeat your depression. You can start with the Thought Catcher we describe in Chapter 5. In this chapter, we build on the Thought Catcher, by explaining how you can examine your thoughts and perceptions using objective evidence. You can then use this new, more accurate evidence to create alternative constructive thoughts. And as well, we provide you with a well-stocked toolkit for repairing distorted thoughts, so that you can fix things and make yourself feel better.

After six months of thoroughly enjoyable retirement, George's golf handicap has decreased by three strokes. He swings his number nine iron and grins as the ball flies down the fairway. He resists renting a golf-cart; walking the course is part of his exercise routine. But today, he notices an uncomfortable tightness in his chest, and then he feels nauseous and begins to sweat. He's suddenly dizzy, and pain radiates from his chest down his right arm. He collapses on the grass.

Five weeks later, after successful heart bypass surgery, George sits at home. Feeling depressed and hopeless, he believes that life is never going to be the same. He can't imagine ever being able to play golf again. His retirement is going be one of further illness, misery, and ever-increasing boredom.

His doctor refers him for a rehabilitation programme at the hospital's physio-therapy gym, and predicts that George is going to be out on the golf course in just a few months. George cancels his rehabilitation appointments. He barely finds the energy to get dressed in the morning, let alone go to the gym. His dreams destroyed, George is nonetheless shocked when he finds himself contemplating suicide.

George experienced a triggering event (his heart attack) that set off a whole host of negative, even catastrophic, predictions about his future health and retirement. Unquestioningly following those thoughts led him directly into depression. However, the good news is that he can restructure his thoughts in ways that will make him feel better. He just needs to practise the series of skills we discuss in this chapter.

You need skills to defeat your depression. You can start with the Thought Catcher we describe in Chapter 5. In this chapter, we build on the Thought Catcher, by explaining how you can examine your thoughts and perceptions using objective evidence. You can then use this new, more accurate evidence to create alternative constructive thoughts. And as well, we provide you with a well-stocked toolkit for repairing distorted thoughts, so that you can fix things and make yourself feel better.

Taking Your Thoughts to Task

As we mention at the start of this chapter, the investigation of depressive thinking begins in Chapter 5 where we show you how to identify thoughts, emotions, and events relating to depression using a Thought Catcher. This allows you to record the events that trigger your emotions and explore the interpretations, or *thoughts*, you have about those events. This tool provides illustrations through various examples of how feelings naturally result from your thoughts. In Chapter 5, we also show you how thoughts can seriously distort reality.

Now, we take the Thought Catcher an important step further and show you how to put your depressive thoughts on trial through a process we call 'Taking your Thoughts to Task'. The purpose of this process (which is also known as *cognitive restructuring*) is to restructure your thoughts and create accurate, believable alternatives. Although the idea of 'Taking Your Thoughts to Task' may appear to be a lighthearted concept being used to describe the restructuring process, keep in mind that the strategy is both serious and powerful.

We suggest that you use the 'Taking your Thoughts to Task' strategy frequently, regularly, and persistently. The good news is that you don't have to spend huge amounts of time on the task. Devoting 10 to 20 minutes, 4 or 5 times a week, is going to give a noticeable boost to your mood within 8 to 12 weeks. And after your mood starts to lift, we suggest that you continue the work for at least another 8 weeks or so to ensure that your new ways of thinking have plenty of practice. As you become more skilled and find it easier, you're likely to discover that you're automatically monitoring all your thoughts, and putting the potentially negative ones to the test for accuracy.

Introducing the restructuring process

Here's a brief summary of the 'Taking Your Thoughts to Task' process for you to review. We give you the complete rundown in the sections that follow.

1. **Catching negative thoughts:** This part of 'Taking Your Thoughts to Task' is made up of using a Thought Catcher to record all your thoughts, interpretations, or perceptions of the event that triggered your multitude of difficult feelings. You also rate the severity of the resulting feelings. (Go to Chapter 5 for more details about filling out a Thought Catcher.)

2. **Putting the thought on trial:** This step involves gathering evidence so that you can prosecute and defend the truthfulness of your thought. We ask you to carefully examine your thoughts and weigh up the evidence to decide if you should hold onto your thoughts because you judge them to be valid, or give them a life sentence because you decide that they aren't valid and are guilty of making you feel unnecessarily depressed.

3. **Coming up with constructive alternative thoughts:** You take this step if you find the evidence shows that the thought isn't valid. You develop an alternative thought that seems believable, but that isn't unrealistically positive. These thoughts often include an element of the original negative thought, but they include credible, positive information as well.

4. **Evaluating your alternative thoughts:** Finally, you test out your restructured, alternative thoughts for a period. It's important to discover if your new alternatives actually feel better than your previous, depressive thoughts. Therefore, this step asks you to rate how you feel when you think of the new thought versus the earlier one.

Persistence is key to 'Taking Your Thoughts to Task', and overcoming negative, depressive thoughts. Practise regularly and keep at it until your feelings of depression start to lift – and then continue practising some more! Be aware that improvements take time. But if things get worse instead of better, consider seeking professional help.

You are likely to get the best results from the 'Taking your Thoughts to Task' techniques by writing everything down. Taking a shortcut by simply following the techniques 'in your head' is a great boost to the work you do on paper, but it *can't* stand alone. Don't underestimate the power of the written word. Writing all the elements down in a notebook helps you utilise the objective part of your mind, which you need for this task. Writing things down increases your chance of both remembering, and even believing them. Also, keeping a written record allows you to regularly review your thought records.

We're not suggesting with the 'Taking your Thoughts to Task' process that negative thoughts and feelings have *no* validity and have to be banished entirely. Before we go any further we need to clear up any possible misconceptions. Consider the following points:

- **Negative thoughts often (though not always) do have a grain of truth.** Acknowledging this truth is important, because denial isn't useful. When things are truly bad and difficult, you're better off finding ways to cope than attempting to rationalise and trying to fool yourself.

- **Sadness isn't the same as depression.** Loss and adversity will make you unhappy, and it's inevitable when such events occur you are going to feel sad. The death of a loved one, loss of a job, severe illness, financial problems, and physical disabilities all present serious challenges and emotional upheaval, and can give rise to profound sadness or even despair.

  Typically, reactions to losses don't cause a deterioration in your basic sense of self-worth, and they do ease over time. It can take a very long time, but the feelings do get better eventually. Refer to Chapter 2 to find out more about the difference between grief and depression.

Catching negative thoughts

It's important to capture any suspiciously negative thought, before you can put it on trial. Think of a time when you felt strong negative feelings such as sadness, despair, guilt, or shame. Where did these feelings begin? A Thought Catcher can tell you by uncovering the links between events, thoughts, and feelings. A Thought Catcher shows you that most of the time, your unpleasant emotions come from the thoughts or interpretations you make in response to events that have happened to you.

To understand the relationship between thoughts, feelings, and events, you need to record your thoughts, plus the events that occurred before them, and also the feelings that followed. Rating the intensity of those feelings in order to find out just how much your thoughts are disturbing you is also a good idea. Refer to Chapter 5 for more information about Thought Catchers and the connections between events, feelings, and thoughts.

Karol's story shows you how to take your thinking to task. We follow Karol throughout this chapter to show you how the process works. First, he identifies his negative thoughts.

Karol, the son of migrant EU workers, wants to train as a teacher in Britain. After successfully completing a teaching assistant's course he commences an access to further education course. His place on a teacher training course at a local university depends on successful completion of this course.

Initial euphoria at the start of the course rapidly gives way to low mood and he reluctantly seeks help after feeling seriously depressed for a month. He isn't sure how his depression started, but he feels it's affecting his sleep, energy, interests, and concentration. He's starting to be late for classes and is given a verbal warning that his place on the course may be terminated after he hands in his first assignment late. At the strong urging of one of his friends, Karol arranges an appointment with the college student counsellor. The counsellor uses a cognitive behavioural therapy approach, as advocated by government guidelines. It has the longest and best established track record for treating depression, and also helps prevent relapse.

The counsellor asks Karol to start noticing the times when he feels especially sad, depressed, and/or upset. Then he asks him to record these feelings on a Thought Catcher that he gives to Karol. After Karol completes the form, the therapist suggests that Karol underlines the most troubling, upsetting thought – the one that stirs up the most difficult emotions. Table 6-1 shows one of Karol's records.

Table 6-1	Karol's Thought Catcher	
Feelings (0 to 100)	*Events*	*Negative Thoughts (or Interpretations)*
Shame (90) Guilt (80) Despair (85)	I handed in my first assignment late and the lecturer threatened to chuck me off the course in front of the whole class. My parents are working so hard to pay for me to train as a teacher and this is how I repay them! I really found it difficult to do the coursework but all the others managed it. Maybe I'm just stupid. I'm not cut out to do be a teacher.	I should never have enrolled on this course in the first place. I couldn't do the work on time because I'm thick. I'll never get a place on a teacher training course. I really worked hard and without learning support I couldn't do it on time and now they're going to chuck me off the course. I look like an idiot to the whole class.

Karol diligently records the specifics of his unpleasant event and carefully rates his feelings. He looks closely at the thoughts instantly passing through his mind after being given the verbal warning. At first, all he comes up with is the thought that it was a mistake to take the course in the first place. However, when he considers the implications for his future and what he thinks passing the access course really means to him, he finds more information to write down under his negative thoughts column. Finally, he reviews his various thoughts and decides that the thought that troubles him the most is the thought triggering feelings of shame, guilt, and despair at being thrown off the course and getting an F grade in the exam, meaning that he's a failure and that he'll never be a teacher.

Putting the thought on trial

After identifying your particularly troubling thought, put it on trial. You are both the lawyer for the prosecution, and for the defence. Your job is to prepare both sides of the case. The depressed mind usually has no difficulty coming up with evidence for the defence of the negative thought (that is, evidence in support of the thought). You're likely to have more trouble coming up with evidence for the prosecution (evidence disproving or making the negative thought useless).

We have a list of evidence-gathering questions to help you prepare the case against the troubling thought (witnesses for the prosecution!):

✔ Do I have any experiences or evidence from my life that contradicts my thoughts in any way?

✔ Have I had thoughts like these in the past that didn't work out as I predicted they would?

✔ Is this event really as awful as I'm letting myself believe that it is?

✔ Is this negative thought illogical or distorted in any way? (Refer to Chapter 5 for a list of common thought distortions.)

✔ Am I ignoring any evidence that disputes this thought?

✔ Is my thought based on facts or my own critical judgements?

✔ What evidence is there to support the thought – or is it just another of those troublesome negative automatic thoughts?

Using a Thoughts on Trial Form (see Table 6-2 for a sample), record the evidence both for and against your problematic thought in your notebook. Divide the page into two columns: 'Defence' (evidence that supports your thought) and 'Prosecution' (evidence against the validity of your thought).

Now we return to Karol to show you how this process works in practice. Karol's counsellor suggests that he puts on trial his upsetting, negative thought (that an F grade in the exam means he's stupid). To do so, he asks Karol to play two roles – first the defence lawyer and then the prosecutor.

Next, the counsellor gives Karol a Thoughts on Trial Form and asks him to fill the form in carefully. Table 6-2 shows what Karol returns to his counsellor after working on both sides of the case.

Table 6-2	Karol's Thoughts on Trial Form
Accused thought: The verbal warning means I'll be chucked out and never become a teacher.	
Defence: Evidence in Support of Thought	**Prosecution: Evidence Disproving Thought**
I've been given a verbal warning. If I get a written warning next time, I could be asked to leave the course.	Well, I suppose one late piece of work and a verbal warning doesn't have to mean that I'll be late with the next assignment.
If I get given a written warning, I'm one step away from being thrown off the course.	If I give the work in on time, I won't get a written warning.
I'm not cut out to be a teacher if I can't hand in the coursework on time without support.	I'm sure that even bright students find it difficult to do the assignments and submit them on time.
This was only my first assignment. If I couldn't hand that in on time, I'm bound to hand the next one in late and I bet the work will be even harder.	
My mother said that I'm just lazy and maybe I'm not cut out to be a teacher. What she really means is that I'm stupid.	

As you can see, the defence case for Karol's thought is stronger than the initial case for the prosecution. Karol's obviously struggling to develop a convincing case for the prosecution, to find *against* the negative thought.

Here's a dialogue between Karol and his counsellor showing how a few of the right questions can make all the difference. Note that the counsellor asks questions, but it's Karol who has to come up with the answers. This technique is known as Socratic questioning, (after the famous philosopher, Socrates) and is key to the way a good therapist helps you find your own evidence and answers.

Therapist: So, Karol, you were given a verbal warning for handing in your fist assignment late and concluded that you're stupid and you're never going to be a teacher, is that right?

Karol: Well, yes. What else could it mean?

Therapist: Think hard about this. Can you come up with any evidence that suggests you're actually quite bright? Anything at all?

Karol: I suppose so. I did get a distinction for my teaching assistant award. But it was an ESOL course and we all got English language support. Anyway, I didn't do my course at a college – I trained at an adult education centre and their standards were lower.

Therapist: That's great about the distinction. Let's come back to the quality of adult education training in a moment. Tell me, do stupid people normally get distinctions?

Karol: Okay. So I got distinction in the internally marked unit, and, with support, I got a distinction on the externally marked one, too. But that was easy. The teachers simplified it all, and we had lots of extra language support. I know I can produce good results if I get lots of help and guidance, so that doesn't count.

Therapist: Wait a second. Please explain that to me. You just said you know your results really don't count? Does this sound a bit like the thought distortion we spoke about earlier, when you *discard positives?* How can you show you understand how to help children to learn and get a **distinction** for your written work unless you've understood the principles and shown you've successfully applied them? And is anyone really able to do that if they actually are stupid?

Karol: Okay. I take your point. Maybe I'm discounting important information. But I still handed in my first assignment late.

Therapist: That's true. You did. And that reminds me, where did you do your teaching assistant course?

Karol: In Croydon. Why?

Therapist: How long have you been in the UK?

Karol: I came here three years ago, and I didn't speak a word of English when I arrived. I got a lot of help with English at my secondary school but I still left without any A*-C grades. My teacher thought I might do well on a vocational course, so I applied to train as a teaching assistant. Why?

Therapist: Is it just possible that English is a little more difficult for you than for some of the other students on your course, because you've only been in the UK for three years?

Karol: I suppose so . . . but I've always been really good at everything I try to do.

Therapist: And when you succeed, does that mean that's because you're just lucky or because you're actually pretty bright?

Karol: I suppose, sometimes, I'm quite bright.

Therapist: By the way, didn't you tell me that some of the other students you spoke to said they'd also found the first assignment really difficult and had to stay up really late completing it, so they could hand it in on time? And don't most of them speak English as their first language? If that's true, maybe you're being a little hard on yourself, to say the least?

Karol: Okay, I see your point. Maybe I am, as you say it, ignoring positive information and focusing on negatives. Perhaps a little more work in English? Maybe I should go to the learning centre and see if I can enroll on a Learndirect course to improve my English?

Armed with this ammunition from his therapist, Karol develops a list of additional evidence for the prosecution. He's looking for evidence against his negative thought which says that being given a verbal warning for failing to hand in work on time means he's stupid and he's never going to get onto the progression course and train as a teacher. His list of evidence for counter arguments to his negative thought is now growing, and includes the following:

- ✔ I did get a distinction for my Teaching Assistant award. Some members of my group got Merits and one only got a Pass.

- ✔ I usually succeed in most of what I do.

- ✔ Because I usually succeed, I probably go to pieces when I don't, because I'm just not used to that.

- ✔ How can I expect to do really well on this access course if I've only been studying through the medium of English for three years? I just need some more guided practice and perhaps I can get some learning support this year.

- ✔ My mother's always criticising me, and says I can't do anything right. Just because she thinks I'm not cut out to be a teacher doesn't mean I'm not going to be a good teacher. Actually, maybe she's trying to get me to drop out of the course and go to work to help support the family. I plan to get an evening job when I'm managing my work better, and pay towards my board and keep, but not yet.

- ✔ I guess even very bright people do hand in work late sometimes. I think I do need to see the bigger picture.

At first, most people find it difficult to come up with good evidence for disproving their thoughts. If that happens to you, try these tactics:

✔ **Take your time.** You can go back to the form over a period of several days if needed. The goal isn't to feel better immediately, but to discover the skill of subjecting your thoughts to careful, objective analysis. And acquiring new skills takes time.

✔ **Carefully review the evidence-gathering questions we list earlier in the section 'Putting the thought on trial'.** Think hard about each question and push yourself to find evidence that contradicts your negative thought.

✔ **Consider seeking help from a professional therapist to get you started.** Professionals can help you see that the vast majority of your negative moods are supported by thoughts that are actually groundless.

After Karol fills in his Thoughts on Trial Form with his new evidence, he's ready to reach a verdict. He declares, with the full support of his therapist, that his thought, 'Getting this verbal warning means that I'm stupid and that I'm not good enough to train as a teacher' is guilty of fraud and deception. He now sees that the thought causes him enormous shame and pain, but with little basis for doing so.

Coming up with constructive alternative thoughts

After finding the thoughts leading to your depressed feelings are guilty of inaccuracy, you need to develop an alternative view, a *constructive alternative thought*. These thoughts do require effort to put together. If a constructive alternative thought is based on falsehood it won't stand up to scrutiny.

Overly positive spins and simplistic dismissals of negative thoughts look very different from reasoned, alternative, restructured thoughts. An *overly positive spin* is an inappropriate attempt to make a bad event or situation seem like a good thing (politicians are pretty good at positive spins). And *simplistic dismissals* are ineffective attempts to minimise the meaning of unpleasant events by denying them and saying they aren't so (this isn't convincing!).

Here are examples of Karol's three types of ineffective replacement thoughts, followed by the later more effective restructured alternatives.

✔ **Unrealistic optimism:** Okay, so I handed the work in late. Next time I'll work harder. I don't need any help – I just need to put in more effort and I'm bound to do really well from now on.

✔ **Overly positive spin:** One verbal warning for late work will only show up on my college record, so the university need never know. I'll still get onto the teacher training course and that's all that matters.

✔ **Simplistic dismissal:** So what? A verbal warning is meaningless. I know I'm bright and I can do the work without any outside help.

✔ **Restructured alternative thought:** A verbal warning doesn't mean that I'm stupid; I've too much evidence to show otherwise. If I hand everything in on time from now on, and I manage to get good grades, I can still get a good reference from one of my tutors, and I should be able to pass the course and get my place to train as a teacher. Handing the work in late has helped me to understand that I still need some support and to work on my English. It's really a good thing because I need really good English if I am going to be a successful I'm intelligent enough to try to access the help and support I need.

After putting your thoughts on trial and going through the painstaking work of finding them guilty, don't next replace them with other equally false, negative alternatives. Rather, continue designing a new perspective based on reason, logic, and solid evidence. Develop a perspective that's a realistic, accurate interpretation of what's occurred in your life, and base any future predictions on this.

Such reflective interpretations include any partial truth contained in your negative thoughts. For example, Karol realised that a verbal warning is significant but it does not show that he is stupid. These interpretations are most effective if they include realistic positive information. In Karol's case, that means including the recognition of his intelligence.

Evaluating your alternative thoughts

If you find your thoughts guilty of deception, and restructure them using constructive alternative thoughts, you've made a great start. But the exercise is only useful if it actually does you some good!

We suggest that after putting your thoughts on trial and constructing alternatives you then rate the outcome. How? Simple. List the feelings you originally rated as arising from your negative thoughts. Then re-rate those feelings to see if they change.

Karol wrote down each of his feelings and found that:

✔ Shame went from 90 to 55.

✔ Guilt went from 80 to 40.

✔ Despair went from 85 to 65.

These ratings show that Karol's work on restructuring his thoughts substantially changed his feelings. However, the difficult feelings didn't go away entirely. And the reality is that you too can expect that some unpleasant feelings are likely to stay with you. You may have to practise this exercise a lot before you find your feelings diminishing to the point that they feel unimportant.

But what if the feelings stay the same or, get even worse? This outcome occurs occasionally, so try not to panic. Consider the following possibilities instead:

- ✔ **You've identified the wrong event.** To check out this possibility, ask yourself what else was going on around the time you experienced the troubling feeling. Possibly, the event you really need to identify was a daydream, image, or thought that had just floated through your mind, and you failed to notice it. If you're able to capture another triggering event that is more likely to have started the downhill slide, start again, and go through the whole 'Taking your Thoughts to Task' process once more.

- ✔ **You've caught the wrong thoughts.** It may be that you've put a thought on trial that's less upsetting to you than another thought about the event. For example, if you're feeling ashamed and inadequate after missing a pass while playing football with your friends, perhaps you thought it was because you were a bit slow to react. So you subject the thought about slow reactions to the 'Taking your Thoughts to Task' process, but find you feel no better after making it ineffective and coming up with a constructive alternative thought.

  But maybe the event involves additional, more troubling thoughts. As well as thinking that you were slow to react, perhaps you were troubled by seeing how upset your teammates were, and by thinking that you've horribly disappointed them and let the side down. If so, you need to take the more disturbing thought through the 'Taking your Thoughts to Task' process. If you don't benefit from 'Taking your Thoughts to Task', be sure to ask yourself if you have additional, more troubling thoughts to catch and put on trial.

- ✔ **You may have additional thoughts that you need to deal with.** We suggested that you to take your most disturbing thought to task. However, you may want to take remaining thoughts through the same process. Do so with any such thoughts if they seem to arouse a lot of unpleasant emotion.

- ✔ **You came up with an unbelievable reflective replacement thought.** Ask yourself if your replacement thought is too much like the overly positive spin or the simplistic dismissal we discuss in the 'Coming up with constructive alternative thoughts' section, earlier in this chapter. Develop a constructive alternative thought that is truly believable.

- ✔ **You sense that you don't want to change your feeling about the situation.** If this concern applies to you, you may want to read Chapter 3, which deals with breaking barriers to change. You may well discover that certain beliefs are indeed blocking your way towards feeling better. If so, it's helpful to work on those beliefs first.

If after working through the 'Taking Your Thought to Task' process, as well as the potential change-blocking beliefs in Chapter 3, and you're still struggling to feel better after a number of weeks, please seek professional help. Get help sooner if you feel hopeless and helpless and can't shift those feelings fairly quickly. This self-help book can still be used alongside therapy, but you shouldn't try to just use it on its own if you are experiencing dark and gloomy thoughts.

Following a model example

We introduce this chapter with a story about George and his bypass surgery, and we now want to end his story on an up note. Recalling George's progress gives another example for you on how to complete the 'Taking your Thoughts to Task' process.

George's cardiologist recently attended a conference featuring discussions about how often depression follows heart attacks and even increases the likelihood of additional heart problems. The cardiologist follows this up and after more research on cognitive therapy, suggests to George that he see a counsellor. George agrees, and after his first session with his counsellor, George decides to put his thoughts on trial. Here's how George makes the most out of the 'Taking your Thoughts to Task' techniques.

First, George fills out a Thought Catcher form, as seen in Table 6-3.

Table 6-3	George's Thought Catcher	
Feelings (0 to 100)	**Events**	**Negative Automatic Thoughts (or Interpretations)**
Despair (85) Hopelessness (85)	Heart attack, bypass surgery, hospitalisation, and the prospect of lengthy rehabilitation	I'm old. I'll never recover from this heart attack. Rehabilitation sounds really heavy going. I can barely get out of bed. And I can never be happy not playing golf again.

George's thoughts that trigger the most despair and hopelessness include the idea that he's never going to recover and that he can never be happy without playing golf again. He analyses these thoughts with a Thoughts on Trial Form, you see in Table 6-4. To do so, he thinks about the evidence-gathering questions (see the section 'Putting the thought on trial', earlier in this chapter, for the list of questions).

Table 6-4	George's Thoughts on Trial Form

Thoughts suspected of being negative: I'm old. I'm never recover from this heart attack. And I can never be happy not playing golf again.

Defence: Evidence in Support of Thought	Prosecution: Evidence Disproving Thought
I've seen good friends fade away and die after a heart attack.	I guess I've also seen people get a lot better after bypass surgery and live a number of good, active years.
Rehabilitation takes months, and that's even assuming it's going to work.	I've thought things looked pretty awful in the past, and they improved. I was convinced I'd never get over losing my wife. It sure was tough, and I still miss her, but I actually have felt happy occasionally since then.
I don't have the energy for rehabilitation; maybe I'll go along to it when I feel a bit better.	I suppose maybe I'm ignoring my doctor's prognosis; he predicts I'm going to recover.
If I don't get better, I'm never going to play golf again.	Maybe I'm trying to reach conclusions based on how I *feel* rather than on the facts.
	They say that energy increases once you just start moving, and that the body deteriorates when you lie around. Maybe that's really so.
	Although it's true that I'm never going to play golf again if I don't get better, I'll certainly never get better at all if I don't get moving.
	Even if I don't play golf again, I do know some friends who seem pretty content, despite their physical limitations.

Based on George's Thoughts on Trial Form, he comes up with a restructured thought: 'The odds are pretty good that, with work, I can recover from this bypass surgery. It won't be easy, but it sure beats the alternative. And if I don't recover to the extent that I hope, I can still find some interesting things to do.'

Finally, George rates the results from his new constructive alternative thoughts by re-rating his feelings:

✔ Despair was at 85; now it's at 30.

✔ Hopelessness was at 85, now it's at 10.

George continues working with the 'Taking your Thoughts to Task' process for several months. He recovers from his surgery and does play golf again. His handicap never gets quite as low as before, but he feels good about the outcome, and enjoys his retirement for a further two decades.

Using a Thought-Repair Toolkit

Using the 'Taking your Thoughts to Task' process that we outline in the previous section isn't the only method for dealing with potentially negative thoughts. We've designed a toolkit for detecting and working out any distortions and twists in these thoughts. You may want to look at each of these tools and try them out on your own thoughts.

See Table 6-1, 'Karol's Thought Catcher' shown earlier in this chapter, and fill a Thought Catcher out for yourself in your notebook. Underline the thought that triggers the most difficult emotions. Then run the thought through one or more of our thought repair tools in the following sections. As with the 'Taking your Thoughts to Task' strategy, the goal is to develop accurate, believable alternative thoughts rather than ones that put overly positive spins on events.

Making it someone else's problem

What? Are we suggesting that you find a way to saddle another person with your problems? Not exactly. This thought-repair tool involves imagining that a good friend of yours experienced the identical event to you, and responded initially with exactly the same thoughts and feelings. Viewing your problem as belonging to a friend allows you to see the thoughts from a different, more objective perspective.

So you imagine that your friend is sitting in a chair next to you, telling you about those negative thoughts. What do you say? Keep in mind that we're not asking you to try and make your friend feel better by lying or distorting the facts. Rather, we think that telling your imaginary friend what you are thinking makes sense. Claire's story illustrates how you can put this tool to good use.

Claire's childhood consisted of a constant stream of criticism from her father; that is, when he noticed her at all. Now, as an adult, she's assistant director of a large recruitment agency. Unfortunately, she has little confidence in herself, and finds fault with almost everything she does. Also, she has an exaggerated view of her mistakes, seeing them as much bigger than they are.

Claire's boss is impressed with her report on a specific project development and he insists that she make a presentation to the executive board of the agency. Though terrified, Claire agrees to the request. She does a credible job, and several board members make positive comments. However, she forgets to distribute the handouts until her talk is over, and one of the members suggests that her presentation would have made even more sense if they'd had the handouts in advance.

Claire feels absolutely gutted. She proceeds to fill out a Thought Catcher (see Table 6-1) and realises that her feelings of shame and self-loathing relate to her unchallenged, negative automatic thoughts, which have decided for her that her performance was an abject failure, and that her job may even be on the line.

Not having a better idea, and although sceptical, Claire agrees to try the tool of seeing her problem as someone else's. She imagines her friend May sitting in an empty chair next to her. May tells Claire about the presentation, concluding that she failed abysmally, and may even lose her job. May adds that, after all, the person responsible for the critical remark was the agency's chair of the board of directors!

To her surprise, when Claire hears those thoughts coming from the imagined May sitting in the chair, she finds different, more reasonable alternative thoughts flowing through her mind. She says to May, 'I beg your pardon! Didn't you hear the boss say that he was so impressed with your report that he wanted you to make the presentation in the first place? And why are you discounting the positive comments made by several of the influential board members? Obviously, forgetting to distribute the handouts in advance was an error. Probably your anxiety interfered with your memory. But other than that, you've got to admit you did a great job!'

You're probably thinking that this strategy is too simple to be credible. How can something this easy possibly work? The tool helps because it allows you to distance yourself from your problem a bit and think it through from another's perspective. After you've done that, you may find it easier to be a little more objective. We certainly find that many people benefit from this strategy.

Having time on your side

It's amazing how much anguish people can experience about the things that happen in day-to-day living. When unpleasant events are staring you in the face, gaining perspective's tricky to say the least.

Putting time on your side is a strategy asking you to view your problem as though you were looking back from a distant, future point in time. You think about how important your problem and your thoughts about it are going to be different in weeks, months, or even years into the future. It's amazing how many of the things people find upsetting look insignificant in the future. Andrea's story shows how she makes use of this tool.

Andrea has a rather serious problem with anger. She's abrasive, curt, and hostile – more so than she realises. She has few friends, and her blood pressure has soared in the past year. She's depressed, and her psychologist tells her that anger contributes both to her lack of friends and to her depression.

Andrea's psychologist suggests that she start using the strategy 'putting time on your side'. She says, 'It's pretty simple, Andrea. What I'd like you to do is notice what's going on whenever you feel angry. Then take a moment to step back and ask yourself a question: how upsetting is this situation going to feel and how important is it going to be a year from now? Rate that importance on a scale from 0 to 100, where 0 represents of no consequence at all and 100 is equivalent to a gang capturing you and threatening to torture you slowly to death over the next two weeks. The 100 rating represents your feelings when the torture's just begun.'

It takes Andrea a while to appreciate the rating scale, and then to start catching her angry moments and stepping back to answer the question. However, as she does so, she discovers that very few of the anger-arousing moments in her life manage to rise above a level of 10 on that 100-point scale a year later. Slowly but surely, she finds her anger lessens.

Putting time on your side works especially well with anger-arousing events. However, it can also put a better perspective on other events that trigger different feelings, such as sadness or distress. See how it works for you.

Testing out your thoughts

Many of the thoughts that disturb you can be put to the test. You can run various behavioural experiments to see if they really hold up under test conditions. We have three such experiments for you to carry out.

Putting negative predictions to the test

The depressed mind makes loads of predictions about the future. And these forecasts are typically gloomy and foreboding. In part, the predictions look bleak because of the various distortions we discuss in Chapter 5, such as filtering out positive information and exaggerating the negative. Thus, positive possibilities are discarded, and negative outcomes are greatly enhanced.

If you're depressed and listen to your mind's forecasts, you're probably going to avoid activities and events holding the remotest chance of unwanted outcomes. Try nonetheless to push yourself to experiment with your mind's forecasts:

- Go to that party and see if you do have as bad a time as you're assuming you're going to.
- Make yourself volunteer to give that speech and see if you survive.
- Call your friend and ask if he wants to have lunch with you even though you're convinced he's going to refuse.

If you plan to use this strategy, your best bet is to test out at least ten of your negative thoughts and predictions. Some of them may very well prove true! But most of the time, the vast majority are likely to prove false. Even when your negative thoughts turn out to be true, the actual experience usually doesn't feel nearly as awful as your forecast predicted. See Chapter 5 for more information about challenging negative predictions.

Doing a survey

You can also test out your thinking by actively collecting data and information. You can carry out a survey of family, friends, or colleagues. For example, perhaps you've just had to accept a post with a lower salary, and you believe that most people see money and status as the measure of a person's worth. Ask a group of friends what makes a person important and worthwhile in their eyes. Is it earning power, prestige, or other qualities, such as honesty, friendliness, and so on? You may be surprised at what they tell you.

Alternatively, if you have a concern specific to a particular individual, you can approach that person and check it out. Robert uses this tool to overcome a consuming worry that his wife is losing interest in him.

Robert notices that his wife has been less interested in sex lately. He assumes that she no longer finds him desirable. So he becomes increasingly distant with her because of his fear of rejection. The consequence is that the more he withdraws, the more she seems to lose interest. He becomes irritable, and the relationship deteriorates further. His psychologist suggests that he ask his wife what's going on. He doesn't want to, but with some persuasion, realises he may as well, because he has little or nothing to lose.

Robert approaches his wife and says, 'You know, darling, I've been missing you lately. We both seem to be working too much. Can we see how we can find more time for us?' He's surprised to find that she misses him too, and has been holding the same negative assumption (that he's lost interest in her!). She explains that work really was intense for a few months, and that her sex drive had indeed waned for a while. But then when her interest returned, it seemed that he'd become distant. This discussion allowed Robert and his wife to make sure that they made time for one another, leading to an improved relationship – and sex life!

If you use this tool, be sure that you don't set your experiment up to fail. Had Robert approached his wife in an accusatory manner, the outcome probably wouldn't have been nearly so positive. How do you think his wife would have responded if he'd said, 'Why don't you ever want to have sex any more? Don't you care at all about me or about our marriage? Or maybe it's because you're having an affair?" When you check something out, do think about what your wording will sound like.

If you unfortunately do come up against negative information when you check things out, at least you then know the score. Even if Robert's wife had said she was having an affair, at least now he knows what's going on, and can decide what to do. We find, time and again that avoidance rarely spares pain in the long run.

Perfecting your acting skills

A final method for putting your thoughts to the test is acting 'as if' you don't believe the thoughts. If you think that you'll be (rejected every time you approach someone, try taking on a new persona for a week or two. Imagine that you're someone who won't get rejected. Think of a person you actually know, or a famous person who you're sure wouldn't be turned down. Act as if you're that person and see what happens when you approach others. Don't take our word for it, try it out. Doing this exercise increases your chances of social success because you put yourself in a position to succeed. And if things don't go well, don't be crushed – just try again with the next person. Go ahead. See for yourself.

Revising your black and white thinking

As we mention in Chapter 5, the depressed mind all too often thinks in all-or-nothing, black and white terms. Perhaps you fall prey to this kind of thinking from time to time? If so, an example is that of thinking that you must achieve perfection, or else you're abysmally and totally inadequate. Similarly, you may think that you must:

- ✔ Achieve everything possible, or else you're a complete failure.
- ✔ Live a totally moral existence, or else you're an unforgivable, guilty sinner, deserving of hell and damnation.
- ✔ Always think of others, or else you're completely selfish.

We aren't suggesting that you can't have high standards for yourself. It's just that the black and white thinking that usually goes with perfectionism sets you up to fail miserably. No one is perfect. See Chapter 7 for more information about the perfectionism belief.

You're likely to benefit from redefining and recalculating your black and white thinking. When you find yourself immersed in this type of thinking (and almost everyone does now and then) try the following:

1. **Carefully define what you're talking about.**

   Clearly define and work out what you mean by any labels you apply to yourself, such as 'failure,' 'loser,' and so on. Without having a clear idea of what these labels mean to you, you can't perform the next step.

2. **Recalculate your new definition on a rating scale.**

   Here's how you do the recalculation: whenever you hear absolute terms in your mind, such as 'always,' 'never,' 'failure,' 'loser,' 'horrible,' and so on, try thinking in terms of a rating-scale. Recalculate and estimate what *percentage* of the time your negative thought is true.

   Thus, if you think that you're a failure, estimate what percentage of the time you've succeeded, versus what percentage of the time you've failed, and consider what failure means to *you*, rather than simply giving yourself a dictionary definition. If you think that you're a horrible person, recalculate and ask yourself what percentage of your actions are truly 'horrible,' as you defined the term in the first step, what percentage are 'good,' and what percentage are 'neutral.'

Few things in life exist in black and white terms. Redefining and recalculating can help you see the subtle, forgiving shades of grey that your depressed mind may have blocked from your sight. When you define your terms, and rate what percentage of time you really are like that, you'll probably find that your recalculated assessment not only feels much better, but more importantly, it more accurately reflects reality.

Eleanor complains to her counsellor that she's a useless mother because her children 'always' play up at school. The therapist asks her to explain what a useless mother is; what does such a mother do that other mothers don't? Eleanor replies that a useless mother is one who doesn't know a thing about parenting, is mean to her kids, and neglects them. The therapist asks Eleanor if that definition fits her, and Eleanor says, 'Well, I guess not totally. I suppose what I really mean is that sometimes I haven't a clue how to handle them.'

Her therapist replies, 'Okay, then instead of asking how often you're a useless mother, because that doesn't fit, let me ask you how often you have no idea at all of how to handle your kids versus how often you reckon you do know what to do?

After a lot of thought, Eleanor decides that she probably knows how to manage her children about half the time. This more realistic redefinition and recalculation of her problem leads to a fruitful discussion of how Eleanor can discover more about parenting, and increase the percentage of time she feels competent in knowing how to handle her children. Eleanor thinks that, with work, she can increase the percentage to 60 per cent of the time, and with further work she's likely to improve on that. She also admits that the children don't 'always' play up at school – only once recently!

Facing the worst

Facing the worst (also known as the downward arrow technique) is one thought-repair tool that's especially important. Cognitive therapy won't work if you stick your head in the sand like an ostrich. Rather, you have to think through the very worst possible implications and potential outcomes of your thoughts, until you reach the most horrible end possibility – and then see how to find a way to deal with that.

Here's how the technique works. Perhaps you're terrified of making a mistake at work. You think through what you fear is going to happen (your manager getting angry), then what? Follow the downward arrow. Perhaps you're going to get a verbal warning → then a written one → be sacked → be unable to find another job → lose the house → divorce → lose your partner and children . . . until your ultimate fear is of having nowhere to live, no friends or loved ones, and being alone and hungry. Pretty heavy stuff, but at least you then know what it is you're *really* worried about!

Dealing with the worst

It's surprising how often people, when exploring their worst imagined fears discover that they *can* cope with them, if they had to. Of course, no one wants to, but you're likely to discover that facing up to your fears is much easier than you think.

Using the downward arrow technique that we describe in the section 'Facing the worst' identify your worst imagined fear by asking yourself what you're most afraid of. Then, ask yourself if your worst fear has actually happened, and what it was like for you? Then move on to some fear-coping questions. These questions include:

- ✔ How likely is it that your worst feared fantasy is going to come true? Give yourself a probability from 0 to 100 per cent likely.

- ✔ If the worst fear actually happens, in what ways can you cope with it? Include all possible options and alternative plans of action. For example, you may consider retraining, or volunteering to work abroad. Think of friends or family – near or far – who may be prepared and able to help get you back on your feet. Include everything you can come up with.

If you get stuck when reflecting on these fear-coping questions, you may find it helpful to review other thought-repair tools, as well as the 'Taking your Thoughts to Task' process we discuss earlier in this chapter. And if anxiety and fear complicate your depression, consider reading *Overcoming Anxiety For Dummies*.

Putting the technique to work

Jack's story illustrates how this process of facing the worst goes. Jack celebrates his 45th birthday with a sense of gloom and doom. He's worked at a high tech chip manufacturing company for the past 15 years. During those years, he's invested 90 per cent of his retirement fund into his company's stock. For a while, that decision looked pretty good to Jack as his fund soared to heights he'd never imagined, well over £2 million.

Then, suddenly, the value of Jack's company's shares plunged so fast that he couldn't salvage anything from his retirement fund.

Jack is understandably devastated – he fears it may be years and years before he can retire. His therapist suggests that Jack identifies his thoughts using a Thought Catcher (see Table 6-1). The event is the collapse of Jack's retirement fund. Jack rates his feelings of despair as 80 and rates self-loathing as 85. Jack records his thoughts in response to the event as:

- ✔ I might not be able to retire before I'm 80 years old.
- ✔ I was stupid to invest so much money in my company.

Of course, Jack and his therapist can work on these initial thoughts to see if they contain distortions and to gather evidence for disproving them. They do so by using many of the techniques we show you in this chapter. However, Jack experiences only a minor improvement in his troubling emotions of despair and self-loathing. Therefore, his therapist asks Jack the following:

> **Therapist:** Even though we can show evidence to the contrary, let's assume for a moment that you really were stupid to invest so heavily in the company and that you won't be able to retire until you're at least 80 years old. What's the worst possible meaning that these thoughts hold for you if they did happen to be true?
>
> **Jack:** It means I'd be ridiculed.
>
> **Therapist:** Okay, and let's say you're ridiculed. What is it about ridicule that feels so awful? What is going to happen next if you are ridiculed?
>
> **Jack:** Everyone is going to see me as an idiot and a fool.
>
> **Therapist:** So if you really are an idiot and a fool, what is it that makes that feel so horrible to you? What's the worst imaginable thing that can happen if that were so?
>
> **Jack:** Everyone I care about is no longer going to love me and may leave me . . . I just know I can't cope with that.

At this point, the therapist has reached some of Jack's truly core fears – abandonment and loneliness. So Jack's thoughts hold even greater meaning for him. He's stupid and can't retire for a long time, and everyone he cares about is going to leave him and he can't bear living on his own without them.

Jack's therapist questions him further, in order to help him gain a better perspective. Jack's answers follow the questions.

- ✔ **How likely is my worst feared fantasy to actually coming true?** Actually, as I consider the evidence, it seems pretty unlikely that my family are going to decide that I'm an idiot and leave me. Even if they thought I did something stupid, I've lots of evidence that they're totally loyal. So I reckon this scenario has about a 5 per cent chance of happening.

- ✔ **If the worst fear actually happens, in what ways can you cope with it?** Yeough! It would be very difficult. But I guess I'd find a way of dealing with the loss. People do. Perhaps I'd join a support group. I could stay in therapy longer. And I could get involved in some useful activities, such as reading and exercise.

- ✔ **If the worst occurs, can you think of any other plans of action?** I'd try to stay in touch with my kids, even if they thought I'd been stupid. I guess I can always find a group of supportive friends. Even if my current friends think that I'm an idiot, it doesn't mean other people are going to think the same because they won't know about what I did with my retirement money. And I could master new job skills or find work in another tech company. Some companies are still taking on staff, and I'm not that old. I do have time to rebuild my finances. Finally, over time, I may find another wife. I'm not that bad looking after all.

Cognitive therapy works best when you don't deny, rationalise, or avoid your worst thoughts. Rather, cognitive therapy delivers maximum results when you deal with your worst-case scenarios directly.

Chapter 7

Discovering the Distorting Perceptions Behind Depression

*E*veryone views the world from different perspectives, which we call *life-lenses*. As you look at your world through your life-lenses, they filter what you see. The correct lenses can make your view clearer, but others distort what you see. Lenses can be clear, grey, cloudy, rose-tinted, cracked, dirty, or distorted.

Andy, the eternal optimist, lands a good job at a marketing company immediately after graduating from university. He cheerfully assumes that he's going to find a solution to every problem and that nothing and no one will ever stand in his way. He feels confident and even superior. He boasts to colleagues about his successes. He buys an expensive luxury car on credit, convinced that his salary is going to increase steadily. He views himself and the world through rose-tinted lenses.

Ralph, also taken on by the same marketing company, is the exact opposite of Andy. Ralph always expects the worst. He anticipates pitfalls and problems that his colleagues can't even imagine. Ralph sees himself as less skilled and experienced than how his colleagues view him. He worries constantly about losing his job. Ralph peers through grey, smoky lenses when viewing life. Not surprisingly, he usually has a bleak and unpromising outlook.

Life-lenses colour your perception of events, yourself, and of people around you. You're probably going to be surprised by how powerful these lenses can be. And you may be totally amazed to discover that both Ralph *and* Andy eventually fall prey to depression. Ralph, who feels inadequate, fails to progress in his career because he lacks confidence. He becomes depressed, which probably isn't surprising given his bleak outlook on life. But Andy sees himself and his world as if nothing can ever go wrong for him. Although some optimism is understandably helpful, Andy actually feels superior to all those around him. Eventually, he's fired for his overbearing insolence and he too quickly slides into depression. Despite their contrasting life-lenses, the outcome is the same for both men. And neither Andy nor Ralph is particularly unusual.

In this chapter, we show you how life-lenses operate, sometimes making you susceptible to depression and other problems, such as anger and anxiety. We help you see which of these lenses may be influencing you, even though you are unaware of it. You probably have a selection of different life-lenses that you use to view different types of events. After discovering which lenses you're looking through, we give you the opportunity to update the outdated, problematic lenses, and find new ones that suit you.

Looking Closely at How You See the World

In Chapters 5 and 6 we discuss how thoughts or interpretations of events can lead directly to depressed feelings. For example, if you visit your mother and she tells you that 'by and large' she feels proud of you for something you've done, you may instantly interpret that in positive or negative terms. Perhaps you see the 'by and large' phrase as just a trivial figure of speech, and take her statement as a sincere compliment. Or, you may take the words 'by and large' as highlighting other areas of your life of which she doesn't approve. If so, you could well have thoughts that you've failed and disappointed her, and your mood falls sharply.

What lies behind those instant thoughts? You guessed it: life-lenses. Life-lenses can be so powerful that they can cause two people to view the same event in totally contrasting ways.

For example, Helen and Olivia go to the same university and each gets an upper-second honours degree. They receive acceptance letters for the same prestigious postgraduate course. In the letters, they're both awarded part scholarships. Helen is ecstatic and phones everyone she knows to tell them the good news. Olivia feels keen disappointment and shame that she didn't get the full scholarship she'd hoped for, and feels that the university has failed to appreciate her talents. Helen is shocked by Olivia's negative reaction. And Olivia can't believe that Helen can be so happy about getting a measly part-scholarship when she also obviously deserves more. What's going on with these two students?

The answer lies in the life-lenses that each of them are looking through. Helen happens to have pretty clear, undistorted lenses through which she views her achievements. Olivia, on the other hand, looks through the life-lens we call 'entitled'. The entitled lens makes her believe that she *must* and *will* always be at the top, and that she deserves the best of everything. Anything less is totally unacceptable. Thus, Olivia's reaction, although perhaps a bit exaggerated, now at least makes sense, doesn't it?

In the following sections, you find out about the 12 life-lenses that are particularly problematic, where these lenses come from, and how they work .

Introducing the problematic life-lenses

Most people don't realise that they look at their world through life-lenses, and they're usually quite unaware of precisely which ones their minds use .

The potential list of possible life-lenses is long. But working with people suffering from depression we have found that there are 12 life-lenses which cause particular problems. Our list covers most of the problematic issues dealt with by mental health professionals.

- **Entitled:** A perspective that you always deserve the best and you feel outraged when your needs go unmet

- **Guilty:** A pervasive sense that you inevitably, usually unwittingly, do the wrong thing, and you deserve punishment for this

- **Inadequate:** A sense that you lack important skills, abilities, or other vital qualities

- **Inferior:** Viewing yourself as insignificant and less important than others

- **Intimacy avoidant:** You don't like getting close to people

- **Invulnerable:** No recognition of the need to take special care because you believe you can come to no harm

- **Without conscience:** Shameless disregard for ethics and morality

- **Perfectionistic:** A belief that you can and *should* do everything perfectly – go to Chapter 5 for more information about the destructive influence of 'shoulds'

- **Scared of abandonment:** Worry that people you care about plan to leave you

- **Superior:** The view that you are far better than others

- **Unworthy:** A sense that you don't deserve good things, or to have good things happening to you

- **Vulnerable:** A belief that the world is a dangerous place, and you are at imminent risk of coming to harm

Remember Andy's rose-tinted spectacles that we mention in the introduction to this chapter? You can see from the list that the rose-tinted spectacles actually consist of two lenses from the following list – superior and invulnerable. In other words, Andy feels both superior to others, and that he is invincible.

Understanding the origins of life-lenses

Who writes the prescriptions for life-lenses, when and where do people go to collect them, and why do they wear them? Knowing the answer to these questions helps you understand that no one deserves blame for having a variety of problematic, distorted life-lenses. After all, who is going to go to the Take a Quick Peek Optical Superstore and ask for a pair of cracked, distorted glasses? We believe that no one wants distorted life-lenses. Nevertheless, people end up wearing them for good reasons.

Generally speaking, the life-lenses through which you see yourself and the world were created in childhood. From infancy onwards, children actively work to make sense out of the activities and actions of parents, friends, teachers, relatives, and others. From a child's perspective, these lenses reflect a reasonable understanding of the events they experience. And during childhood, they seem to make pretty good sense.

Thus, people who look through a guilty lens probably had parents who criticised them frequently and harshly. Naturally, a child comes to the conclusion that they must be to blame. Similarly, people with the entitled lens were probably spoiled as children, receiving excessive praise and even flattery.

The world inevitably changes as people mature and enter adulthood, but the perspective they hold often remains constant. For example, a boy who is always hearing how inadequate, inferior, and unworthy he is, quite possibly isn't going to go on hearing those messages as an adult. However, he continues to look at the world through the same old lenses. As an adult, because of his long-held distorted views, he may interpret comments from others as criticism, even if that's not intended.

Although events later in life may shape or reshape a person's view of themselves, childhood is usually when the most difficult, distorted perspectives are formed.

Seeing the world through cracked life-lenses

Now, to show you precisely how these lenses operate, here's an example of how viewing the *exact same event* through different lenses leads to totally contrasting thoughts and feelings (refer to Chapters 5 and 6 for more information about the interconnections between events, thoughts, and feelings).

Imagine you're giving a presentation to a group of colleagues. You feel slightly nervous at the start, but quickly relax and gain confidence as you get your point across. After the talk, a colleague comments, 'I noticed you were a little nervous up there.'

Depending on your particular life-lens or perspective, your reaction to the comment may lead to very different thoughts and feelings. Table 7-1 illustrates how these lenses work.

In Table 7-1, you may notice that the final lens, 'good enough,' wasn't on the list of problematic lenses listed earlier. If so, you observed correctly. That's because some lenses are not distorted, or "cracked" and do give a clear view of yourself and the world. We discuss clear lenses in the section on 'Seeing Clearly: Replacing the Distorting Lenses' later in this chapter.

Table 7-1	How Life-Lenses Lead to Contrasting Thoughts and Feelings	
Event: You give a talk, and a friend says that you looked a little nervous.		
Life-Lens: Definition	**Thoughts (or Interpretations)**	**Resulting Feelings**
Inadequate: I'm not very bright or good at anything.	I'm never going to be a good speaker. I shouldn't even try. Everyone thinks I'm a twit and an idiot. How stupid can I be?	Shame Despair
Scared of abandonment: I really worry about whether people like and approve of me. Eventually, everyone leaves.	My friend won't want to associate with me any more. No one else is going to, either.	Worry Anxiety Isolation
Superior: I'm better than others and therefore I look down on them.	My so-called friend is trying to undermine me! Who is he to say something like that? As if he could do any better. I never thought much of him anyway.	Anger Rage
Good enough: I know and accept that I have both strengths and weaknesses. I like to do well, but I can learn from mistakes too.	My friend is right; I did feel nervous, and it probably did show a bit. I don't particularly like looking nervous, but I'm sure I can improve my performance with practice.	Mild, Short-lived Distress Optimism

Same event, different perspectives. When viewing life through various lenses, people can't help but see starkly contrasting pictures. This process explains why people have such conflicting thoughts and feelings when facing the same situations.

The difference between a life-lens, or a perspective, and thoughts about events (refer to Chapter 6 for more information about distorted thoughts) is that you apply the same lens to a variety of situations, whereas your thoughts are generally more specific to a particular event. Thus, if you have the guilty lens, you're likely to end up having a range of different, guilt-related thoughts when you make any errors, big or small, as opposed to thoughts of being unloved as a consequence of your mistake.

For example, Lionel's life-lens, of seeing himself as inferior, causes him to have a multitude of thoughts, which in practice actually do him a disservice in a variety of different situations. At parties, he has thoughts about how poorly others regard him, so he tries to blend into the background. At work, he fails to put himself forward for promotion because he doesn't rate his own abilities, and also thinks that others at his level are loads better than him. At the neighbourhood association meetings, he's loath to participate, because he assumes that no one is going to take him, or his ideas, seriously. Though his thoughts in each situation are different, they all relate to his one lens, the perspective that he's inferior to others.

Uncovering Your View

You're now probably curious about which life-lenses you are looking through. All is about to be revealed. Discovering your life-lens can unearth the root cause of much of your emotional distress – depression as well as other troubling feelings, such as anger, anxiety, and worry.

Awareness is the first step on the path towards change. Changing a problematic lens is difficult unless you first identify the lens (or lenses) you're dealing with. You need to find out the specific lenses that may be causing trouble in your life. And just like people having short and long-sightedness, the lenses that shape your perspective also exist as contrasting opposites, as you can see in Table 7-2.

The Problematic Life-Lenses Questionnaire in Table 7-2 contains a description of what we've found to be some of the most important distorted lenses. Take your time and don't rush this questionnaire. Before going through this questionnaire, please note the following:

- ✔ **Answer as honestly as possible.** Sometimes, people readily spot how they think they *should* answer, and reply in that way rather than with an honest self-appraisal. Self-deception isn't useful.

- ✔ **Base your answer on how often you feel and react in situations that relate to each lens.** For example, if you frequently *feel* that you are inadequate, but know that in reality you are adequate, answer on the basis of how you *feel* when your adequacy comes into question, such as when you're asked to give a presentation.

✔ **Take your time.** Reflect on various events and situations that have happened to you and that are relevant to each lens. For example, in answering questions about being scared of abandonment, versus avoiding intimacy, think about the relationships you've had, and how you feel and react to those close to you.

✔ **Don't worry about inconsistencies.** The lenses come in opposite pairs, and you may find yourself using first one, and then the other of the opposing pairs. Thus, if you're a perfectionist, you may also feel inadequate if you make a mistake. Or, if you normally feel unworthy and undeserving, you may find yourself feeling angry and entitled when your needs unexpectedly go unmet. People often go from one to the other of a pair of opposing lenses, so don't worry if you think that you appear to be a bit inconsistent.

✔ **Answer on the basis of how often each lens describes you.** If some aspects of the description apply and others don't, just underline the aspects that describe you and rate yourself on them, noting how often they apply to you.

✔ **Use a scale of 0 to 4 to rate the frequency.** Use **0** if the lens almost never describes you, **1** if it does occasionally, **2** if it does sometimes **3** if it usually describes you, and **4** if it almost always describes you.

Table 7-2	Problematic Life-Lenses Questionnaire
Lens	*Opposite Lens*
_____ **Inferior:** I feel I am less significant and important than other people. I see others as better than me. I feel like I don't fit in because there's something lacking. about me	_____ **Superior:** I feel like I'm far above other people. Truly, few are my equal.
_____ **Unworthy:** I just don't feel like I deserve to have good things happening to me. I feel uncomfortable whenever someone does something nice for me.	_____ **Entitled:** I deserve the best of everything. I expect to have almost anything I want. If my needs unexpectedly go unmet, I feel angry.
_____ **Scared of abandonment.** I need lots of reassurance to feel loved. I feel lost without someone in my life, and I worry about losing those I care about. I feel jealous and cling to my loved ones because of my fear.	_____ **Intimacy avoidant.** I don't like to get close to anyone. I'd just as soon stay away from any emotional involvement. I don't need anybody in my life.
_____ **Inadequate:** I feel like I'm not as talented or skilled as most other people. I just don't measure up. I don't like taking on things I've never done before if they look difficult.	_____ **Perfectionistic:** I feel like I must do everything perfectly. And if I want something done right, I'd better make sure I'm the one to do it.

(continued)

Table 7-2 *(continued)*

Lens	Opposite Lens
_____ **Guilty:** I feel guilty and that I deserve to be blamed. I worry about whether I've done the right or wrong thing. I hate hurting anyone else.	_____ **Without conscience:** I don't let any such nonsense as morality and conscience stand in my way if I want to do something.
_____ **Vulnerable.** Bad things happen all the time. I worry a lot about the future. I'm scared. The world feels very dangerous.	_____ **Invulnerable.** I'm invincible. Nothing can hurt me. I have superb luck. The world treats me well. I never worry about taking risks.

Any life-lens that you rated as 2 or higher, in terms of how frequently it describes you, probably gives you problems now and then. You have to appreciate that these life-lenses can make you susceptible towards negative feelings and to depression. Even if you've overcome your depression by working on your troubling thoughts discussed in Chapters 5 and 6, you're likely to find it useful to do further work on these lenses. That's because if you change your life-lenses, you can lessen the likelihood of depression reoccurring in the future.

Don't despair if you rated many of these life-lenses as frequently applying to you. We find that working slowly but surely, most people can tackle multiple lenses in just the same way as they deal with one or two.

Challenging Life Perspectives

Assuming you're fully aware that you're looking through distorted lenses, now what? We recommend that you take one distorted lens, or perspective, at a time, re-cut it, and then clean and shine it up. Not always an easy task! Life-lenses are manufactured out of long-lasting, emotionally intense material, hardened through the years. Therefore, you need to go slowly and take your time.

If the task of re-engineering your life-lenses ends up being too difficult, we've found that many people can at least put their old, distorted lenses away in a drawer for a while. You may still find yourself using your old lenses occasionally, but as time goes by your old lenses are no longer going to be the only way you look at yourself and the world.

You can expect the task to take time if you've been depressed for a long while, or if you've been experiencing recurring depressions. However, with patience and diligence, you can succeed. If you start to waver, take a look at Chapter 3, which deals with breaking barriers to change.

Avoid trying to go to the opposite extreme in your approach to change. For example, if you have the inadequate lens, you won't solve the problem by setting your sights on perfection. Having the perfectionistic lens is the opposite extreme, and can be as troublesome as the inadequate lens. Similarly, if have the scared of abandonment lens, avoid the temptation to believe that you need no one in your life (the intimacy avoidant lens). Later in the section on 'Seeing Clearly: Replacing the Distorting Lenses,' we show you how to make up a prescription for a lens that's halfway between such opposites.

Finding self-forgiveness

Finding self-forgiveness is a crucial step that ultimately leads to removing and replacing your distorted life-lenses. All too often, people beat themselves up for having distorted perspectives. Punishing yourself merely drains you of much needed energy for making difficult changes. It's like running a race and hitting yourself on the head with a hammer at the same time because you haven't yet reached the finishing line.

Instead, we suggest that you explore ways of forgiving yourself, thereby freeing up your energy for better purposes. An approach that has been proved to be helpful to many of our clients is called the 'Childhood Review.'

The Childhood Review asks that you look back over the emotionally important events in your life, particularly from the perspective of how they may have contributed to the origins of your life-lens. For example, if you have the scared of abandonment life-lens, look back on your life for possible causes, such as:

- ✔ Parents divorcing when you were very young
- ✔ Emotionally rejecting parent(s)
- ✔ Being left alone for long periods of time at an early age

After identifying likely causes, ask yourself if those life-disrupting events may have shaped the development of your life-lens. If so, try going easy on yourself. Appreciate that everyone is, in a sense, at the best place that he or she can possibly be, given each person's unique life history, genetics, biology, culture, and other such factors.

Focus on what you can do about future changes rather than beating yourself up over a past that you can't change.

Separating then from now

Your life-lenses are largely shaped by emotionally intense events in childhood. As an adult, when you look at current life experiences, the lens makes you see occurrences from the perspective of childhood events, as if they are now happening all over again. You may find it useful to compare and contrast the events triggering your problematic life-lens with how you viewed the world in your childhood. When you do, take into account that your reaction probably has more to do with events from long ago than with what's happening now.

Eileen repeatedly runs into trouble with her guilty life-lens. When she makes the smallest error or social blunder, she feels overwhelmed with guilt and self-loathing. She takes the Problematic Life-Lenses Questionnaire (see Table 7-2) and becomes aware of the extent to which she struggles with one particular lens.

Eileen's therapist suggests that she fills out a Then and Now Form to help her appreciate that her reaction relates more to the past than the present. He suggests that Eileen writes down her problematic life-lens in the left column; in the middle column records one or more images from her childhood that may have contributed to the development of the lens; and, finally, writes about the event currently triggering her guilty feelings in the right-hand column. Table 7-3 shows what Eileen does with the Then and Now Form.

Table 7-3	Eileen's Then and Now Form	
Problematic Life-Lens	*Childhood Image(s)*	*Current Triggers*
Guilty: I worry about whether I've done the wrong thing. I can't stand hurting anyone else.	Mother constantly tried to make us kids feel guilty. She repeatedly called us ungrateful, lazy, and worthless. She told us we were ruining her life.	When I forgot to pay my coffee fund contribution for two months, I felt really guilty and sick to my stomach. My boss told me it wasn't a big deal, but I couldn't forgive myself.
	The priest in our church bombarded us with messages that we'd all end up in hell if we committed sins. I was terrified and believed him for years.	I found a £20 note in the car park, and kept it instead of handing it in. I felt like I'd committed a mortal sin and broken one of the Ten Commandments.

Problematic Life-Lens	Childhood Image(s)	Current Triggers
	My father stopped me from going out with boys until I was 18. He said that all boys wanted was sex and sex was disgusting. He made me think that I was perverted for having any sexual feelings.	When I had a brief fantasy about our neighbour, I felt guilty for weeks. And yet I know that I'd never have an affair.

As Eileen reviews her Then and Now Form, she realises that the events in her present-day world pale into insignificance compared with her vivid images from childhood. Yet, the current events call up almost identically unhappy emotions. She starts reminding herself that her reactions that she's experiencing as so intense because of her earlier history. She starts saying things to herself, such as, 'I feel exactly like I did when I was 13 years old, and my father yelled at me for looking at a boy. Let's face it – a brief fantasy, which I've no intention of acting on, is pretty insignificant compared with my father's outrageous behaviour.'

Try using the Then and Now technique with your problematic life-lenses. You may need to repeat the exercise many times, but as you do, you're probably going to find your life-lens cutting down the impact on your emotions.

Carrying out a cost/benefit analysis

Many people would be willing to change their problematic lenses sooner than they do, but are held back because they believe the lenses protect or benefit them in some way. At first sight, you may think that idea sounds unlikely. For example, why is someone going to think that feeling unworthy is in any way beneficial?

One of the reasons life-lenses feel beneficial is that people believe in the view, and they fear the consequences which may arise if they discard the lens. We give you a couple of illustrations of how such concerns play out for several different lenses:

✔ **Entitled:** Someone with this lens fears that if they give up feeling entitled to everything they want and need, this means that they're not going to get what they want.

✔ **Inadequate:** If a person with this lens decides that he is in no way inadequate, but is the equal of others, he may start taking risks, such as volunteering to lead a project at work. But he doesn't do so because he's absolutely convinced that his inadequacy lens is true, and if he does volunteer, that he's going to fail miserably if he tries to discard the view of inadequacy.

✔ **Superior:** A person who feels that he stands far above others fears that letting go of this lens is going to cause him to be seen as the opposite – totally inferior to others.

✔ **Unworthy:** If a woman with this lens decides to discard it and believe that she's truly worthy of good things, she's likely to fear that others may see her as outrageously greedy and self-centred because, she believes that others really do know that she doesn't deserve those things.

We suggest that you carry out a careful cost/benefit analysis of each problematic life-lens that distresses you. Start by filling out the benefits side and list every possible advantage to having the lens. Table 7-4 shows you what Thomas sees as the benefits.

Thomas has a vulnerable life-lens. Having been abused in childhood, he now worries constantly about every imaginable danger – financial losses, terrorism, car accidents, threats to health, and more. He goes to great lengths to protect himself and his family. He saves every possible penny, he controls the family's diet, exercises religiously, and he imposes strict curfews on his children. Thomas lists the benefits for his vulnerable life-lens in Table 7-4.

Table 7-4   Thomas's Benefit Analysis of the Vulnerable Life-Lens

Benefits	Costs
I always steer clear of danger and maximise safety	
I'm less likely to be hurt.	
I can plan for dangers and what to do when (not 'if') they arise.	
I do a pretty good job of protecting my family.	
We all just might live longer because of me.	

Table 7-4 contains a pretty impressive list of benefits, doesn't it? Thomas had little difficulty coming up with his list of benefits for his lens. What value is it to him to discard his vulnerable life-lens? To find out, Thomas works on developing a list of costs for his vulnerable life-lens. With quite a bit of effort, he manages to identify a number of important costs. You can see his revised cost/benefit analysis in Table 7-5.

Table 7-5	Thomas's Cost/Benefit Analysis of the Vulnerable Life-Lens
Benefits	**Costs**
I take loads of precautions to maximise safety.	My wife says I'm like a jailer and that she can't stand it.
I'm less likely to be hurt.	My daughter got so angry with her curfew that she ran away from home for three days.
I can plan for dangers and what to do when (not if) they arise.	We never do anything for fun because I feel a need to save every penny I make.
I do a pretty good job of protecting my family.	I had a car accident in spite of all my extra care. Perhaps I was a even a hazard to others as I drive so slowly.
We all just might live longer because of me.	Sometimes, I wonder whether living longer is that important, if everyone is so unhappy.
	Only eating healthy foods still didn't prevent me from getting prostate cancer.
	I think that my absolute obsession with safety is probably making me and the entire family miserable.

After Thomas finishes his cost/benefit analysis, he feels more motivated to remove and replace his problematic life-lens. No matter which lenses cause you problems, a cost/benefit analysis of each lens can help you do the same. You're probably going to want to use all the lens-replacing strategies we discuss in the following section. A cost/benefit analysis can help you see the value in making the effort.

Seeing Clearly: Replacing the Distorting Lenses

If you've reached the point where you know that your old, distorted lenses aren't doing you much good, then now's the time to try out some new ones. When you look for new lenses, giving them a new name – one that's more flexible and balanced – is helpful. For example, instead of *inferior* or *superior*, you can design a lens you call 'equal to others.' Or instead of *invulnerable* or *vulnerable*, you may come up with a lens you call 'reasonably cautious.'

Hold on to the fact that the process of removing and replacing old lenses isn't quick or easy. The good news is that you can succeed with patience and hard work.

You need to proceed with care and attention because acting against the distorted perspective you've been seeing through your lenses is like being in a foreign country where you are driving on the opposite side of the road. The ingrained, habitual side of your mind says to drive on the left, and the clear-headed, adaptive side says to drive on the right. Preventing the old habit from automatically taking back control means keeping your mind on the task – no doubt you or some one you know has had experience of driving in Europe!

We have four separate strategies that are likely to help you remember which side of the road to stay on. Remember to drive slowly and watch the road signs. You may find that one of these strategies works for you, or you may find it helpful to use two, three, or even all four.

Looking through contrasting lenses

You can feel overwhelmed with the effects of distorted life-lenses but it's not impossible to find another, clearer lens that's been lying in waiting, neglected, in some corner of your mind. Nearly everyone has access to other reasonable, logical, and less distorted ways of thinking. Nonetheless, you may not have explored that area of your mind for quite a while.

The Looking Through Contrasting Lenses tool is an effective way of getting in touch with the clear-thinking, logical, level-headed side of your mind. (And we do believe that everyone's mind has a clear-thinking side.) This type of thinking increasingly develops as children grow up. Sadly, all too often it goes into hiding when depression sets in. Sometimes, looking for the clear lens feels like searching for a contact lens that flew out of your hands onto the carpet. Though you think it's disappeared, be assured that you can find clarity if you just keep looking for it.

Here's how looking through contrasting lenses works:

1. **Place two chairs facing each other. Label one chair with the distorted lens that your mind uses all too often, and label the other chair as the clear lens that looks at events logically and objectively.**

2. **Sit in the chair labelled distorted lens first and talk aloud to the imagined you sitting in the chair labelled clear lens.**

   Tell that logical, clear side why you have every right, and indeed *should* be feeling as bad as you do. Argue forcefully!

3. **When you run out of arguments, swap chairs and sit in the clear lens chair. From this clear side, tell the negative, distorted chair all the reasons why the arguments you just heard are invalid.**

   Use evidence, data, and logic. Point out any distortions you heard from the distorted lens chair.

4. **Keep swapping chairs until you've run dry of all the arguments on both sides.**

   Notice how you *feel* in each chair. Ask yourself which chair feels stronger and which side most reflects reality.

Perhaps the Looking Through Contrasting Lenses tool sounds somewhat silly, and a little muddling. But rest assured that psychologists have used various versions of this technique for decades for one key reason: it works! If the strategy sounds a little confusing, perhaps Jessica's story can help to clear things up for you.

Jessica has felt depressed for about four months. About two months ago, she started reading self-help books. In the last three weeks, she's noticed a significant lifting of her mood, but then her mood plummets again. Her boyfriend says that he has to go away on a four-day business trip. Jessica's mood plunges steeply downward. She tells herself that she must be crazy to believe that her depression is getting better, and face up to the fact that she's really a hopeless case .

Jessica realises that her scared of abandonment life-lens has led to her intense feelings of hopelessness. Here's how the Looking Through Contrasting Lenses tool works out for Jessica in tackling her scared of abandonment lens:

Scared of Abandonment Life-Lens chair (Talking to the Logical, Clear Life-Lens chair): 'Why did you even bother to hope? You're a loser, and you know it. Jamal makes loads of out-of-town trips. One of these days he's going to find someone else, and that's going to prove that you're a loser who's never going to have a successful relationship. Besides, the fact that your depression has returned also shows that Jamal is eventually going to leave you. After all, who'd want to stay with someone who's always depressed?'

Logical, Clear Life-Lens chair: 'Did you really think that your depression is going to go away, like that, and stay away for ever? It doesn't work that way – you've read that in any number of books. Jamal's stuck with you through thick and thin for over a year now. He says that he wants to spend his life with you. He's concerned about your depression, and he says that he's going to do anything it takes to help. Why not believe him?'

Scared of Abandonment chair: 'Well, you've had other boyfriends who left you after they said nice things. Why is Jamal any different? Remember how hurt you were when Simon dumped you?'

Logical, Clear chair: Hold it right there! Firstly, you know that a couple of those guys who left were actually pathetic nobodies; and you didn't really want them any more than they wanted you. And yes, you were hurt when Simon left. But let's face it, most of your friends have had a great guy leave at some point or another. It doesn't mean that all men are going to walk out. Natasha broke up with five guys over the years, but then she got married four years ago, and things are still looking just great for them. Besides, you know that you practically drove Simon away because of your fears and your desperate need for reassurance. Don't do that again!

Scared of Abandonment chair: 'But I won't be able to stand it if Jamal leaves me! I'd die.'

Logical, Clear chair: 'Well guess what? You felt hurt, but did you really die when Simon left? Did you? What have you got to lose by hanging in there, trusting, and not pushing Jamal away?'

Scared of Abandonment chair: 'I guess you have a point, but I'm afraid.'

Logical, Clear chair: 'Of course, you're afraid, but you can handle it. Hang in there with me and let's try something different for a change.'

Repeated practice with the Looking Through Contrasting Lenses tool is an effective means of convincing yourself that the new, clear lens is more accurate and also feels better to look through than the old, distorted life-lens. Repeat the exercise every time you waver in your attempts to use the new way of looking at yourself and the world.

Trying a new look

This strategy for finding clear life-lenses is like going clothes-shopping. One of the most common ways people decide what they like in clothes is by looking at friends, acquaintances, and models for ideas. If you see an outfit that looks good on someone else, you may decide you'd like something similar. Then what do you do? You try it on to see what it looks like and what it does for you.

If you have a life-lens that isn't giving you the results you want, look around for someone you know who has a clear lens that would suit you. We call this the New Look Technique. Trying on a new lens is surprisingly, pretty straightforward:

1. **Find someone you know who seems to look through a clearer lens than you do.**

2. **Give that new, clear lens a name and decide what it means to you.**

3. **Try on the new lens just like you'd try on a new outfit.**

Howard's story illustrates how to use this approach. Howard hardly looks like someone who'd fall into depression. He got his membership of the Royal College of Orthopaedics eight years ago and now is nearing the top of his profession in terms of both income and prestige. However, in the past six months, he's been waking up at 3 a.m., unable to go back to sleep. His energy drains away, his appetite disappears, and he loses interest in sex.

Howard's wife persuades him to get help for his depression. Though he isn't convinced that he's depressed, he agrees to see a psychologist. After four sessions, the psychologist manages to get Howard to accept that he really is seriously depressed. And much of his depression seems to stem from his perfectionistic life-lens that causes Howard to work excessive hours and beat himself up relentlessly for even the most trivial of mistakes.

Howard berates his psychologist: 'You don't get it, do you? I can't possibly stop being a perfectionist; I'm a surgeon for crying out loud! If I don't go over every detail time and again, patients could die!'

'Yes,' Howard's psychologist agrees, 'but do you know any colleagues who work hard, do an excellent job, and yet aren't so completely driven by perfectionism?'

When pushed, Howard manages to think of his friend Michelle. She's a successful surgeon too, but she doesn't work the hours that Howard does. And Michelle doesn't appear to beat herself up over tiny details. Howard agrees to try out Michelle's life-lens.

Having done the first step in the New Look Technique, Howard moves onto the next step of naming the new lens. He certainly can't consider looking through a lens labelled 'adequate,' yet he knows that the perfectionist view is destroying him. He settles on a perspective that he decides to call 'productive and proficient.' He defines this new lens as meaning that he wants to be highly competent and work hard, but not nearly as driven and obsessed as before. Howard tries on his new life-lens for a week. Thus, he essentially tries out acting 'as if' he is his friend, Michelle. After a fortnight, he decides that he likes this new lens a whole lot more than his old one, and – lo and behold! – he hasn't lost a patient.

With the New Look Technique, you find someone you know who has a different lens from you. You try on their lens, and give yourself the option of going back to your old one if it feels better.

Taking direct actions

Now comes an even scarier approach – *behaving* (rather than thinking) in ways that directly go against the perspective seen through your distorted life-lenses. Although it may feel a bit frightening, Taking Direct Actions against your lenses isn't complicated. What you do is:

1. **Ask what your old, distorted life-lens has been causing you to do/ not do that's self-destructive, not useful, or fails to give you what you want.**

2. **Make a list of a few different things to do – actions that are likely to lead to long-term benefits.**

3. **Start doing them, one at a time.**

Starting with small steps is always a good idea. You've been looking through your old life-lenses for a long time; there's no rush!

Adelaide's scared of abandonment life-lens causes her to hang on so tightly to every new relationship that invariably her partner ends up feeling smothered and eventually leaves. Her distorted lens results in the very outcome she fears most. Adelaide feels lost without someone in her life, and her cost/benefit analysis (see 'Carrying out a cost/benefit analysis' earlier in this chapter) tells her that her scared of abandonment life-lens is doing far more harm than good. She then makes a list of self-destructive behaviours that her life-lens has typically directed her to do:

- ✔ If I'm in a new relationship, I phone or text the guy frantically several times every day asking for reassurance.

- ✔ I do almost anything to keep from being alone, including sometimes going to the pub and letting myself get picked up.

- ✔ I wear really sexy outfits and make sure I attract guys because I so hate being alone.

- ✔ I neglect my friends.

Adelaide decides that she wants to do something different to her past patterns. After looking over her list she thinks of some things she can do to change:

- ✔ I'm going to phone a female friend once a week and meet up with her, rather than always brooding about men.

- ✔ I'm going to spend at least three evenings a week at home and plan a range of activities to occupy the time I'm alone.

- ✔ I'm going to quit trying to find guys in bars and stop wearing sexually overt clothes.

- ✔ If someone does come into my life, I'm going to force myself to call him no more often than he calls me and I'll get a couple of my friends to help me on this one.

Adelaide works hard at carrying out her new actions. Sometimes she succeeds, and sometimes she doesn't. But by frequently reviewing her list, she manages to maintain her focus on where she's headed. Slowly but surely, she starts to see the world through a new life-lens that she decides to call 'intimacy comfortable.' For her, intimacy comfortable means discovering that she's fine when she's by herself, and equally so when she's involved in a relationship.

Taking direct actions simultaneously allows you to take off your old lenses and put on new ones that let you to see life from a different perspective. It's not that easy when you first start, but you're likely to find this approach rewarding in the long run.

Writing a letter to the source

When you were a child, did you ever try on lenses at the opticians, finding everything looked out of focus and telling the optician that you couldn't see? Now imagine the optician saying to you, 'These new glasses have lenses which were made specially for you. That's how things are supposed to look! Give the glasses time, eventually they'll feel just right.' And, because you were a child, imagine you had no option but to go on wearing them. And even though you fiddled with them, you just couldn't make them right.

Later in life, you'd figure out that you'd been had by that optician. And you're likely feeling angry about having been forced to wear the wrong lenses for years. Writing a letter to the optician can't change what's happened, but it does allow you to release your pent up feelings, set the record straight and let the other person see things from your point of view.

That's what the Writing a Letter to the Source exercise is about. Have a go at writing a heartfelt letter to the person or persons most closely linked to the development of your distorted perspective. Include details about what the person did and how you felt. After pouring out your emotions, tell the person your plans for creating a new, clear-sighted life-lens – your plan for positive change.

In the majority of cases, you won't actually post the letter to the source. If you do decide to send your letter, give yourself time to think over the decision. And discuss your intention with a trusted friend, minister, or professional. Make sure that you've thoroughly thought through the advantages and disadvantages of sending the letter.

If the source that you're directing your letter to is one or both of your parents, you may feel reluctant to express anger. Perhaps you feel guilty and think that it's wrong to express such feelings towards a parent, even if you don't plan to send the letter. You may be tempted to defend your parents' actions. It can be useful to write about your anger and distress nonetheless. You also may benefit from finding forgiveness for the source of your life-lenses. But forgiveness usually comes only after first letting the steam escape and evaporate from the boiling emotional caldron.

Adam looks at the world through an inadequate life-lens. As a child, his father had no patience for teaching Adam anything; instead, he got fed up with Adam whenever he made the smallest mistake. For his entire adult life, Adam has shied away from acquiring new skills because of his fear of looking clumsy and stupid. He even hires a carpenter to put up shelves in his lounge, rather than attempting to put them up himself. When his wife says that they need to get out more, and suggests dance lessons, he feels like crawling under a stone and going into hiding. Nonetheless, Adam decides to try writing a letter to the source. Figure 7-1 shows the letter he writes to his father.

Dear Dad,

I remember how so many times you'd get red in the face and walk off in frustrated disgust whenever you tried to teach me something. It didn't matter what it was, your temper had about a six-second fuse. What did I do to deserve that abuse? Do you know how ashamed and humiliated I felt when you expected me to master things on the first attempt, whether it was riding a bicycle or hammering a nail?

I remember I wore clip-on ties for years rather than ask you to teach me how to tie a tie. I felt like a stupid geek wearing them, but that was a lot better than watching you explode again. And then there's the fact that you were always out at the weekends. Most of the time you didn't even manage to get off work to go on holiday with the rest of us. What was that about? I concluded that you didn't want to be around me.

But why were you so close to my older brother, Kevin? I imagined that he was so much smarter and cleverer than I. I can't even express how hurt and angry I feel about all those times.

It's funny but much later in life I learned that you spent time with him and ignored me. I am actually pretty intelligent. I guess I can't make a piece of furniture like you can, but I can do an awful lot of things you can't. I'd like to see you try writing those magazine articles I write every week. I'm being promoted to Senior Editor next week, by the way. Not that you'd care or ever show any recognition of something I do.

Well, I must say that it feels good to get some of these issues off my chest for once. I realize that you must have your own problems, and that some deficiency of your own kept you from ever connecting with me. I think perhaps you lost as much as I did – maybe more.

At any rate, I'm sick of feeling like I'm not good enough. So let me tell you what I plan to do now. I'm going to go to the Home Warehouse and take an evening class in DIY. And if I don't get it at first, I'm going to take it again. And again – until I master some things and feel better about myself. And, incredibly, I'm going to take dance lessons with my wife. I know that I'll feel just like I did when I was six years old and you screamed at me for dropping a hammer, but I'm going to keep at the lessons no matter what. I'm not going to live the rest of my life feeling like a complete geek and a klutz.

Perhaps someday you'll dig down deep and show interest in me and my life. And possibly not. Either way, I plan to move on and overcome what you instilled in me.

Love,
Adam

Figure 7-1:
Adam's
letter to the
source.

At first, Adam feels guilty when he starts writing his letter to the source of his life-lens. But he realises that he has no intention of actually sending it and that he has a perfect right to feel the way he does. Note that he includes not only his feelings of anger, shame, and humiliation, but also his plan for choosing and putting on a new life-lens. If you've struggled long enough with a destructive life-lens, try the Writing a Letter to the Source exercise.

If you want even more ideas for how to 'find and replace' problematic life-lenses, we recommend *Reinventing Your Life* by Jeffrey Young and Janet Klosko and *Why Can't I Get What I Want?* by Charles Elliott and Maureen Lassen.

Schemas: The astonishing power of life-lenses

Psychologists have another term for what we are calling life-lenses – *schemas*. Schemas work like lenses. They're the mind's way of organising and making sense out of the bewildering onslaught of information it's receiving.

Schemas can be useful, because they allow us to take shortcuts in interpreting a vast amount of information. However, these mental frameworks also cause us to exclude relevant information in favour of information that confirms our pre-existing beliefs and ideas. Schemas can contribute to stereotypes and make it difficult to hold onto new information that doesn't conform to our established schemas. They are thought to be the central and enduring themes in a person's life. Schemas reflect deep, difficult to change views of ourselves, others, and the world. They also refer to a broad organising structure that significantly influences our moment-to-moment experiences .

Schema-focused therapy, a form of CBT, particularly developed by the clinical psychologist Jeffrey Young, is a psychological therapy that has been found to be very useful in treating chronic depression. There's a great deal of research and clinical work on schemas, which demonstrates how using distorted schemas laid down in early life can affect the mood of adults and how it is possible to work to successfully modify long-established schemas.

In a famous experiment, volunteers wore glasses that literally turned their world upside down. After much discomfort and confusion the volunteers eventually reported that they saw the world the right way up through their glasses. The brain had taken the inverted image seen by the eye, and turned it the right way up. The only problem was, when the volunteers took their glasses off, their perspective remained inverted! Eventually the brain switched the inverted view (which was still being seen even without the glasses) back to the right way up. Just goes to show the influence your brain has over what you see – even to turning your world upside down, just to make it look right!

Chapter 8

Amending Your Memory

· ·

In This Chapter

▶ Understanding how your memory works

▶ Looking at how depression affects your memory

▶ Caring for your memory

▶ Investigating strategies for improving your memory

· ·

Depression is bad enough. You feel absolutely awful. Your sleep may be disturbed, your appetite practically non-existent, and nothing seems like fun any more. Is worse to come? Well, you can add memory problems to the mix – a serious lessening in your ability to remember such things as names, dates, tasks, and even shopping lists.

But why single out memory as a special concern? Mainly because a misbehaving memory messes up your everyday life. Also, when you notice memory problems, beating yourself up for having the problem is all too easy. And you certainly don't need any more triggers for negative thinking than depression is already giving you.

Depression and memory impairment go hand in hand. Here's the good news – when your depression lifts, your memory is likely to improve. But in the meantime, there are a number of techniques for making your memory perform better for you, which may in turn lift your spirits.

To appreciate how depression affects memory, we talk about how memory works, and then describe the different kinds of memory. Next, we show you the ways depression can wear down and disrupt your memory. Although being a bit forgetful is perfectly normal, we explain how to recognise if you have a problem and if your memory is in need of help. Finally, we give you sound strategies for dealing with memory problems and boosting your memory skills.

Making Sense of Memory

Think back to when you were a child. What's the earliest memory you can recall? Do you remember where the event took place, who was there, and what you looked like? Good. Now try to remember what you had for lunch today, a fortnight ago. What? You can remember something that happened way back in the mists of time, but you can't remember something that happened only two weeks ago?

This little exercise proves that memory processes are complex. You can't remember *everything* that happens to you. We're pretty sure you were awake and paying attention to what you ate two weeks ago. But you probably don't remember the food on your plate unless it was unusual, special, or important to you in some way.

Scientists agree that all memory begins with how you view incoming information, or an event, using one or more of the senses. Many factors determine the perception that forms a memory and whether you're going to recall that memory. Briefly, here are the most important processes involved in memory:

- **Immediate memory:** Think of immediate memory as a multi-sensory recording, including all your senses – sound, vision, touch, taste, and smell. The recording of each moment is briefly held in your immediate memory, but then most of the detail quickly dissolves. Right now, you're reading these words, but your senses are also aware of the temperature of the room you're in, the sounds of cars going by, the level of light, and the comfort of your seat. You can turn your attention at will to any of those sensations, but most of them are never really brought into your awareness.

  Your lunch two weeks ago was in your immediate memory for a short time. Unless something unusual occurred, such as choking on a fish bone, the memory of your lunch is probably never going to be transferred from your immediate memory to long-term memory (which we describe later). Instead, the memory is going to dissolve and be lost for ever.

- **Working memory:** When you pay attention to information, your working memory (a temporary holding zone) allows you to use, manipulate, build up, or send the information into long-term storage. Working memory is like a blackboard in your brain where memories are constantly being rubbed out and new ones being chalked up. Without working memory, you'd be unable to solve many types of problems that involve thinking about more than one idea at a time. Here's an example: say all the letters of the alphabet (which you now retrieve from your long-term memory) that rhyme with the word *me*. To search for these letters, you have to use your working memory to picture all the letters, scan through them, and work out if they rhyme.

✔ **Long-term memory:** Most of the information that passes through immediate memory and through working memory is quickly forgotten. But when the brain places a memory into long-term storage, the memory then lasts a while – maybe even a lifetime. When asked to recall the alphabet, you (hopefully) have no problem remembering the letters. But unless you're a schoolteacher, you probably haven't had to specifically practice writing or reciting the letters in order since you were a kid. You can thank your long-term memory for keeping this little nugget of infrequently-used information on file. Your long-term memory can store huge amounts of information; it's what most people think of when they use the word *memory*.

✔ **Retrieval:** You have billions of memories stored in various places in your brain. But sometimes you can't easily find those memories. When you can't remember someone's name and then a couple of hours later it just seems to pop into your brain, you've had a retrieval problem. Retrieval (or *recall*) is the process of pulling stored information into conscious awareness. The earlier memory failure is actually a retrieval problem.

When all's well, the brain processes, stores, and recalls memories with efficiency and ease. However, memory can be subject to many disruptions, including those caused by neurological injuries or diseases, problems with concentration, drugs, alcohol, and emotional disorders. Depression can also be one of these disruptions, and it can temporarily damage the sophisticated memory system.

Depressing Disruptions

Depression fills you with sadness. Your ability to think clearly can be clouded by feelings of hopelessness, helplessness, guilt, and low self-esteem. But depression also affects your ability to think clearly by having a negative influence on all aspects of your memory. In the following list, we describe the ways that depression affects each aspect of memory. (For more on each aspect, see 'Making Sense of Memory', earlier in this chapter for experimental evidence of depressed versus non-depressed memory.

✔ **Immediate memory:** Depression decreases your ability to pay attention to what's going on around you; you may not even notice important information. Things that you normally pay attention to may just slip by.

An overwhelming depression slows **Piotr** down and he practically crawls through his morning routine. He notices the time and realises that he's going to be late for work. Piotr starts searching frantically for his keys. He tosses papers aside, digs in his briefcase, and scurries from room to room. 'Damn, damn, damn,' he fumes, as his rising panic and irritation grow. Suddenly, his hand discovers the keys, in his pocket, where he put them just minutes earlier. 'Damn, damn, and double damn!' Everyone probably experiences something like this from time to time, but Piotr is having this problem almost every day. His immediate memory is impaired.

✔ **Working memory:** Depression disrupts your ability to concentrate and hold onto information. Your problem-solving ability sharply declines.

Throughout her company, colleagues know **Isabella** as an energetic, kind, and intelligent manager. Lately, she has been experiencing a lack of energy, a poor appetite, and a huge decrease in her usual enthusiasm for her job. Today, she's chairing a meeting with six other managers to work on solving a company problem. She begins the meeting by asking the managers to report on their understanding and views of the situation. She expects to find a solution easily once the problem has been examined from all sides. But as the meeting progresses, Isabella finds it increasingly difficult to listen and hold onto the various ideas in order to compare and contrast them. Her mind floods with negative thoughts. At the end of the presentations, she realises that she doesn't have a clue how to approach this problem. Her working memory isn't working very well.

✔ **Long-term memory:** Depression makes acquiring new information much harder. Tasks such as studying for an exam can become extremely difficult. Concentrating is more difficult, and the information just doesn't seem to stick. Information refuses to be properly filed into the memory's retrieval storage system – your long-term memory.

The cold, slushy, dreary days of winter are especially depressing to **Eric.** His mood matches the long dark days of the season. But this winter seems worse than past years. Eric loses his job at a building society, deepening his depression. The job market looks terrible, so he decides to change careers and move into accountancy. He gathers all the study materials, thinking that it doesn't look too difficult to train in this field, but finds that he can't remember anything of what he reads. He's never experienced this kind of problem before. He reads through the books twice, and keeps notes. He takes a practice test and fails miserably. His struggles add to his depression. Eric is having trouble storing new information in his long-term memory.

✔ **Retrieval:** Depression makes recalling information like dates or doing the shopping without making a list more difficult. Previously known names, faces, and facts are harder to remember. Happy events are particularly difficult to recall. When you're depressed, you're more likely to come up with sad and depressing memories, because depression floods your brain with negative memories. You may actually have trouble remembering whole periods in your life when you were happy.

'I'll never find Mr. Right' **Emma** complains to her friend Heather. 'Every time I think someone's nice, I find out he's married, or just not interested in me. And even the guys who seem interested are only after one thing: sex. I've never had a good relationship. They all fail miserably. I may as well just give up once and for all.'

TECHNICAL STUFF

Picturing the depressed brain

Researchers are certain that depressed people have real problems with memory. Exciting new brain-imaging techniques are now helping scientists see what depression looks like in the brain. With this knowledge, they're beginning to understand the complicated relationship between mood and memory.

One explanation for poor memory during depression may be found in increased levels of *corticosterone,* a hormone that's released when people experience severe stress. Corticosterone levels increase during depression. Research in Canada and California has found that high levels of this hormone significantly increased depression-like behaviour and impaired rats' ability to retrieve information previously acquired or stored in long-term memory. Another possible explanation for poor memory may be the decreased levels of the brain chemical serotonin found in depressed people. *Serotonin* helps regulate attention as well as the ability to be interested in pleasurable activities.

When the body is under stress, it produces extra quantities of a hormone called cortisol. In the short-term, this helps you deal with difficulty and danger. But long-term raised levels of cortisol can be harmful. Usually, cortisol levels are highest in the morning, and then steadily decreases. For depressed people, there's a different pattern. Often they've had long periods of uncontrollable stress, which goes with higher cortisol levels. This seems to affect the transmission of the brain chemical serotonin. The result can be clinical depression. Physical illness can also disrupt cortisol patterns, and therefore also have an effect on attention, memory, and depression.

Other research suggests that people who have suffered from depression may have a smaller *hippocampus,* a key area in the brain that is important for storing information and recall. There is a theory, that the stress hormone *cortisol* may have toxic effects on the hippocampus.

Heather is astounded. She remembers plenty of men who were interested in Emma, and she recalls several long-term, stable relationships that Emma actually broke off. Emma has more dates than anyone in her circle of friends. In fact, Heather has always been jealous of Emma's ability to attract the opposite sex. What's going on? Emma is suffering from depression. She really can't remember the good times.

Forgiving Forgetfulness

When you experience memory problems as a result of depression, worrying about these problems may deepen your depression, adding to your forgetfulness. If you're depressed, don't be too surprised if you forget where you parked your car, can't remember a specific word or someone's name, or if you misplace everyday items. Getting upset about minor memory problems can easily make you even more depressed.

For example, following a serious car accident, one of the authors of this book, Elaine, suffered post-traumatic shock. One of the distressing symptoms of her shock was what she calls 'holes in her head' – memory problems. On one occasion, a friend rang to ask why she'd missed their lunch meeting. Elaine was astonished; she had no recollection whatsoever of making plans to meet her friend. But rather than beating herself up for her memory lapse, Elaine forgave herself. She accepted that her friend was telling the truth, gave herself permission to nonetheless be unable to recall their plan, even with prompting. Elaine's approach lessened the additional stress and misery of getting angry with herself about a perfectly normal and forgivable event.

Try going easy on yourself, telling yourself that your memory 'hiccoughs' are because of your depression. These memory problems are likely to be resolved when your depression lifts. You can also begin to take a more active approach in beefing up your memory, using the tips and techniques we provide in 'Assisting Your Ailing Memory', later in this chapter.

An underlying disease or disorder sometimes causes poor memory. A certain degree of forgetfulness is a normal part of aging, too much stress, or depression. But really bad memory may be a sign of a more serious problem. If you notice any of the following symptoms, make an appointment for a complete check up with your GP:

- ✔ You become confused when performing activities you're very familiar with, such as doing the washing or cooking.

- ✔ You get lost when going to places you regularly visit, such as the post office or the supermarket.

- ✔ You get *disoriented*, unsure about where you are or what you're doing, for more than a brief moment or two.

- ✔ Your memory problems begin to significantly interfere with your everyday work or relationships.

Your doctor may find that a treatable, physical cause is at the centre of these problems, or may alternatively decide that your memory problem is due to depression, too much stress, or anxiety.

Assisting Your Ailing Memory

So, you have a few problems with your memory. If you're depressed, you probably don't have lots of enthusiasm for any strenuous exercise that can help improve your memory. So we're going to give you some quick, simple tips and techniques to help you cope until your depression lifts and your memory improves.

If you're ready for some advanced memory training, browse the shelves at your local bookshop. Books like *Improving Your Memory For Dummies,* by John Arden, (Wiley) can really help.

Putting pen to paper

 Acknowledging that you have a problem with your memory, and then taking steps to work on it is a great start. Keep a daily planner next to you at all times, and make sure that you use it. Write down everything you need to remember. List your appointments, what you need from the shops, names of people you recently met, and things you want to get done. Check your daily planner often.

If you use a personal organiser, do make sure that you update it regularly with all your important appointments and daily reminders. Sophisticated technology can be very useful for people with memory problems. For example, some electronic devices ring scheduled alarms to remind their owners to check their calendars, take their medication, or perform other daily chores. On the other hand, you may find that good old-fashioned pen and paper suits you better.

Consulting your daily planner whenever you sit down for a meal or a cup of coffee or tea can help avoid the embarrassing experience a number of people of reported. There you are having just finished dinner at home, and the phone rings. It's your friends saying 'Is there a problem? We were expecting you for dinner an hour ago – remember? We arranged this weeks ago. Have you forgotten?' Flustered and embarrassed, you mumble a feeble-sounding excuse, grab coat and bag, and race off to 'enjoy' a second dinner without mentioning that you're absolutely stuffed – in more ways than one!

Developing routines

Picture the scene: You finally managed to force yourself to do some shopping, and now you're absolutely shattered. You push your shopping trolley out of the supermarket exit and, suddenly, you can't remember where you parked. You feel such a fool, and are ready to burst into tears. This situation can happen to anyone. But when you're depressed absentmindedness becomes more of a problem, making you feel even more awful, and it can give you yet another reason for feeling bad about yourself.

Try this way of getting round this type of situation. Every time you go shopping, try to park regularly at the end of the row, to either the right or left of the entrance. Alternatively, always choose a particular place on the top floor of the car park, which is usually the least crowded. If you have a favourite shopping centre or supermarket, take some time to select a rarely used space. Park there, even when other spaces nearer the entrance are free. Parking in the same spot increases your chance of remembering where you left the car. It also has the additional benefit of making you walk a little further, by choosing a spot some way from the entrance (see Chapter 10 for information about the benefits of exercise for depression).

Developing habits and routines for other instances of absentmindedness can also help. For example, put up a decorative hook or get a basket for your car and house keys, and make sure that you always put your keys there. Don't forget to write these tasks down in your daily planner (see the earlier section 'Putting pen to paper').

Smelling (and touching and seeing) the roses

Most people experience the world through sight, sound, touch, smell, and taste. Memory experts have discovered that when you use more than one sense, your ability to remember something improves. For example, when you listen to several instructions, you're more likely to remember them if you also see them in writing and then write them down yourself.

When you need to remember something, try to experience it with as many senses as possible. For example, if you want to remember the address '10 Greene Street', picture ten people mowing grass beside a residential road. Using both the image and the smell of the green grass helps plant the address in your memory.

You can also use a familiar melody to help you remember information – just like children do when learning the alphabet. Just change the lyrics of a song to include the information you want remember. But don't forget, one of the very best ways to remember something is to write it down. Writing and singing involve using more than one of your senses.

Using your senses in this way is great for improving memory. But beware the limitations of this technique. When you want to remember the names and faces of people you meet, reaching out and tracing the shape of their faces (or any other part of their anatomy) probably isn't a good idea. And tasting people you've just met is really *not* advisable!

Talking sense!

University of Michigan psychologist Oscar Ybarra examined the relationship between memory and cognitive ability and social engagement. He studied more than 3,000 Americans between the ages of 24 and 96. He also studied 2,000 people from the Middle East. He found that, across cultures, the more people talk to others, the better their memory and cognitive functioning.

Does this mean that if you start talking to people more, your memory is going to improve and your IQ is going to sky rocket? Well, it's not that easy. We can't conclude from this study that social engagement causes improved memory or prevents your memory from declining. It may be that people with good memory tend to get together with friends or family more often, and that people with memory problems or depression tend to stay away from other people. So don't feel like you have to become a social butterfly. On the other hand, the more support you get from others, the better you feel. And getting together with other people can be an excellent alternative to withdrawing deeper into your depression.

Remembering names

Are you having difficulty in remembering names? Do you forget someone's name only seconds after being introduced? If so, try this: next time you're introduced to someone, use their name at least three times when you have another conversation with the person. 'Hi, Ryan, nice to meet you, Ryan. So, do you live locally, Ryan?'

Try looking directly at the person and taking a mental photograph. As you make eye contact, use the person's name again in conversation. When you turn away, picture the person's name, face, and anything interesting you discovered about them. Repeat the name to yourself several more times, and then go and write it down on the daily planner or key it into your personal organiser (see the earlier section 'Putting pen to paper').

Biting off no more than you can chew

Chunking involves grouping or organising large amounts of information into small units. Doing so greatly helps your memory. Here's an example of how chunking works.

First, read the following numbers and then close your eyes and try to remember them.

632895745

You may find this exercise is difficult. An excellent technique for remembering strings of unrelated numbers is to put them together in shorter units or chunks. Now read the following numbers and then close your eyes and repeat them.

554–759–823

Did you do a little better this time? Your brain, and immediate memory in particular, finds it easier to hold onto greater quantities of small parcels of information than storing one large amount of information.

Decreasing multitasking

Do you ever talk on the phone at the same time as answering your email? Do you sometimes listen to the news while you're reading the newspaper? The modern world encourages, and sometimes demands, multitasking. However, when you're depressed, your ability to pay attention is put under pressure. And multitasking makes heavy demands on your attention.

Understand that, during a time of depression, your concentration may not be as good as usual. If you need to remember something or figure out something new, do so in a quiet setting. Make sure that you concentrate on only one thing at a time.

Following through

Do you have several uncompleted projects hanging over you? The stress of knowing that you have unfinished business may increase your negative mood. When you're having problems with your memory, chasing up progress on several different fronts becomes especially difficult.

Whatever you start, make sure that you finish it. Don't begin another project until you've finished the one you've already begun. Alternatively, you can finish a portion of your project and then plan ahead for a later time, place, and space to tackle the rest. For example, with something as time-consuming as your tax return, you may want to break it down into logical pieces, rather than doing it all at once. And finally, make sure that you plan far enough ahead, so that within your plan you are giving yourself enough time for your project.

Food for thought

The food you eat and drink can affect your memory. Eating lots of fruit and vegetables may help you remember more, as well as allowing to you hold on better to the memories you already have. In 2000, research presented at the Society for Neuroscience showed that rats who were fed a diet of spinach performed better on tests involving memory and learning than did rats who ate a more typical rat diet. Although the results are preliminary, this study supports the theory that the *antioxidants* (substances that destroy harmful oxidants which adversely affect your body) found in fruits and vegetables can neutralise the free radical molecules (the byproducts of oxidation) that are thought to contribute to the cell damage and memory loss associated with aging.

Letting it go and reviving recall

One of the most annoying memory problems can be forgetting a word or name in the middle of a conversation. You know that you're going to remember it tomorrow, or in a couple of minutes, but it's on the tip of your tongue and yet won't come out of your mouth! You feel so silly, and the more you try to remember it, the more infuriated you get with yourself.

Stop, take a deep breath, and relax. Tell yourself that it happens to us all, and that remembering the word isn't really that important. Let yourself start thinking about something else. Then, a little later, take some time to think about any associations you may have with that name or word. Most likely, you're then going to find that you remember it. And, whatever else you forget, don't forget to remind yourself that depression disrupts memory!

Part III
Actively Combating Depression: Behaviour Therapy

'It was a suggestion by his workmates to get him out of his bed and out of his depression.'

In this part . . .

Depression stops people in their tracks. Inactivity and a sense of inertia often go hand in hand with depression. This part explores how to change your behaviour, so you can get moving again. Just taking a few initial steps can look like an insurmountable barrier. So we start this part off by showing you how to climb over the obstacles to activity constructed by your mind. Then we explore Exercise Avenue, a great route for improving mood. Next, we encourage you to reconnect with pleasurable activities – whether you feel like doing so or not. Finally, we provide a step-by-step method for solving some of life's most troublesome, irritating problems.

Chapter 9

Don't take it Lying Down!

*I*n this chapter, we give you the tools for putting together an action plan to get you moving again. We then explain how depression reduces motivation, and offer you exercises for overcoming your inactivity. Right now, you may think that just reading a few pages of this book isn't going to help you deal with the overwhelming lethargy you're feeling. But try to be patient, and give our suggestions a go. After all, you've got nothing to lose by reading on a bit further.

Depression drains your confidence, energy, and motivation. If you're seriously depressed, you're probably feeling that you can't carry out even the basic tasks of daily living.

The clock chimes 1, 2, 3, and then it's 10 a.m. Tears stream down Paul's face; he's still in bed. Waves of shame wash over him. Another wasted weekend. He feels like a lazy, good for nothing failure. He just can't face even simple day-to-day tasks. Crushing sadness paralyses him. He's a prisoner of depression, unable to escape. The pain deepens, with each day worse than the one before. 'When is it going to end? How can I end it?' he sobs.

If you've hardly moved for several days and have thoughts of profound hopelessness or death, you need to go and talk to a professional. If making an appointment feels too difficult, ask a friend or family member to help you. You can also pick up the phone and get help: call a crisis line, such as the Samaritans, NHS Direct, your GP, your local Community Mental Health Resource Centre, or your nearest hospital Accident and Emergency department. National phone numbers are listed in the Appendix.

Acting on Action-Blocking Thoughts

Doing the dishes, putting out the rubbish, paying bills, and mowing the lawn – not everyone's cup of tea, but when you're feeling depressed finding the necessary motivation to tackle such chores can be a major problem.

Struggling with depression can make everyday living feel like you're walking in thick, deep, gooey mud. A kitchen with a few dirty dishes may as well be an Army mess hall, paying the monthly bills feels like doing three years of tax returns at once, and taking out the rubbish is the equivalent of climbing Mount Everest.

When you're battling depression, you're likely to neglect important tasks. And that's perfectly understandable. However, putting off necessary chores can set off a multitude of negative thoughts and guilty feelings, sapping any motivation you have and deepening your depression. We call these thoughts *action-blocking thoughts*, and they include any negative thought about your inability to act, or about the futility of doing so. These thoughts can stop you from getting started, or can even stop you dead in your tracks.

If you find yourself thinking action-blocking thoughts, take a close look at the action blockers. You may well find that your inactivity is built on flimsy foundations. Examining your action-blocking thoughts can help you escape their tenacious grip and break the cycle of inactivity. Otherwise, you can all too easily find your mood humming along to the tune of that downward spiral 'The less you do, the worse you feel; the worse you feel, the less you do' – second verse, same as the first . . .

In the following sections, we highlight four common action-blocking thoughts and expose their central flaws. When you can let go of the action-blocking thinking that is holding you back, you can start overcoming your inactivity.

I just can't be bothered . . .

When you're feeling okay, you don't usually lack motivation – and even on those occasions when you don't feel particularly keen on doing something, somehow the desire to get started just seems to arise from nowhere.

Motivation rarely appears spontaneously in the midst of depression. When you're depressed, it's important to get into action. Behaviour changes first, and feelings, second. Taking action actually creates motivation.

Just a few minutes more . . .

This thought, like the previous one about motivation, is seductively inaccurate, and is based on faulty thinking. When you're feeling exhausted, believing that more rest is going to help recharge your batteries is only too easy. Some people then spend more and more time in bed, trying to kid themselves that if they just get enough rest, they're going to be ready to tackle those tasks they keep on shelving. But feeling energetic never happens, because too much rest causes muscles to weaken and fatigue to deepen.

To function properly, you need a healthy balance of activity and rest. Activity (unless it's unusually excessive and prolonged) actually recharges the body giving you drive and energy. The vital key to overcoming fatigue and inactivity is to work on getting started, and just taking one small step at a time.

Why try, when I'm just going to fail . . .

Of course you're going to fail! Everyone fails. Bet you can't think of anyone we know that doesn't fail from time to time? So what's the problem with this view? Depression refuses to acknowledge normality which is that no one succeeds at everything, every time. Depression invites all possible negative predictions, and failure is one of those predictions. But by starting off small, and breaking tasks into do-able steps, you can effectively minimise failure.

A lazy person – that's me!

Labelling yourself *lazy* only makes getting started more difficult. The problem with labels is that they can grossly exaggerate and can stick. When you're depressed, you really do feel tired and you have far less enthusiasm than usual for accomplishing necessary tasks.

Psychologists know that people don't succumb to depression as a result of laziness. Out of the thousands of studies we've seen on depression, we can't think of a single one that shows laziness as a cause. Getting started on tasks when you're feeling low is hard enough; don't add the burden of guilt and shame by attaching the *lazy* label to yourself.

One Step at a Time: Recording Activity

Keeping an Activity Record is the best step you can take if you have severe depression and you're neglecting important responsibilities or chores. The technique is straightforward and simple. (See Table 9-1 for a sample Activity Record.)

1. **Get out your notebook and list each day of the week in a column on the left-hand side of a page.**

   You can also use a daily planner if you prefer.

2. **Identify and write down one previously neglected activity a day, for the coming week.**

   Make your activity something small at first!

3. **After completing the activity, write down alongside it on the right-hand side of the page how the activity went and how you feel after finishing it.**

This exercise is about giving yourself credit for getting started, not on how brilliantly, or otherwise, the activity went.

Is simply recording your activities going to increase your motivation? Surprisingly, yes. We find that any activity focuses attention and helps to get you moving. You also notice how much better you feel afterwards, which makes it even more likely that you're going to tackle the next activity on your list for tomorrow, when you get there.

Kathleen's story gives you an example of how to keep an Activity Record. Kathleen is slowly sinking into depression. For the past month, she's been spending most of her weekends in bed. Her mind is full of self-loathing. Although she somehow makes it into work most days, the minute she gets home, she collapses. Her diet consists of cold cereal and dry crisp bread, because she hasn't the energy to do the shopping, or to prepare anything even if she buys it. What little fresh food there is invariably goes off before being eaten, and is slung out, making her feel even worse.

Kathleen's best friend, Becky, notices her worsening mood and weight loss. Becky is worried about Kathleen, so she pops round to see her. She asks Kathleen what she's been eating, because she sees that the fridge is practically empty. Kathleen tells her, 'Mainly just dry cereal.' 'And what are you going to do when you run out of cereal?' Becky asks. Kathleen shrugs her shoulders and replies, 'Dunno! Guess I'm just going to stop eating. I don't really care.'

Becky suggests that Kathleen starts an Activity Record and briefly explains how to do it. She says, 'I'm going to pop round again in a couple of days. I expect to see food in the fridge. If you don't start getting moving just a little, and if you're not feeling better pretty soon, I'm taking you to your doctor.'

Kathleen reluctantly agrees, because she knows that Becky's not kidding. At first, Kathleen thinks that she can't find the motivation even to start an Activity Record. She's also convinced that she's too lazy, and that even if she does make the attempt, she's probably going to fail. However, Kathleen trusts Becky so she reckons that she has little to lose by giving the exercise a go. Table 9-1 shows Kathleen's Activity Record for the first week. Notice that the Activity Record in Table 9-1 doesn't include any huge projects.

Table 9-1		Kathleen's Activity Record
Day	*Activity*	*Outcome*
M	Order a take-away from the local restaurant whose menu came through the door, and which says it includes delivery.	Well, I did it. I didn't feel like eating most of it, but I spoiled myself with a wicked chocolate dessert. It actually tasted pretty good.
T	Go to the corner shop and pick up a couple of things for dinner, and some cereal and milk just in case I really can't face cooking.	This was a lot harder. I didn't want to go in, but at least there wasn't much of a queue. When I got home, I didn't cook, and just had the cereal. It did taste better with fresh milk than just dry.
W	Go to the bank. I've been putting that off for quite a few weeks.	It felt surprisingly good to get that done. I even decided to microwave the food I bought yesterday. It wasn't too bad at all.
Th	Go to the post office and get stamps so I can post the letters and bills off.	This wasn't as hard as I thought it was going to be. Admittedly, I did have to force myself to do it, but I guess that's okay.
F	Pay any remaining outstanding bills, and start looking at what can go onto direct debit.	I was just too tired; I couldn't get myself moving. Maybe the direct debit decisions are going to have to wait. I'll try something less ambitious tomorrow.
Sa	Pay remaining bills. Do a supermarket shop.	I've actually paid all my bills on time this month! What a relief. I really get so angry with myself when I keep on putting things off and results in exorbitant interest charges plus late penalty fees. I feel so good. And I actually did the supermarket shopping!
Su	Phone Becky with my report, before she checks up on me!	I have to admit I felt pretty good telling Becky what I've done so far. I've a long way to go, but it's a great start.

When you develop your Activity Record, select small, manageable goals. None of them should take more than 20 or 30 minutes at first. After getting started, you can think about including slightly bigger tasks.

Kathleen didn't do everything she set out to do each day. So don't worry if you also don't complete everything. Celebrate your successes and forgive your failures. If you don't complete an item, think about putting it onto the list for the next day. But if you still don't do it the next day, then perhaps the task is more than you can handle right now. Put it to one side for the next week or so.

If you find yourself unable to get started on your Activity Record, or don't feel a little better after using the record for a couple of weeks, think about getting help from a professional.

Conquering 'Can't' Thoughts

Your mind is constantly buzzing with thoughts about yourself, other people and about the future. Even if you're not suffering from depression, many of your spontaneously occurring thoughts in no way reflect the reality of what has happened, is currently happening, and is going to happen. In the following section, we review specific 'can't' thoughts and ways to defeat them. Throughout this book, and especially in Chapters 5, 6, and 7, you can find more information about the many ways that thoughts distort your view of the world, and what you can do to change the distortions.

Depression can greatly magnify negative thoughts. One of the most common thoughts we hear from our clients when discussing the idea of taking action is, 'Well, I'd really like to, but I just *can't*.' If you've ever had that thought, you most likely truly believe that you're incapable – because of basic inadequacy, incompetence, or depression itself – and you're genuinely convinced that taking action is beyond your ability. Read on to find out how to banish activity-sapping thoughts.

Thinking through your thoughts

When you regularly tell yourself that you're incapable of accomplishing specific tasks, we call this type of thinking 'can't do-itis'. Although this diagnosis may sound a bit fanciful, we assure you that its effects aren't. Through repetition alone, 'can't do-itis' can become a fixed belief that you eventually see as a fundamental truth. Consider the following common thoughts:

✔ I can't remember a thing.

✔ I can't think clearly.

✔ I can't possibly clean out the shed; it's just too much.

✔ I can't concentrate on anything.

✔ I can't motivate myself to do anything.

✔ I just can't function any more.

✔ I can't do anything right.

Do they sound familiar? They do to us! On some days, can't thoughts can just keep on going round and round in your head.

Not that long ago, author Elaine was feeling a bit low, and heard herself saying through tears, 'I just can't face it!' She then sniffed miserably and admitted, 'Actually, I know that I *can* face it – but I really don't *want* to!' Having realised that she wasn't *unable* to act, but was *choosing* not to, Elaine proceeded to break the task down into a number of smaller, less scary, potentially do-able chunks. Then she did just the first tiny bit of the task, successfully. Having disproved the 'can't do-itis', Elaine was then able to tackle the next bit of the task, and so on.

Perhaps you're thinking that putting can't thoughts to the test may work for the authors of this book, but it won't work for you when you're terribly depressed. If so, you may be interested to know that the majority of our depressed patients also think at first that the strategy isn't going to help them. Nevertheless, when they try it, they almost always discover that testing out can't thoughts helps.

Testing out behavioural experiments

You can prove once and for all that each of your can't thoughts is false by showing evidence to the contrary. Here are some ideas you can use to test a few of the can't thoughts we list in the section 'Thinking through your thoughts'.

✔ **I just can't function any more.** Breathing is practically all you have to do to disprove this idea! But as well as breathing you can further test yourself by getting out of bed, pouring yourself a glass of water, drinking a few sips, and doing a couple of small activities, such as brushing your hair or your teeth. If your 'can't thoughts' start to interfere, focus and concentrate intently and solely on the movements of your body while you're performing the task. Make a daily habit of disproving that you are incapable of moving: make an Activity Record that lists a new task each day (see 'Taking One Step at a Time: Recording Activity', earlier in this chapter).

✔ **I can't remember a thing.** We have our colleague, Dr Steve Hayes, to thank for this idea. Try remembering this number sequence – 1, 2, 3. Now pretend that we're offering you a million pounds (don't forget that we said 'pretend!') if you can remember '1, 2, 3'. We're willing to bet that if a million pounds were really on the table, you'd remember that sequence a few minutes from now. (If not, we suggest that you see your doctor, because something other than depression may be going on.)

If you can pass *this* test, you can probably find many more examples of things you can remember. And if you can remember something – anything – then you can you use this to disprove your 'can't thought'. At the same time, please realise that depression does cause a certain amount of difficulty with memory. If you want more help with your memory, flick to Chapter 8.

✔ **I can't possibly clean out the shed; it's just too much.** Start by cleaning out one very small corner of your shed. After getting that done, consider cleaning another small area the next day. Perhaps in a few more days you can tackle two or three small spaces. That's how seemingly impossible tasks get done – one small bit at a time.

When you're depressed, your mind can sabotage your efforts to improve how you're feeling by focusing on the whole task facing you – making it feel as though you must get the task done in one go. For example, if you picture all the miles you're going to walk in the coming year, and you believe that you must walk the entire distance today, we bet you probably won't even feel like starting.

Break tasks down into very small, achievable chunks. You can conquer 'can't do-itis' by identifying a small bit of whatever it is that you think you can't do, and then going ahead and doing just that.

Checking Out Your Negative Predictions

Your mind can sabotage your plans for taking action in another clever way – by assuming that catastrophes are a certainty. When depression takes hold, these negative predictions seem increasingly believable and horrible. You may feel as though your horoscope consistently says, 'Today is absolutely not the day for trying new things. Retreat, withdraw, and stay passive. Don't take any action.' And your 'horror-scope' never gets updated.

If you're hearing similar dire predictions from your mind's fortune-teller, perhaps it's time to test out such misguided advice.

If you get stuck when it comes to tackling important tasks, try using our Negating Negative Predictions technique, to conquer your catastrophising. Use this technique initially for just one week. You may find that it helps you to get moving and also helps in shifting your depression. Take the following steps and check out the sample chart in Table 9-2.

1. **For each day of the week, write down one or two tasks you've been avoiding.**

   Try to think of small, do-able projects. If you choose a larger project, break it down into small pieces to be tackled over a certain period. Then do it just one bit at a time.

2. **Make a stress prediction for each task.**

   Predict (on a 0 to 100 point scale) how much stress you think that the task is going to cause you. For example, do you reckon that paying the bills is going to feel incredibly difficult? If so, you may want to predict the stress factor as 70 or even above.

3. **Make a boost prediction for each task.**

   Rate (on a 0 to 100 point scale) how much of a boost you reckon you're getting in terms of satisfaction, confidence, and a lifting of your mood when you've completed the task. For example, if you think that paying bills is going to result in a mild to modest boost in satisfaction, mood, or confidence, you may want to rate the expected boost at around 25 to 40.

4. **Record the outcome (or your actual experience) on your chart for both the stress and boost categories.**

   After finishing the task, write down how much stress and aggravation you *actually experienced* from doing the project, plus how much of a boost you got in terms of increasing your feelings of satisfaction, confidence, and improvement in your mood.

Amelia, a university professor, has been depressed for the past month. She starts arriving to work late and sinking on to the sofa the moment she gets home. She eventually drags herself upstairs to bed after a night spent watching what she calls mindless TV. Important tasks, such as preparing lectures, marking exam papers, paying bills, and shopping, start mounting. Amelia decides to try the Negating Negative Predictions technique. Table 9-2 shows you her chart.

Table 9-2	Amelia's Negating Negative Predictions Chart				
Day	Task	Pre-dicted Stress	Experienced Stress	Pre-dicted Boost	Experienced Boost
M	Household shopping	50	25	10	20
T	Mark one exam question	70	20	10	30
W	Do the dishes	45	10	5	20
Th	Finally call Thomas to talk	50	5	20	60
F	Pay bills	75	30	25	70
Sa	Mow lawn	50	50	15	50
Su	Plant flow-ers	40	10	25	60

As you can see in Table 9-2, Amelia consistently predicted that her activities would involve more stress and hassle than she actually experienced. The stress was only as great as she expected in one case – and that was because the lawnmower kept cutting out. Although not every task gave her a huge boost in satisfaction, confidence, and mood, the kick that she experienced was always far greater than she imagined it was going to be. After one week, Amelia still felt depressed, but she at least experienced a small lift in her mood from the exercise. And that lift made it easier to take on new tasks.

If you're like most other people with depression, you're likely to experience results similar to Amelia's. You find yourself predicting activities to be more stressful and less rewarding than you actually find them to be. Why not try out the Negating Negative Predictions exercise for two weeks?

We didn't include any fun activities in the Negating Negative Predictions exercise. Did we leave out fun activities because we think that you shouldn't or can't enjoy yourself if you're depressed? No. We excluded these activities because we believe that finding renewed pleasures is so important that we devote all of Chapter 11 to this topic.

Giving Yourself Credit

As well as the action-blocking thoughts, 'can't do-itis' and negative predicting that we explored in the previous section, your depressed mind has another way of stopping you dead in your tracks. Consider this: you eventually manage to get yourself to finish something you've been putting off for quite a while. Then your mind proceeds to rubbish your success with the thought, 'Well, sure I did that, but so what? Any fool could've done that!' As this thought shows, depression not only spoils quality of life but it also tries to sabotage efforts you make to overcome it.

When you hear your thoughts telling you to belittle your accomplishments, think about an alternative perspective. Doing the shopping when you're **not** suffering from depression, perhaps doesn't look like much of an achievement. But if you did the shopping despite having a broken leg, are you likely to value the achievement more highly?

Okay, so you don't have a broken leg. But the effect of depression is much the same. Depression makes everything harder to do than when you're in a good frame of mind. As we point out in Chapter 2, depression drains the body of energy; saps enthusiasm, sabotages sleep, and can cause confusion.

 Given the wide range of physical and mental effects of depression, accomplishing any task in this condition is a remarkable feat. Therefore, don't forget to give yourself a big pat on the back for getting things done when you're depressed. It's very important that you give yourself credit, by congratulating yourself for each and every effort you make – big and small.

The technique of 'three pats on the back' a day can set up your new, productive habit. Note down three things you've managed to do each day, no matter how small or seemingly insignificant. You're likely to find that keeping and reviewing this record is going to help in lifting your mood.

Chapter 10

Exercising to Lift Depression

. . . .

In This Chapter

▶ Answering the 'Why exercise?' question

▶ Finding motivation in all the right places

▶ Fitting an exercise programme into your life

▶ Choosing exercise you can live with – and enjoy

. . . .

*I*n this chapter, we show you how a fitness programme designed to fit snugly into your lifestyle can substantially improve your depression, your physical health, and even your quality of life. Exercise drives out depression. When depression tries to tell you that you can't get started, we explain how to talk back to your depression and draw up a plan for overcoming your lethargy. And we help you choose the type of exercise that's just right for you and your lifestyle.

At 4 a.m., **Patricia** wakes up and can't get back to sleep. She knows that lack of sleep affects her performance at work, which makes her even more upset, and that, in turn, makes getting back to sleep even more difficult. This early waking has just got to stop. Yesterday, even her boss commented that she looked tired. Patricia tosses and turns for the next two hours and then finally gets up at 6 a.m. What a miserable way to start the day.

Depression runs in Patricia's family, and she herself has been on and off medication for the past five years. Her doctor tells her that she's probably going to need to be on antidepressants for life. But lately, the medication alone seems ineffective. Her depression worsens. First, her doctor increases the dosage; when that doesn't work, he suggests adding another drug to improve her response to the medication. Patricia is worried about both short- and long-term side effects of both drugs. She asks her doctor about other therapies for depression. He suggests regular exercise. (And we agree!)

But as much as we urge exercise, it serves as just one piece of the puzzle. If you try repeatedly, and still find you just can't get into exercise, don't beat yourself up. This book is bursting with many other ways of overcoming depression.

Introducing Endorphins Into Your Life

Who doesn't want to feel good? There are so many ways of feeling great: laughter, a delicious meal, making love, dancing, or perhaps a walk in the great outdoors are just a few examples. But what is it about these activities that actually makes people feel good?

The answer lies, in part, in the brain. The brain has special receptors that receive *opiates*, drugs such as heroin and cocaine that relieve pain and bring about a heightened sense of wellbeing. The human body produces its own natural substances, called *endorphins* that function like opiates in the brain. Endorphins produce a similar 'high' to that produced by heroin and cocaine: except endorphins are legal substances – and safe! You can generate endorphins through exercise and doing activities you enjoy. Endorphins bring about a feeling of pleasure and wellbeing that may well hinder depression.

You can increase your production of endorphins by having sex, eating chocolate, consuming spicy foods, and, you guessed it, engaging in exercise. And although you can try to boost your endorphin level by sitting around eating chocolate all day or having non-stop sex, it's pretty obvious that these approaches aren't advisable. So you're left with exercise.

Regular exercise stimulates endorphin production and also tones up your whole body. Exercise improves your cardiovascular system, reduces the risk of various cancers, decreases the risk of diabetes, and balances your cholesterol ratio. As well, exercise gets rid of excessive adrenaline that can cause anxiety and other problems. It's a fact: The right sort of exercise makes you healthier.

Research suggests that exercise can help in easing depression. As yet, it isn't clear if one particular type of exercise works better for lessening your depression (or if all types of exercise work equally well). Although we don't recommend exercise as the only answer to dealing with major depression, you're likely to benefit enormously from *regular* exercise.

Always check with your doctor before beginning an exercise programme – especially if you're overweight, over the age of 40, or have health problems. You also need to see your doctor if you experience serious pain, dizziness, nausea, or other troubling symptoms after exercising, because these symptoms aren't generally normal after moderate exercise.

Ungluing Yourself from the Sofa

Exercise can help you feel better emotionally and physically, but there's just one problem: depression tries to point you in the exact opposite direction, telling you to withdraw, retreat, and hibernate. So when you're depressed, you can feel paralysed. Ordinary living takes extraordinary effort, and you may feel like staying in bed and pulling the covers up over your head.

The mere thought of starting to exercise may sound utterly impossible when you're in the midst of depression. You can barely put one foot in front of the other; how can we possibly suggest that you start exercising? The depressed mind comes up with thoughts that stifle initiative and motivation. These lethargic, demotivating thoughts may be telling you that you can't possibly succeed in carrying out an exercise plan. We know you may feel this way. Please understand that we don't underestimate the difficulty of overcoming the fatigue that's brought on by depression. Nevertheless, we believe you're going to find that the benefits of exercise outweigh the effort you put in.

You *can* talk back to these dark thoughts that try to stifle activity. You can start by subjecting them to scrutiny and analysis. Ask yourself if there's an alternative perspective to your depressed mind's point of view. Is your mind exaggerating, distorting, or making negative predictions without any real basis? If so, try to substitute the negativity with realistic alternatives. You need to identify and provide counter-arguments to any negative thoughts that come into your mind, and then get that body moving!

In the first column of Table 10-1, we list the five thoughts that most frequently get in the way of reasonable, alternative viewpoints and prevent you from getting active. If you find yourself thinking negative demotivating thoughts, argue back with alternative, motivating thoughts such as the ones in the second column. (Go to Chapter 9 for other ideas on how to overcome action-blocking thoughts.)

Table 10-1	Defeating Demotivating Thoughts
Demotivating Thoughts	*Motivating Thoughts*
I'm too depressed to exercise.	Although that's how I *feel*, it doesn't mean its true. I can test this thought out by going for a ten-minute walk.
I can hardly get out of bed; I can't possibly exercise.	Another interesting, typically depressed thought. But I do get out of bed every day. And, if I can get out of bed, I know logically that I can push myself to do a small amount of exercise.

(continued)

Table 10-1 *(continued)*

Demotivating Thoughts	Motivating Thoughts
Exercise isn't worth doing.	That's how it feels, but the evidence says otherwise. Exercise helps people feel better. I know I read that somewhere . . .
I don't enjoy exercise.	True. But I don't have to turn into a fitness fanatic. I can benefit from even a small amount of exercise.
I don't have time to exercise.	I make time to brush my teeth daily. If something is really important, I can find a way to fit it in a few times a week.

After identifying your demotivating thoughts and arguing against them, you may still feel unmotivated. And a few demotivating thoughts may linger. Realise that thoughts are just thoughts – they're not necessarily true.

To show you how thoughts aren't facts, we have a short exercise for you to do. (If you have a physical problem stopping you getting up and down easily try thinking up an exercise you can do sitting down that helps you conquer your demotivating thoughts.)

1. **Sit down in a comfortable chair.**

2. **Say out loud, 'I can't stand up!'**

3. **Forcefully say out loud, 'I can't stand up!' ten more times.**

4. **Now stand up.**

Did you manage to stand up? Your mind told your voice to say 'I can't stand up', but you did (or at least, we assume you did). The point of this seemingly silly exercise is to show your negative thoughts simply aren't always true.

You may find yourself thinking things that are inaccurate or untrue, and then act as though they really are just that. For example, we bet that you've heard quite a few people say, 'I can't stop smoking.' Indeed, giving up smoking is incredibly difficult; and at times, it may seem impossible. Yet *millions* of people who make that statement eventually do manage to quit. Of course, when the smokers think that they can't stop, they truly believe it. And when you're depressed, you fully believe the thought that says you just can't exercise.

Thoughts are just thoughts – many thoughts born of a depressed mind have no more reality than 'I can't stand up', or 'I can't stop smoking'.

Easing Into Exercise

With any luck, you can convince yourself that it may well be easy to start exercising. But that doesn't mean that exercising itself is going to be easy. Depression really does sap your body's energy, so we suggest that you start your exercise programme gently and ever so slowly.

Most exercise gurus preach the importance of exercising for at least 20 minutes, three to five times a week. You may have read recent guidelines recommending that you exercise for at least one hour each day. We don't know about you, but we certainly don't have a spare hour a day. Research shows that doing *any* exercise is far better than none, so even ten minutes, three or four times a week, can help. And you can ease your way into the world of exercise with activities that barely seem like exercise at all:

- ✔ Park a little farther from your workplace.
- ✔ Choose the space in the car park furthest from where you want to go.
- ✔ Take the stairs rather than the lift or escalator.
- ✔ Do a few brief exercises during work breaks.
- ✔ If you use a cordless or mobile phone, walk while you talk.
- ✔ The next time you go shopping, walk a bit further through the shopping centre.

Walking a little farther, taking the stairs, and moving around more all make a good start for your exercise programme. Then, if you want, you can add a little more activity to your daily routine. To get the maximum benefit from exercise, work your body a little harder each day.

The following list shows you three decisions you have to make when designing your exercise programme. For each, start small and build up slowly. And remember that you're not competing with anyone, so don't compare yourself to others if you go to the gym.

- ✔ **Frequency:** 'How often am I going to work exercise into my life?' As a start, consider planning to exercise twice a week.
- ✔ **Intensity:** 'How fast and how far am I going to walk, or run? How heavy are the weights I'm going to use?' At first, we suggest the answer be 'not very' to all of these questions.
- ✔ **Time:** 'How long do I want to exercise each time?' Try starting with just ten minutes.

Weighing Up Your Exercise Options

What type of exercise is going to work best for you? We can honestly say that we have no idea. And you may not know either. So we recommend that you review the various exercise options and pick one that looks the most appealing at first sight (or even just the one that looks the least horrible!).

In this section, we look at strength training, aerobic exercise, and yoga – three of the most popular exercise options. If you want even more info on all the possibilities that are out there, check out at your local health club or sports centre, or pick up a copy of *Fitness For Dummies* by Suzanne Schlosberg and Liz Neporent (Wiley).

Whatever type of exercise you go for, try it out for at least two weeks. If you find that type of exercise isn't for you, choose another. You may have to experiment a little, but you're likely to find an exercise soon that works well for you.

The goal isn't to become an accomplished yoga master, or to win an international dance competition, or even to become an Olympic champion. You only need to increase the intensity of your exercise slightly to start feeling the benefits.

Lifting depression's heavy weight

Strength training involves building muscle. You can do this through weight-lifting with free weights or by using weight machines. However, you don't actually need to use machines or weights at all. You can try the following strength-building exercises that don't need any special equipment:

- ✔ Lunges
- ✔ Push-ups
- ✔ Sit-ups
- ✔ Squats

You may think that strength training is only for body builders or for younger people. Not so. Many studies show that strength training provides incredible benefits at almost any age, perhaps even more so in older people. Strength training appears to improve mood, reduce the risk of falls, enhance memory and thinking ability, and prolong life.

Consider the possibility of a personal trainer, who can tailor strength training exercises that are just right for you. If you pay your trainer in advance for a discounted rate for a block of sessions, the desire not to waste your money is a powerful motivator (as is of course, having your very own trainer).

At first, you may find you're not too sure about your decision to work out. You may discover that muscles you didn't even know you had are aching. But within a month, you are very likely to begin feeling the difference made by your new, healthy habit.

Strength training can easily lead to injury if you aren't careful and don't know what you're doing. We recommend that you first talk to a trainer at your local gym or read a book on the subject, such as *Weight Training For Dummies* by Liz Neporent, Suzanne Schlosberg, and Shirley Archer (Wiley).

Working your heart and lungs

Aerobic exercise (or *cardiovascular exercise*) is one of the easiest exercise programmes to start. This type of exercise increases your oxygen intake and speeds up your heart rate. (*Aerobic* means 'with oxygen'.)

Aerobic exercise has a positive effect on your body. As well as improving your mood, aerobics can:

- Reduce bad cholesterol and raise good cholesterol
- Increase energy
- Reduce blood pressure
- Improve lung capacity
- Reduce anxiety
- Reduce the risk of breast and colon cancer
- Reduce the risk of diabetes

Walking is the most basic form of aerobic exercise. To turn it into an even more effective aerobic exercise, all you have to do is increase your walking speed so that your heart rate goes up. Of course, you can also do other aerobic activities, such as jogging, skating, cycling, dancing, and even aerobic workouts – at home with a DVD or video, or at an exercise class. Basically, an activity qualifies as aerobic if it speeds up both your heart-rate and your breathing to the point where you feel a little winded, but you can still say a short sentence without gasping for breath.

Health care professionals often recommend that you establish a *target heart rate* for your aerobic exercise. You can find out your target heart rate zone by first subtracting your age from 220. That number represents your absolute maximum heart rate, a rate you want to avoid going above. Your ideal zone lies between 0.5 and 0.8 of your maximum heart rate, depending on your fitness level. Your doctor can help you determine your fitness level and your ideal zone.

Relaxing and strengthening with yoga

Practising yoga may conjure up images of bodies being twisted into impossible-looking contortions. Or maybe you visualise rows of robed monks seated cross-legged on mats, chanting 'Ommmm. . . '

Nowadays, you're more likely to find practitioners of yoga dressed in the latest gym gear, straining and sweating at a local health club. And although some people with highly advanced yoga skills may twist their bodies like pretzels, most yoga exercises don't require such awesome flexibility.

As with many exercise routines, you won't know how you feel about yoga unless you try it. You can take yoga classes at your local health club or a Buddhist centre, or even by attending an adult education centre. You can also find all you need to know about yoga by reading *Yoga For Dummies* by Georg Feuerstein and Larry Payne (Wiley), or exercising with a video or DVD, such as *Basic Yoga Workout For Dummies* by Sara Ivanhoe.

Chapter 11

Rediscovering Healthy Pleasures

*W*hen you're feeling depressed, everything seems flat and lifeless. Food doesn't taste as good, music doesn't soothe you, and comedians aren't the least bit funny. Even the activities you used to enjoy seem pointless. So, what can you do to bring back pleasure into your life?

In this chapter, we talk about the beneficial effects of pleasure on your mood and body. Next, we help you rediscover a few of your favourite activities from a time when you weren't depressed, and even find some new ones. We explain why we believe enjoying life is your natural right. And even though you may believe you've lost the knack of having fun, we show you how to defeat your negative predictions and start enjoying yourself again.

Taking Fun Seriously

When depression overtakes you, managing the normal demands of daily living seems impossible. You may not even feel like getting out of bed. Having fun's totally out of the question, even frivolous.

Nevertheless, we suggest that you take a serious look at pleasure. Why? First, because pleasure lifts mood. Although the effect may initially be only temporary and slight, you're likely to find that with time and persistence pleasurable activities can help you overcome depression.

As well as the positive effects of pleasure on your emotional and mental states, pleasure can also have positive physical benefits, such as:

✓ Reducing chronic pain

✓ Decreasing risk of heart attacks

✓ Improving overall health

✓ Increasing immune function

✓ Prolonging life expectancy

Second, pleasure helps reduce stress. People who do enjoyable activities typically feel happier, more relaxed, and calmer. After taking all these factors into account, the pursuit of pleasure isn't in the least bit frivolous. Consider pleasure-seeking an essential activity for getting your life back on an even keel.

Identifying Activities You Enjoy

When you're depressed, you may not even be able to remember what fun and pleasure feel like. And coming up with a list of possible pleasurable activities may seem unimaginably difficult. Don't worry – this section helps you get started.

If you're feeling depressed, take a look at the fun things we list in this section. Obviously, not all of these activities are going to appeal. However, we suggest that you circle each of the items that you currently or *used to* find enjoyable. You can rank the activities: from the ones that appeal the most down to the absolutely unthinkable. Then think about which activities are possible for you. For example, if you currently don't have a partner, making love may not be at the top of the list this time round!

The Associates for Research into the Science of Enjoyment (`www.arise.org`) carried out a survey of adults from all over the world and what gave them the most pleasure. It seems that simple pleasures provide the most enjoyment. These activities include:

✓ Drinking a glass of wine

✓ Eating chocolate

✓ Entertaining friends

✓ Exercising

✓ Going out for a meal

✓ Having a cup of tea or coffee

✓ Making love

✓ Playing with children

- Reading
- Shopping
- Spending time with family
- Taking a hot bath or shower
- Watching TV

If you've ever been to France and gone into a bread shop, it probably won't surprise you to discover that the French have a particular fondness for indulging in pastries. Italians rank sex high on their list of pleasures. And Brits apparently really enjoy a nice cup of tea and drinking alcohol (No! You don't say!).

If nothing on the previous list captures your imagination think about choosing from the good things in life that appeal to the senses, such as:

- Eating spicy foods
- Having a massage
- Listening to music
- Looking at beauty in nature or art
- Smelling fresh flowers
- Spending time in a sauna or steam room
- Strolling through the great outdoors

Possibilities for enjoyable activities include experiencing the great outdoors, while indoor activities can be equally great! Here are some suggestions:

- Camping
- Cinema/video/DVD
- Dancing
- Hiking
- Theatre, concerts, musicals
- Reading groups
- Participating in sports
- Playing games
- Playing with pets
- Spectator sports
- Travel and holidays

Pain or pleasure? Some like it hot

You may have heard the perhaps surprising survey results concluding that curry – a spicy dish with meat, fish, or vegetables – is now Britain's most popular meal. According to David Smith, on the website Curryhouse.co.uk, the most popular curry in UK restaurants is Chicken Tikka Masala. While many imagine this to be a typical Indian dish, David Smith, says that Chicken Tikka Masala is actually a restaurant invention created in the UK by Bangladeshi restaurateurs, and one he calls 'A true hybrid and a recent chapter in the long history of curry.' He quotes Brent Thompson, who is highly knowledgeable on the subject of curries and has lived in India :'the term curry itself isn't really used in India, except as a term appropriated by the British to generically categorise a large set of different soup/stew preparations ubiquitous in India and nearly always containing ginger, garlic, onion, turmeric, chilli, and oil (except in communities that eat neither onion or garlic, of course) and which must have seemed all the same to the British, being all yellow/red, oily, spicy/aromatic, and too pungent to taste anyway' .

In New Mexico, pain is considered a flavour! The pain comes from the hot chilli sauce that chefs liberally pour – the hotter the better. At a New Mexican restaurant, 'Red or green?', is a question referring to the colour of the pepper in the sauce. The gourmet replies 'Which is hotter?'

Newcomers and visitors don't understand this, and many plates stay untouched after the first bite or two. Visitors frantically attempt to ease the pain (solutions like sour cream or honey work well). Diners sit bewildered, watching other, more experienced chilli enthusiasts wolf down huge quantities of fiery foods. But if they're willing to try the food again many people do find themselves, like the local population, actually craving chillies.

Science has discovered a cause for the craving of hot, spicy foods. Chillies are addictive. Here's why: when you bite into something peppery, *capsaicin* (the portion of the chilli that makes it hot) is released into your mouth. When capsaicin contacts the nerves in your mouth, pain signals rush to your brain. The brain releases a flood of *endorphins* (go to Chapter 10 for more about endorphins), blocking the pain and also inducing a state of wellbeing and pleasure. The brain also releases endorphins when you take part in the other pleasurable activities, we describe.

Vanquishing the Joy Destroyers

When you're wrestling with depression, putting pleasurable activities back into your life isn't all that simple. In fact, you may experience the very opposite when trying to reintroduce them. Recognise any of the following?

✔ **Feeling guilty:** This occurs when you believe that pleasure is wasteful, frivolous, undeserved, inappropriate, unproductive, or even downright sinful. We explain more about guilt in the next section.

✔ **Negative predicting:** Depression increases the likelihood that you see future events as bleak and joyless. You can find out more about negative predictions in 'Tackling self-fulfilling prophecies', later in the chapter.

You aren't going to get very far in your attempt to backer-introduce pleasure into your life if guilt or negative predicting are getting in the way. Here are some suggestions to unblock your path to progress.

Getting to grips with guilt

Guilt can be a good thing. When you do something truly wrong, guilt tells you not to do it again. And knowing that you're probably going to feel guilty can stop you from acting in ways that are unhealthy or morally wrong. Guilt functions as a moral compass, *when it works effectively.*

When you wave a magnet around a compass, the needle spins wildly. In the same way, too much guilt causes the needle on your moral compass to wave about wildly, and then point you in the wrong direction. Out-of-control guilt grossly exaggerates real or imagined wrongdoings. For example, excessive guilt may tell you that a single bar of chocolate is a sign of uncontrolled gluttony. Also, guilt may make you feel that you are undeserving of pleasure.

Excessive guilt is a key feature of depression. You not only feel low and miserable, but guilty as well. The combination of guilt and depression limits your ability to experience happiness, because depression drains you of the energy needed to enjoy life and guilt tells you that you don't deserve to feel good in the first place.

Increasing your awareness

Increasing your awareness of how guilt can influence your decision to take part in in the good things of life is critical. When guilt starts to interfere with those activities designed for enjoyment, certain thoughts may repeatedly run through your mind. Do any of the following thoughts sound familiar?

✔ I'm not good enough; I don't deserve to be happy.

✔ I feel that pleasure is a frivolous waste of time.

✔ If I beat myself up enough, I just may become motivated to do something more productive.

✔ I *should* have done things differently (there are about a million or so variants of this thought).

✔ I'm a loser. Pleasure's for the successful.

✔ I'm a burden to the people I care about.

Putting yourself down brings on powerful feelings of guilt. But how can you tell if your guilt is indicating an appropriate, healthy response based on a well-functioning moral compass, or is excessive, encouraging self-criticism and self-defeating thoughts and actions? Actually, identifying the specific type of guilt you're experiencing isn't that difficult – as the following section shows.

Guilt isn't *always* inappropriate. For example, it's perfectly reasonable to feel guilty if you have done any intentional, unnecessary acts that cause harm to you or someone else. But appropriate guilt has a time limit. Prolonging the bad feelings beyond this actually intensifies your depression. Holding onto guilt simply leads to negative thinking and self-criticism.

Breaking guilt's grip and reclaiming pleasure

Ask yourself if your pleasurable indulgences are really deliberate, harmful behaviours. If they are, perhaps a little short-term guilt may remind you to watch out for such behaviour in the future. But before you reach that conclusion, be sure to ask yourself the following Guilt Querying Questions:

- Was my indulgence aimed at harming myself?
- Is it possible that a little enjoyment can be a good thing rather than a bad thing?
- Is it possible that I'm magnifying the 'awfulness' of my indulgences?
- Am I blaming myself for something that I have no control over?
- Am I telling myself off just for having normal human imperfections?
- Where is it written that I *should* have done something different?

Here's an example of how you can put the Guilt Querying Questions to use. Connie works as a nurse at a busy hospital. The stress of working long hours (which are filled non-stop caring for and dealing with the needs of patients) builds up and up for her. The shortage of healthcare workers in her community pushes her to accept extra work shifts on a regular basis. She has little time for friends or fun. Her fatigue and loneliness gradually turn into depression.

Some close colleagues notice Connie's deteriorating mood. They advise her that she needs to do something for herself once in a while. Their suggestions include:

- Drinking wine
- Eating chocolate
- Having a massage
- Seeing a musical
- Renting an up-lifting DVD or video

As Connie mulls over her colleagues' suggestions, negative thoughts churn through her mind. She thinks, 'Great, I'm already ten pounds overweight, just think of how fat I'm going to get eating chocolate and drinking wine all day. And I'd feel horribly guilty spending my hard-earned money on something as self-indulgent as a massage. Massages are for the wealthy. So that leaves going to a musical. In my mood? Bet I'll hate it – and then the ticket's just another waste!'

Connie feels guilt *in advance* of indulging in a few simple pleasures such as eating chocolates, drinking an occasional glass of wine, or having a massage. After answering the Guilt Querying Questions we list earlier in this section, Connie's feelings of guilt alter slightly:

- **Was my indulgence primarily intended to harm myself?** Connie's response: 'Well, actually I haven't even done it yet. But my intention is to enjoy something, not to harm myself.'

- **Is it possible that a little enjoyment can be good rather than bad?** Connie's response: 'I suppose I rarely give myself any freedom to indulge in much of anything. What's so awful about a little pleasure? I'm starting to sound like my mother! I've read in that Dummies book that pleasure's actually good for the body and mind.'

- **Am I magnifying the 'awfulness' of my indulgences?** Connie's response: 'I suppose an occasional chocolate, glass of wine, or massage doesn't exactly mean I'm a mass murderer. Even Benjamen Franklin argued the benefits of taking all things in moderation.' She then says thoughtfully, 'Everything in moderation, including moderation.'

- **Am I blaming myself for something that I don't have control over?** Connie's response: 'Well, in the case of my weight, I admit it's down to so many factors – genetics (most of my relatives are overweight), insufficient exercise, daily lunches courtesy of the pharmaceutical sales reps, processed foods, too much fast food, to name but a few. Just a couple of sweets or a glass of wine really makes little difference.

- **Am I telling myself off just for having normal human imperfections?** Connie's response: 'Hey, at least I'm good at beating myself up! If I stop a second and think about it, everyone has their flaws. Ten pounds of extra weight isn't exactly the very worst thing I could imagine.'

- **Where is it written that I *should* have done something different?** Connie's response: 'I use that word *should* on myself a lot. Maybe I *should*, oops, I mean maybe it *would be better if* I replaced that word. Although diet books don't exactly recommend eating chocolate and drinking wine, most of them advise modest indulgences and say that there are hardly any foods falling in the "absolutely never" category.'

We hope that you also are going to seriously review the Guilt Querying Questions and come to Connie's conclusions about healthy indulgences. We believe that you really do deserve a reasonable amount of pleasure in your life. You don't need to earn the right to pursue happiness – indulging in a few enjoyable activities can be a powerful tool for fighting depression, if you give yourself the permission to use it.

If you answer the Guilt Querying Questions we list earlier in this section and guilt is still blocking you from seeking enjoyment, please read Chapters 3, 5, 6, and 7. These chapters give you more information about tackling the guilt that accompanies depression and robs you of the ordinary pleasures of everyday life. It is up to you to grant yourself the right to experience pleasure.

Tackling self-fulfilling prophecies

You may find after selecting a few enjoyable activities, you then dread the thought of doing them. You start seeing them as a burden. Depression creates a fog that obscure your ability to think clearly about the future.

Lucas graduates with a degree in architecture and immediately finds work he loves with a small firm in Northampton. Then the economy takes a nosedive, his firm restructures and he's made redundant. Around that time, Lucas breaks up with his girlfriend of four years standing. Understandably, he feels miserable, has less energy, and his sleep's disturbed. His counsellor suggests Lucas lists activities he found pleasurable in the past. He comes up with:

- ✔ Cycling
- ✔ Clubbing
- ✔ Badminton
- ✔ Spending time with friends

Negative thoughts then flood Lucas's mind. He predicts his friends will get fed up with him – he's dull and boring since his depression. He'll hate cycling now he's so unfit. And he decides he can't afford to go out clubbing.

If you're experiencing even a mild depression, beware. Your predictions of the future are most likely to be unreliable. Because pleasure seems impossible when you're down, anticipating enjoyment is particularly difficult to do. Press on and try to ignore your mind's pessimism.

If you find it difficult to pay attention to your negative predictions about activities that are meant to be fun, you can combat your mind's gloomy forecasting with an activity called Firing Your Mind's Faulty Forecaster. Slt down, grab a pen and paper, and make a chart like the one in Table 11-1. You're going to be surprised how helpful this activity can be.

1. **Pick three or four small, potentially pleasurable activities.**

   You don't have to view these as truly pleasurable – yet. Just try choosing easy(ish) ones to tackle, or some that you enjoyed in the past.

   If you have good, valid reasons for not engaging in a particular activity (other than low expectations of pleasure), don't select that item.

2. **On a point scale of 0 to 10, rate the amount of pleasure or fun you expect to get out of the activity.**

   Zero represents expecting absolutely no fun, 5 is anticipating moderate enjoyment, and 10 means expecting the activity will be utterly fantastic. We don't predict many 9's or 10's while you're feeling depressed.

3. **Perform the activity – just do it!**

   This is the hard part. Even if you rate an activity as 0 or 1 on the pleasure scale, push yourself to do it anyway. Your mind may resist with negative thoughts. Short circuit those thoughts and move that body of yours.

4. **After doing the activity, rate how much pleasure you actually experienced and briefly describe your reaction in words.**

   If you complete this exercise, you're likely to find that you experienced more fun and enjoyment from activities than you predicted. Invalidating your predictions may encourage trying some more pleasurable activities. The more pleasure you experience, the less depressed you're going to be.

Checking back in with Lucas, he has four activities on his pleasure list. None of them sound particularly exciting to him, so he tries the Firing Your Mind's Faulty Forecaster exercise. Table 11-1 shows Lucas's results.

Table 11-1	Firing Your Mind's Faulty Forecaster	
Activity	*Forecasted Fun*	*Experienced Fun*
Cycling	2	4 – I wasn't quite as unfit as I'd feared. Being outdoors felt good.
Clubbing	4	2 – the music was loud and lousy, and the drinks were too expensive.
Badminton	3	5 – I was pretty rusty, but it felt good being back at the old club.
Spending time with friends	3	6 – I had a surprisingly good experience.

While in three out of four cases, Lucas experienced significantly more fun and pleasure than he anticipated, in one case, he actually did have a pretty rotten time. Experiencing less pleasure than anticipated can occur for many reasons – Lucas,' financial concerns turned out to be quite realistic.

Also notice that Lucas didn't have the greatest time in the world with any of the activities; this is normal, because depression seriously dampens the experience of joy and your ability to have fun. However, if Lucas continues to pursue pleasurable activities, the amount of fun he has is very likely to increase slowly over time.

Like Lucas, you may have less pleasure than you anticipate occasionally. For example, you arrange a walking weekend, only to find it's rained off. Or, you go to a party and find that you feel uncomfortable or awkward. But be aware that the more pleasurable activities you try, the greater the probability you'll start experiencing pleasure.

Depression is a formidable enemy. Adding pleasure to your life is a small but significant step in fighting your depression. Give fun a chance. Remember that finding out how to have fun once again takes time and patience. Start with an activity that's going to give pleasure but doesn't isn't too demanding Your very favourite activities can wait until you are stronger.

Chapter 12

Handling Life's Headaches

In This Chapter

▶ Developing an effective problem-solving game plan

▶ Applying problem-solving skills in your life

Depression has a nasty way of slowing down and clogging up your brain's problem-solving machinery. When you're depressed, your problems can quickly grow from molehills to mountains, paralysing you and filling you with hopelessness. This then increases your depression, clouding your ability to find a way out of what is troubling you.

But despair not – here's the good news. Developing more effective problem-solving strategies helps defeat depression. This chapter shows a new approach to problem–solving - one you can easily apply to real-life problems.

We give you an all-round game plan for tackling problems that come in all shapes, sizes, and colours. Adele's story is typical of the problems that people with depression face. But getting the hang of a new game plan is much easier if you have examples, so we use Adele's story throughout this chapter to help you follow the game plan and hopefully score a victory over your problem.

Adele married Eddie, a self-confessed computer geek, when they were both 19. Come their 25th wedding anniversary, Adele realises that she's seriously bored with the marriage. She and Eddie don't talk to each other much any more – their life together feels boring and stale. Trying to discuss her feelings with Eddie, he's simply not interested, becoming increasingly distant and evasive the harder she tries. The months pass by, Adele slowly slides into a deep depression. She thinks seriously about divorce or having an affair - neither option appeals to her. She feels stuck, and can't see a way out.

Read on to see how Adele takes up CRICKET to help tackle her problems . . .

Devising Life's Problem-Solving Game Plan – CRICKET

In recent years, the problem-solving approach to fighting depression has gained wider popularity owing to research showing its effectiveness. The aims of the problem-solving approach, when applied to depression, are to:

- ✔ Uncover life problems that may be contributing to depression
- ✔ Figure out how depression lessens chances of finding solutions
- ✔ Develop effective problem-solving techniques
- ✔ Prevent relapse by improving coping skills

To make our problem-solving plan easy to remember, we give it the acronym CRICKET. The CRICKET game plan guides you through a series of steps. These steps help you to find effective solutions to your problems and then try them out.

- ✔ **C** stands for the central *core*, or the problem itself. The core includes how you see the problem and its cause(s), your feelings about the problem, and your beliefs about trying to solve it. For example, you may believe that the problem simply can't be overcome. That belief is part of the core of the problem.

- ✔ **R** stands for running through the *routes* – these are all the available routes or options you can take to approach the problem creatively.

- ✔ **I** is for *investigating* the outcomes that carrying out each option creates.

- ✔ **C** involves committing to a *choice* about which option you want to try.

- ✔ **K** refers to not *kidding* yourself by saying you 'can't decide'. Remember that no decision is still a decision – you're deciding not to change.

- ✔ **E** stands for your *emotional plan* for carrying out your option, because some choices may need courage.

- ✔ **T** stands for the *test* match – testing out your option. You carry out your plan, review the outcome check if it produced the desired result, and work out what to do next, if your plan proved unsuccessful.

The CRICKET problem-solving game plan doesn't guarantee success. But the approach does give you a better way of thinking through your problems. A thorough analysis helps improve your chances of discovering and putting in place the best possible solutions. CRICKET helps ease your depression by increasing confidence and building problem-solving skills.

In the following sections, we examine each of the steps in your game of CRICKET. Like many of the exercises throughout this book, most of the steps require putting pen to paper (or fingers to keyboard), so get out your note-book or switch on your computer.

If the problems in your life seem utterly hopeless and overwhelming, and you can't imagine even attempting to tackle them, please seek professional help before attempting to make use of our problem-solving game plan. The plan may still help you, but you're likely to need professional help in carrying it out.

Identifying the Central Core (C)

The first step in CRICKET involves a careful examination of your problem:

1. **Come up with a description of your problem.**

   Carefully consider what your problem is actually about. If has several strands, try to home in on which is the most important. Focus on the first key issue, then write down all you can about what's relates to it.

   Adele (who we describe at the beginning of the chapter) decides the quality of her marriage is a bigger problem than her boredom – though boredom plays a big part in her life. So she decides to initially focus on her marriage. Adele realises she and her husband haven't any common interests. Lovemaking is practically non-existent- their evenings are usually her slumped in front of the TV while husband Eddie plays on his computer. Adele wants a change, but doesn't know what to do.

2. **Reflect on your feelings about the problem.**

   Reflecting on all the feelings you have about a given problem is important. Doing so helps you to understand the impact the problem is having on your life.

   Adele identifies the overpowering feeling of boredom as a major problem in her marriage. Identifying other feelings is tough, because she tends to think that she doesn't deserve much from life and that she has no right to have particular feelings, such as anger. (Refer to Chapter 7 for looking at different ways of viewing the world). Adele decides that as well as boredom, she also feels resentment and anger towards her husband, plus anxiety at the possibility of her marriage breaking up and facing a life alone as a 44-year-old divorcee.

3. **Consider the likely causes of your problem.**

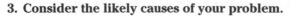

Depression may mislead you when you're working out the possible causes of your problem. Depressed minds often assume that the person who has the problem is also the cause. Although that person often bears some responsibility, considering all other causes is important. Sometimes understanding the whole range of causes points towards solutions.

In Adele's case, she first blames herself for being an inadequate, uninspiring wife. But thinking things over she realises actually she's been trying to improve things, but Eddie's always rebuffed her. She decides another cause may be the emptiness they've both felt since their second and last child left home for university six months ago. Finally, she realises she and Eddie have few friends or a social life, even more so since their friends Natasha and Sean moved to Torquay last year.

4. Search for information about your problem.

The chances are that you're not the first person experiencing your particular problem. Read around the subject. Whether the problem's to do with finance, relationships, career, sex, in-laws or difficulties with your children,, there' probably a wealth of information and advice on it. In Chapter 4 we suggest ways to evaluate trustworthy sources. Consider talking to an expert in the area of your problem for further advice.

Adele picks up *Making Marriage Work For Dummies* by Steven Simring, Sue Klavans Simring, and Gene Busnar (Wiley), and *Relationships For Dummies* by Dr Kate Wachs (Wiley).

5. Consider the importance of your problem.

Ask yourself how much this problem really matters Will solving it actually help? If so, how much? Rating the problem on a scale of 0 (no importance to you whatsoever) to 100 (nothing in the world is more important).can indicate what effort to put into solving your problem.

Adele realises that the quality of her marriage matters to her a great deal. She rates the issue as 75 on a 0 to 100 point scale. She decides that it's most certainly worth putting in considerable effort to get her marriage on a happier footing.

6. Check out solution-interfering beliefs.

After following the preceding steps, you need to ask yourself if you have any beliefs that may be interfering with your attempts to solve the problem. The beliefs you are holding can even stop you from taking action and become part of the problem itself.

Adele realises that she has five major beliefs that may getting in the way of her problem-solving. You may be experiencing similar ones.

Table 12-1 lists the five beliefs we've identified which most commonly interfere with problem solving. We offer positive alternative ways of considering those beliefs, to help finding solutions.

Table 12-1	Common Solution-Interfering Beliefs and Positive Alternative Views
Solution-Interfering Belief	*Positive Alternative View*
My problems are too huge to solve.	Sure my problems are large, but they don't have to be solved all at once. People solve big problems all the time. It just takes persistence.
I don't think my problem is solvable.	Well, I suppose that's possible. But in that case I'm going to have to start figuring out how to live with it. However, I won't know whether it's solvable until I try everything I can first.
I'm not a good problem solver.	Well, I haven't always tackled big problems easily in the past, but that doesn't mean I can't start now. The CRICKET problem-solving plan looks pretty straightforward. ANyway, what can I lose by trying?
I prefer to let problems solve themselves.	Yes, I suppose that could happen – and pigs might fly! My experience is problems persist or even get worse if I don't do something about them. *No* decision is still *a* decision!
If I try and fail to solve my problem, I'm just going to feel like an even bigger failure. It's better not to try.	And of course if I don't try, I'm guaranteeing failure. Besides, if my attempts fail, I just may discover something from the process and then have another go, strengthened by knowing more.

If you find that your beliefs are blocking the your way of solving the problems in your life, write them down as in Table 12-1. Look for positive alternative views that challenge those interfering beliefs. If you try this, but and have difficulty coming up with alternative views, flick to Chapters 5, 6, and 7 for more information on dealing with problematic thoughts and beliefs.

Running Through the Routes (R)

Step two in our CRICKET problem-solving game plan helps you find possible solutions for your problem. The following sections point the way to designing creative solutions.

Write down absolutely any option that come to mind. Don't listen to your internal critic saying, 'That's a really daft idea!' Now really isn't the time for evaluating your ideas, you're doing that later. Sometimes the silliest solution leads to another idea, which proves realistic – and Yippee! It works!

Letting go

Trying too hard to solve a problem, can sometimes bring you up against a brick wall. Too much effort can stifle creativity. Just give the process time; don't push yourself. You've probably been working on it for quite a while, so taking a little longer solving it won't hurt, but in fact, it may just help.

First, we suggest relaxing your mind and body as a means of tapping into and harnessing your creative potential. We have a quick relaxation technique you can use for this purpose:

1. Place your hand on your abdomen.

2. Take a slow, deep breath, and watch your abdomen expand.

3. Hold that breath for a few moments.

4. Slowly breathe out and let your shoulders droop.

5. As you breathe out, say the word *relax*.

6. Repeat this exercise ten times. Focus on the physical sensation of this exercise, especially your breathing.

Practising this relaxation technique several times a day for five days in a row helps you to calm your mind and body. If it doesn't work for you, take a look at Chapter 18 for more ideas on how to let go. Also, if you suffer from anxiety as well as depression, you may want to read *Overcoming Anxiety For Dummies* by Elaine Iljon-Foreman, Laura Smith, and Charles Elliott (Wiley).

You may find other letting-go strategies more helpful, so feel free to experiment. Some people find a slow, steady, rhythmic exercise like jogging, or using a running, rowing or cycling machine frees their mind to think creatively. Other exercises like walking, weight-lifting, or yoga (go to Chapter 10 for more ideas) are also potentially helpful. Alternatively, try a recreational activity that you enjoy as a means of letting go (refer to Chapter 11 for a list of activities that help in easing depression). A warm bubble bath is also an excellent way of inspiring creative thinking.

Letting go as a way of finding creative solutions is often a very successful technique. But it does mean that you have to stop forcing your mind to find the answers, and this can be tricky.

Thinking visually

Many people find that their creativity starts flowing more easily when they get into visual mode. Start by relaxing (you may want to use the quick and easy relaxation techniques we describe in the previous section) and picture your problem in your mind. See yourself, in your imagination, actually putting into practice the various ways of tackling the problem. Let the ideas float around; you don't have to settle on any one in particular.

Designing a flow chart is a very useful visual aid in problem-solving. Put each component of your problem in a separate box. Write down possible solutions to each component, then draw arrows from the solutions to the relevant component of the problem.

Adele draws her marital problems on a flow chart. She write down each thought about her struggling marriage in a box, and then develops individual solutions. See Figure 12-1 to discover how Adele approaches her problem.

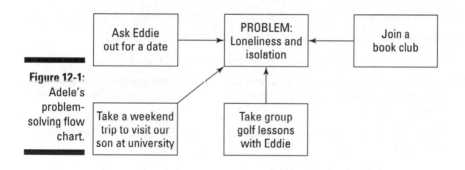

Figure 12-1:
Adele's problem-solving flow chart.

Permitting playfulness

We fully appreciate that your problem may be very difficult to solve. However, allowing yourself to play with ideas is important. Ask yourself if tunnel vision is what's keeping you stuck. Play with the most absurd solutions imaginable. Play allows you to forget about the usual rules and lets you break out of the box.

One way to play around is to design solutions that appear are totally opposite to your first ideas. For example, Adele has a difficult marriage. One solution she considers is having an affair. Then she considers the opposite. Having an affair with her husband! 'That's ridiculous!' she initially thinks to herself.

But then she realises it just may be worth trying. What if she imagines he's a man she's just met and finds attractive (after all, she did find Eddie very attractive years ago, and he hasn't really changed all that much!). Then she can plan how to attract him.

Listing all your options

As you play with all your options for dealing with your problem, list absolutely everything that you come up with. Don't leave any ideas out at this point. After writing your list, review the list and see if further thought gives rise to any more ideas.

Adele lists options for handling her marital problems. As you can see, her options cover possibilities that range from productive to downright destructive:

- ✔ Have an affair.

- ✔ Have an affair with my husband.

- ✔ Get a divorce.

- ✔ Ask for a temporary separation so that I can clear my head.

- ✔ Seek marriage counselling, if I can persuade Eddie to go.

- ✔ Work on my own to improve our marriage by showing more caring and affection, as well as by working on not being on the defensive (see Chapter 14).

- ✔ Take off on an exotic overseas holiday . . . and don't tell anyone where I'm going.

- ✔ Focus on making myself happy outside of my marriage. I could develop new hobbies, find a more interesting career, expand my social circle, or find volunteer work.

- ✔ Indulge in more alcohol.

- ✔ Stop whining and try to put this whole thing behind me!

Your list of possible solutions to your problem, like Adele's may also contain many options. Concentrate on listing the widest range of solutions you can think of. And don't judge your ideas as 'good' or 'bad'.

Investigating Outcomes (1)

Taking your ideas from the preceding 'Running Through the Routes(R)' section , list them in the 'Options' column of a two-column table, as shown in Table 12-2. Next, label the second column 'Likely Consequences and Outcomes'. Then think through each option. List the possible outcomes or consequences and for each one, rate the probability of the consequence or outcome happening in that way, on a 0 –100 point scale, where 0 is almost totally impossible and 100 represents almost complete certainty.

Table 12-2 lists Adele's options, likely consequences and the outcomes she predicts for each. This example gives an idea of how to start your own table.

Table 12-2	Adele's Options and Likely Consequences and Outcomes
Options	*Likely Consequences and Outcomes*
Have an affair.	Fun and excitement (55); guilt (95); sexually transmitted disease (5 or less if I'm careful); eventual destruction of my marriage (60)
Have an affair with my husband.	Fun and excitement (65 because of no guilt, but it may be less intense than a real affair); possible rejuvenation of my marriage (55); complete rejection from my husband (60)
Get a divorce.	Some relief from the struggle (75); sadness and loss (80); eventually, a new and better relationship (30)
Ask for a temporary separation.	Clear my head to see what I really want to do (35); increased distance from my husband (55); increased chance my husband will have an affair (35)
Seek marriage counselling.	Improvement in the marriage if he agrees (65); anger and rage from Eddie because he's always been against this idea (50); rejection by Eddie (30); divorce if it doesn't work (55)
Work on my own to improve our marriage.	Improve marriage (30); damage marriage in some way (10)
Go on an exotic trip and tell no one.	Fun and excitement (85); guilt (99); end my marriage (99)
Increase my own happiness through new activities.	Be happier (70); become more independent (40)
Drink more.	Temporary decrease in pain (65); become addicted to alcohol (50); increase pain in the long run (75)
Quit whining and try to forget the problem.	Increased dissatisfaction (90); marriage will improve on its own (1)

Doing this exercise highlights whether a single, simple solution stands out as the obvious choice. But all too frequently, the best options aren't so obvious. So, in the next section, we help you make an informed decision.

Committing to a Choice (C)

After going through the first three steps of the CRICKET problem-solving game plan, you can choose your option(s). Make a commitment to yourself.

For this fourth step in the CRICKET problem-solving game plan you need to carefully think through all the options. You may be able to quickly zoom in on the one, two, three, or perhaps four best possibilities simply by reviewing the likely consequences of each. Pay close attention to your feelings about each one. Does thinking about the options make you feel hopeful, distressed, anxious, calm, angry, sad, relieved, eager, or perhaps some combination of these feelings? Noticing your emotions in this way may give you more information.

Realise that the option you choose for dealing with your problem can be a combination of several options. Your options don't have to be mutually exclusive.

Adele picks three options that appear to have the best chance of helping her unhappy marriage:

- ✔ Do everything I can on my own to improve the marriage.
- ✔ Increase my own happiness by exploring a new career.
- ✔ Find out about marriage counselling.

After further reflection, Adele begins to think that marriage counselling has the best chance of saving her marriage, but she has a problem: she's very worried that Eddie is going to be furious if she yet again suggests counselling. Is this the choice she really wants to make?

If, like Adele, you find yourself stuck with the dilemma of which option to act on, here are two more strategies that may help – 'Being your own best friend' and 'Choosing sides'. You need a couple of chairs for both of the exercises. Yes, chairs – just go with us on this one.

Being your own best friend

There's a true friend that you can always call on for another perspective – 24/7. That friend is . . . you! This technique may be one of the simplest in this whole book. But don't let the simplicity fool you. We find the 'Being your own best friend' technique is surprisingly useful. Try it!

Sit down in a chair and place an empty chair facing opposite you. Imagine a close friend of yours is sitting in that chair. Your friend happens to have pretty much the same problem as you do; she came up with the same choice for a solution, but dreads carrying it out. Start talking to your friend. Talk out loud. When you're finished, ask yourself if the advice sounds like it's just what you happen to need.

You may think that this idea sounds too simplistic, and also wonder how it can possibly help given you haven't yet settled on an option. The technique helps because it gives you some emotional distance from your problem, helping you let go your fixed mind-set.

Adele tries this technique. Here's the imaginary conversation she has with her friend:

> 'Much as working on your marriage on your own sounds like a great idea, I doubt you're going to succeed unless you combine it with marriage counselling. Sure you're scared! But do you really have anything to lose by trying? What are the odds that your marriage is going to sort itself out if you don't have some marriage counselling? Pretty unlikely, I reckon. Sure Eddie gets angry, but what's new? It's happened loads of times before, and you've always survived. Though he's always totally rejected the idea in the past, try one last time. If he still refuses, then maybe you need to hear that and consider other options.'

Adele finds this exercise helpful, but she still doesn't quite feel ready to carry out her decision to ask Eddie to go to marriage counselling. She needs one more technique – 'choosing sides.' You can also try this one.

Choosing sides

The 'Choosing sides' technique, like the preceding 'Being your own best friend' technique, asks you to place two chairs facing each other. Label the first chair as representing one side of your argument and the second chair as representing the other person's side. Sit in Chair No.1 and imagine the other side of your argument is sitting in Chair No.2. Argue with the other side, out loud, and as forcefully as you can. When you run out of arguments, swop chairs, then argue on behalf of the other side of your argument.

Are you going to feel a little silly doing this exercise? Quite possibly. But do have a go. You may be surprised at how useful you find this exercise. Psychologists have recommended this approach for decades, and clients continue to report that it helps them reach difficult decisions.

Here's what Adele's dialogue sounds like when she tries the 'Choosing sides' technique to help her decide whether marriage counselling really is the best option for her. She labels Chair No.1 'Get Counselling' and Chair No.2 'Don't Do It'.

> **Get Counselling chair (speaking to the Don't Do It chair):** 'Look, you know that counselling has the best chance of succeeding. You've made a few attempts on your own, but they haven't worked. You've reviewed the likely consequences, and you know that getting help looks better than anything else.'

> **Don't Do It chair:** 'Okay, sure. I thought about it carefully, but the bottom line is that I don't think I can cope if counselling fails and I end up divorced. The loneliness and sense of loss would be overwhelming.'

> **Get Counselling chair:** 'Oh, so that's what's holding you back! Well! First, who says marriage counselling is going to fail? The odds aren't that bad if you combine it with your own efforts. You already found those ideas in the books you've read encouraging. With the help of a trained professional, it just may work.'

> **Don't Do It chair:** 'Sure, but if Eddie rejects the idea, I'm just going to feel even more frustrated and angry. Then that'll increase the likelihood of divorce. Bottom line is – I don't think I can bear it.'

> **Get Counselling chair:** 'So you think that taking no action to deal with the problem has a better chance of success? I doubt it! If your marriage is really on the rocks and heading for divorce, surely it's better you find out now than later? And who says you won't be able to bear it? People get divorced every day, and most manage to get through it.'

> **Don't Do It chair:** 'But I'd hate it.'

> **Get Counselling chair:** 'Aha! Now I get it! Of course you don't like the idea of divorce! I don't know many people who would. But that doesn't mean you wouldn't be able to cope. You were okay on your own before you met Eddie, and you can do it again. Being single may not sound too great right now, but there are other men are out there, you know.'

> **Don't Do It chair:** 'Okay, I get your point. I wouldn't like a divorce, but life would probably go on. Somehow I'd find the courage to carry this option out . . . I think, anyway.'

Adele feels more resolved in her decision to seek marriage counselling after trying out the 'Choosing sides' technique. Nevertheless, she still quails at the thought of approaching Eddie.

Don't Try to Kid Yourself (K)

If you decide *against* choosing an option for dealing with your problem, kidding yourself that this is because you can't make up your mind won't work. Admit it! You are in fact making a choice – you're choosing to live with your problem 'as it is'.

You've been through the first four steps (CRIC) and have reached what seems to be the best decision. But you're oh so scared! As the popular advert says – DO IT! Don't try and kid yourself that you can't decide – if you DON'T do it, then admit, you HAVE nonetheless decided . . . either to do nothing, or something else – but no way can you kid yourself you aren't making any decision. It's helpful reminding yourself that if the first decision doesn't work out the way you'd hoped, at least that rules that one out for now – and there's no reason why you can't subsequently try something else!

As you can guess, some options for solving problems can result in unpredicted reactions. Remember, it's quite possible to both be pretty certain that your decision is the right one, but still feel really scared at the prospect of carrying it out. If that's the case for you, you may need an emotional plan for helping you proceed. And we just happen to have one for you in the 'Easing Your Emotions' section that follows.

Easing Your Emotions (E)

When you choose the option(s) that look like they having the greatest chance of helping to solve your problem, troublesome emotions may still threaten to sabotage your best intentions. This step in the problem-solving process is best viewed as an aid to help you in carrying out your choice of option.

If you are feeling very uncertain about what option to choose, go back through the suggestions in 'Running Through the Routes (R)', 'Investigating Outcomes (I), and 'Committing to a Choice (C)' earlier in this chapter. Possibly you're still going to come up with the same solution, and be feeling worried and uneasy about committing to it, but we assure you that your uneasiness is a normal, common feeling. And, given the circumstances, it can be handled with this problem-solving step.

Most solutions to difficult problems require a certain amount of courage to implement. If the solution was easy, you'd have done it ages ago. After all, we did say *difficult* problems.

Here are two simple techniques that can help you settle your nerves and quell the queasiness in the pit of your stomach as you anticipate acting on your solution – rehearsal and self-talk.

Holding the dress rehearsal

Imagine what a West End musical would be like if the musicians, cast, and stage crew didn't rehearse the show. The performance is likely to be a disaster. The performers have stage fright,no one knows what they are supposed to be doing. It probably wouldn't take long for the audience to start voting with their feet! Rehearsals not only enhance performance, they also help to deal with anxiety and apprehension.

If your problem-solving option involves coming face to face with someone or makes you feel anxious, a rehearsal may help. You can rehearse your plan:

- ✔ In your mind
- ✔ In front of a mirror
- ✔ Through role-playing with a trusted friend
- ✔ By writing out a script and using it in any of the above situations

Practising self-talk

You may be thinking, 'Talk to myself? You think I'm crazy?' Actually, most people talk to themselves,but seldom try controlling the content of their self-talk rather just going along on autopilot. If you're anxious or depressed, your self-talk usually contains negative predictions and self-defeating arguments.

The short positive self-statements in the following paragraphs are no cure for depression, nor do they work for long-term issues and problems. However, they can sufficiently motivate you to work through the difficult moments.

You can decide to select new, more productive content for your self-talk. To counter-argue against your negative thinking, you may first need to rehearse the script out loud. Write down short, simple, positive statements. Possibilities include:

- ✔ What I'm about to do is the right thing to do.
- ✔ This is really hard, but I can do it.
- ✔ I really have considered all the options.
- ✔ I have the right to do this.
- ✔ Just do it.

Adele decides to ask her husband Eddie to see a marriage counsellor as the first step towards solving the marital problems she's facing. She makes an appointment for an evening when they're both free. She then rehearses how she's going to approach Eddie with the idea, and chooses the self-talk coping phrase, 'I can handle whatever reaction he has.' She uses this phrase like a mantra, repeating it over and over in her mind as she approaches her husband.

Testing Out Your Solution: The Test Match (T)

Okay, now you've worked through the previous sections, you've gone through all the problem-solving steps except the final one. You've described the problem situation, chosen an option, and you're ready to roll. The time's come to go out to bat in the great Test Match of you versus your depression.

The chances of solving your problem are much greater having done your homework. But CRICKET doesn't come with a label " success guaranteed. After implementing your solution, then review how it worked. Carefully consider what did or didn't go according to plan. Perhaps all's well and the problem's resolved. But if the problem or remnants of it remain, back you go to the drawing board and start working on a new CRICKET game plan.

Here's how Adele's CRICKET game plan works out:

> Adele repeats, 'I can handle whatever reaction he has' in her mind as she walks into the study where Eddie's sitting at the computer. 'Eddie, can we talk for a few moments?'
>
> Eddie swivels to face her and replies, 'Okay, but not too long, I'm in the middle of something.'
>
> 'This won't take very long. I've been worried about our marriage; neither of us seems very happy,' Adele begins.
>
> Eddie interrupts her, 'Speak for yourself. I'm not unhappy. Women! They're never satisfied. What more do you want? This isn't paradise; it's real life.'
>
> Adele, who is now close to tears, continues, 'I'm not asking for the moon, Eddie. I want us to be closer. I've made an appointment with a marriage counsellor. It's next Thursday at 6 p.m. Please come with me.'
>
> 'Forget it. I'm not going to some touchy-feely, inquisitive therapist.' Eddie's voice rises. 'And I'm just fed up with you frittering away all my hard-earned money. I'm not going to waste my time talking about this!' Eddie turns back to his computer and ignores Adele.

Darnn! Adele went through all the steps, but still had a disappointing and upsetting result. It takes her a couple of days to recover, but she works out a new CRICKET game plan. This time she decides to go to counselling on her own and explore her other options with the help of the counsellor.

After several sessions, the counsellor helps Adele see that part of the problem in the relationship has been that Eddie won't participate and Adele is left to make decisions on her own, which have implications for Eddie. Adele explains this to Eddie, and concludes by saying that if he chooses not to go for joint counselling, the only alternative she can see is for a temporary separation. She gives Eddie a week to consider what he wants to do.

Eddie reluctantly decides to go to marriage counselling. To his surprise, they make excellent progress, using many of the techniques you can find in Chapter 14. Over the next few months, Eddie realises how much he values Adele. Both commit to making their marriage ever stronger.

If you or someone you care about is depressed, practically all problems loom larger than life, while solutions seem amazingly elusive. Take the time to prepare a game plan. See if playing the game of CRICKET might just work for you.

Part IV
Adjusting to Changing Relationships

In this part . . .

Interpersonal therapy is another widely researched approach to the treatment of depression. The evidence shows that it works. In this part, we cover key elements of interpersonal therapy, including how to deal with change, transitions, grief, and loss.

Depression also interferes with important relationships with friends, family, and colleagues. We give you tips and tools to enhance your relationships. We review ways to prevent you becoming cut off, showing you how to build bridges, and communicate more effectively with others. With these tools, your relationships can become a source of support rather than just another set of the problems that drag you down.

Chapter 13

Working Through Loss, Grief, and Mourning

. . . .

In This Chapter

▶ Understanding the different types of loss

▶ Overcoming your grief

. . . .

*H*ave you ever stood at the kitchen worktop with tears running down your face when slicing up onions? If so, you're experiencing your body's natural response to something that's causing you discomfort and distress. As you're well aware, your body also produces tears in response to your emotions – such as the overpowering feelings brought on by loss and grief. Tears frequently can take the edge off sorrow – helping to calm or even wash away painful feelings.

Weeping is a normal reaction to grief and loss. However, sometimes grief takes hold and disrupts life in major ways. Grief can trigger depression (go to Chapter 2 for a description of the types of depression). Loss may bring on depressed feelings without you being aware of the cause. Events in the past may be continuing to trouble you much more than you realise. Even if you haven't experienced a major loss in decades, looking at unresolved grief and loss may shed light on why you're experiencing feelings of depression now.

In this chapter, we explore powerful responses to loss. We discuss various types of losses you may be experiencing and how you react to them. If you're feeling depressed, do any painful feelings stem from one of these losses? Working through your grief may help lift your depression. We offer a variety of ways of doing this, whether the emotion is one of normal, uncomplicated grief, or has been triggered by a profound, traumatic experience.

Losing What's Important to You

Everyone experiences loss of one kind or another during their lives. People grieve about all different types of losses. Yet the response to each particular loss varies between people. There are no hard and fast rules for predicting how someone is going to react when something awful happens. And there's no right or wrong way to handle loss. Some people seem to bounce back surprisingly quickly, while others remain stuck in prolonged, intense grief.

If your grief lasts for months without a break, if you're overwhelmed by thoughts of yearning and loss, if you have thoughts that the life is pointless, or if you feel worthless and excessively guilty, you may have a complicated grief and/or a major depressive disorder (Chapter 2 gives more information about grief and various types of depression). If you have any of these symptoms, please ask for professional help.

We can't possibly give you a complete list of the types of losses that lead to grief, but the three major kinds are:

- Death
- Life transitions
- Relationship loss

In the following sections, we discuss death, life transitions, and relationship loss in detail. There is no right or wrong way to deal with such losses. Understanding how each event affects you is what's important. With awareness, or insight, you can draw on your resources for coping. In the 'Working Through Grief' section, later in this chapter, we give you ideas for handling these losses effectively.

Dealing with death

Death is never easy to deal with. Even people with strong religious convictions feel great sadness upon the loss of a loved one. Unexpected death is generally more difficult to accept than death following a prolonged illness. But the period of anticipation before the loss isn't the only factor affecting the response to death. For example, the person's age, the difficulty of the dying process, whether there was an opportunity to say goodbye, and the amount and type of support from friends and family available to the bereaved person all contribute to the reaction in complicated ways.

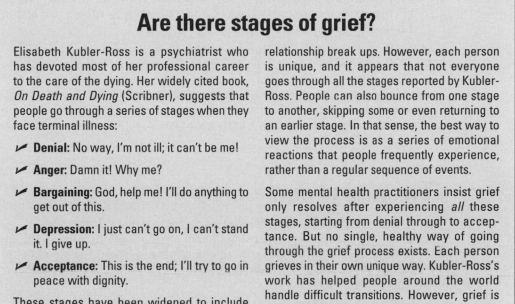

Are there stages of grief?

Elisabeth Kubler-Ross is a psychiatrist who has devoted most of her professional career to the care of the dying. Her widely cited book, *On Death and Dying* (Scribner), suggests that people go through a series of stages when they face terminal illness:

✔ **Denial:** No way, I'm not ill; it can't be me!

✔ **Anger:** Damn it! Why me?

✔ **Bargaining:** God, help me! I'll do anything to get out of this.

✔ **Depression:** I just can't go on, I can't stand it. I give up.

✔ **Acceptance:** This is the end; I'll try to go in peace with dignity.

These stages have been widened to include reactions to other types of loss, such as death of a loved one, loss of physical health, or relationship break ups. However, each person is unique, and it appears that not everyone goes through all the stages reported by Kubler-Ross. People can also bounce from one stage to another, skipping some or even returning to an earlier stage. In that sense, the best way to view the process is as a series of emotional reactions that people frequently experience, rather than a regular sequence of events.

Some mental health practitioners insist grief only resolves after experiencing *all* these stages, starting from denial through to acceptance. But no single, healthy way of going through the grief process exists. Each person grieves in their own unique way. Kubler-Ross's work has helped people around the world handle difficult transitions. However, grief is complicated, takes many forms, and isn't easily categorised.

Your relationship to the person plays a huge role in how the loss affects you:

✔ **Death of a life partner:** This type of loss is often thought to be one of the most difficult to get through. It requires major adjustments.

✔ **Death of a child:** Most experts believe that of all losses, this probably involves the most painful, lengthy recovery. Somehow it feels as though it's against the laws of nature for a child to die before the parent does.

✔ **Death of a parent:** The difficulty of this loss hinges on many factors, such as the age of the parent and child at the time of the death, the nature of the relationship, and unresolved issues. Sometimes the grief is actually intensified if the relationship was stormy and conflicted.

✔ **Death of a friend or relative:** Again, the difficulty of dealing with the loss of this type of relationship varies considerably.

✔ **Death of a pet:** The attachments people form with their pets can be very strong. Pets can become special family members. Others may not fully appreciate or understand the intensity of the bereavement that the loss of a pet can bring, especially when the person losing the pet is childless, by choice or otherwise. This lack of understanding by others can add to the sense of isolation.

✔ **Death of a stranger:** Sometimes a traumatic event witnessed by uninvolved parties can cause grief reactions. For example, when a drunk driver kills a child, it may bring back painful and vivid reminders to an already traumatised family who lost a child years before. Or witnessing a violent crime may also have an enormous impact on the observer. There are also issues surrounding whether you could/should have attempted to intervene.

Changing with the times

Change is the only certainty in life. Nothing ever remains completely the same. You play many roles, often simultaneously, throughout your life: parent, child, employer, employee, student, spouse, partner, to name but a few. Much of the way people see themselves comes from such roles, and these roles change over time.

People also define themselves according to their self-image. You may see yourself as someone who is consistently healthy, strong, important, attractive, and so on. Yet, both roles and self-image frequently change due to unavoidable circumstances. When these changes take place, the transition may or may not be smooth.

You may not always fully appreciate the impact that the passage from one role or self-image to another can have on your sense of self and wellbeing. When the transition involves a loss (and many transitions do), grieving or depression can result. Sometimes the transition is obvious, such as when you lose a job; other transitions can be more insidious, such as the loss of safety and security because of an alarming increase in the crime rate where you live.

No one responds in exactly the same way to these life transitions. As with death, no right or wrong response exists. Transitions that frequently cause difficulty include:

✔ **Leaving home:** Adolescents and young adults often look forward to the day when they can leave home. However, when it finally dawns, they often experience loss, and can be quite surprised by this. No longer can they turn to their parents for instant advice and support. They may feel a loss of connection, and of the comparative freedom from responsibilities that often accompanies childhood. Another related loss comes when a person leaves full-time education. Moving on from the familiar routines and friendships of secondary school or college/university and taking on new roles can mean assuming some quite daunting responsibilities.

✔ **Getting married:** You may wonder why marriage is included as a troubling transition. For most people, marriage is a joyous, but sometimes nerve-wracking time of life. Yet marriage includes losses, which occasionally lead to unexpected feelings of depression. It means give up your identity as a single person. You may lose contact with single friends. Like leaving home, marriage can require relinquishing a certain amount of freedom, in this case that of being single.

✔ **Becoming a parent:** Another joyous occasion! But bringing a newborn into your life also means some loss of freedom, plus more stress...and exhaustion. Bringing up a baby is costly both financially and time-wise. Say goodbye to weekends of rest and relaxation.

Feeling highly emotionally charged after having a baby is normal for both parents. However, depression in women after childbirth can become serious: this condition is called *postnatal depression.* Go to Chapter 2 for details about postnatal depression and the need for prompt treatment.

✔ **Changing jobs:** Whether you're starting your first job, changing jobs, getting a promotion or demotion, or going through redundancy or dismissal, changes in your career and in your everyday activities involve stress and loss. A first job leads to a loss of free time. A promotion can lead to overwhelming responsibilities. Demotion, re-deployment, redundancy, and dismissal can mean loss of income and status.

✔ **Going to jail:** Being convicted of a crime and then imprisoned gives rise to many, self-evident losses.

✔ **Experiencing major economic and political changes in society:** An example, is the 2008 credit crunch which is having serious effects. Repossessions and bankruptcies are soaring, some people are having to postpone retirement, and many are experiencing financial problems. Usually, no one feels very sorry when political leaders go or are forced out. However, in some countries, new regimes can bring on the loss of freedom, economic hardship, or possibly war. These changes can disrupt families and lives in devastating ways.

✔ **Moving home:** Whether you move elsewhere in the same city or further afield, the process can be exciting, but it also comes with losses. You may lose ties with your friends, the familiarity of your home and neighbourhood, and the sense of a shared history with a place you've cared about for a long time.

✔ **Dealing with an empty nest:** Parenting is a loving relationship, but one in which the usual goal is to foster independence and eventual departure. You do your job as well as you can- then your children leave you. You may experience both the loss of the children, and of your parental rolet.

✓ **Suffering a chronic illness:** The diagnosis of a chronic can turn your world upside down. You lose a measure of control over your life; suddenly the health care system takes charge of significant aspects of your daily living. You can be shocked at how dependent you've become. Also, your financial situation, freedom, and status may well suffer.

✓ **Aging:** You'd probably rather be old, when you consider the alternative! Nevertheless, aging inevitably highlights the certainty of death. Along with the threat of loss of life itself comes the loss of loved ones, plus changes in status, independence, appearance, and wellbeing.

Everyone expects and experiences change over the course of a lifetime. But depression may be an unexpected and unwelcome consequence. If you feel intense sadness or depression, and you can't figure out why, review the recent transitions in your life. Ask yourself if any of the issues we discuss in the previous list may be part of the problem.

Breaking up is hard to do

Losing someone through the break up of a relationship or divorce can also trigger deep grief. Unfortunately, society gives far more support to those who lose a loved one through death than those who lose someone through ending a relationship. Typically, we anticipate people picking themselves up, dusting themselves down, and "simply" starting all over again. Society assumes that within a fairly short period of time, people experiencing break ups are going to just get on with life, successfully forming new relationships. The intensity of grief that is felt after a break up may catch people by surprise and overwhelm them. After a relationship ends, feelings of loneliness and isolation can take hold. Yet when people consider breaking up, they too often fail to appreciate the potential magnitude of the disruption and loss. Thus, they make thoughtless decisions about leaving loved ones. Anger, lust, or boredom may fuel the decision to end the relationship.

When you break up with your partner, you may well experience a variety of losses:

✓ **The relationship:** You may lose companionship, affection, mutual hopes and fears, support, being a couple, love, and sex.

✓ **A vision of the future:** Most people who begin a serious relationship together have an expectation concerning the future of the relationship. In the case of partners with children, the vision of being a secure family unit crumbles when the relationship ends.

✓ **Family and friends:** Bonds with the family of the lost partner are often severed. Mutual friends may choose sides.

- ✔ **Finances:** Whether the money is spent on solicitors, therapists, and/or setting up two households, divorce or the break up of partners who live together can run to megabucks.

- ✔ **Status:** Sometimes people owe their status to their partner's job or position. The author Elaine remembers an association of the wives of a particular profession, (which is going to remain nameless). At their social gatherings, the wives wore a name badge with their name – and their husband's role within the organisation!

- ✔ **Ego:** Your ego may suffer, especially when you feel like you're being rejected. However, even when leaving is your own decision, feelings of failure and guilt can take you by surprise and overwhelm you.

There's no right or wrong way to handle grief after a break up or divorce. Giving yourself permission to feel whatever feelings come up can help you deal with the loss. If those feelings swamp you or last for ages, we provide strategies helping you deal with your distress in the rest of this chapter.

Working Through Grief

As we describe earlier in this chapter, death, divorce, break ups, and loss of status frequently lead to feelings of grief. That's to be expected. However, such grief can sometimes takes root in your life, disrupting happiness and wellbeing far beyond the typical six to twelve months grieving period. When grief is enduring, people often lose sight of the source of their unhappiness. So, if you're feeling depressed, we suggest you consider whether any recent or past losses in your life may be contributing to your low mood. (Go to Chapter 2 to check out the differences between grief and depression.)

Experiencing continuing or complicated feelings about losing a loved one may mean you need professional help. Especially if your efforts at self-help including practising the ideas in this book aren't bringing you much relief, or if you have severe depressive symptoms (refer to Chapter 2 for a discussion of the symptoms of depression).

If you decide you're carrying a burden of unresolved grief, do consider how you can lighten your load. Think through all your options. You may decide to explain your situation to trusted friends or family. Let them know that you're going to need some extra looking after during this period. Try asking for their support and help. Perhaps request others give you a hand with day to day matters, or even let go of a few responsibilities. Though you may not be suffering a physical illness, or even feeling sick, do give yourself the same care and attention as you'd give someone who is having similar difficulties. Remember that depression affects both physical and mental and wellbeing.

When you're ready to go to friends and family for assistance, you may wonder if they'll understand your problems and be able to help, especially if your grief concerns a loss from the distant past. You may want to explain that you're trying to work through your grief on your own, and if you don't progress enough through your own efforts within a short period, you're going to get professional help. Tell them you realise your loss happened a long time ago, how it's taken you by surprise, and how much it's still troubling you.

Be aware that bereavement saps your energy. Getting better takes effort and time – you can't rush the process. While you're at it, don't forget to take care of your physical health:

- ✔ Eat healthy foods.
- ✔ Exercise on a regular basis.
- ✔ Make sure that you're getting enough rest.

Before tackling the difficult task of dealing with your grief, be reassured your goal is to help you get back into the business of living a productive, happy life. It isn't to make you forget about your painful losses, nor to make you give up caring about the absent person or other losses in your life.

Sometimes people say that they are likely to feel consumed by guilt if they overcame and resolved their grief. Again, working through grief isn't about 'getting over it' in itself. You're always going to feel the loss, but you can refocus and renew your spirit. You deserve to love and laugh again.

Working through grief may actually lead to an initial increase of low, difficult, and painful feelings for a short time. This is perfectly natural. But if you find that your depression has significantly increased, and that you're having feelings of hopelessness or thoughts of suicide, you need to get an immediate assessment from a professional.

In the following sections, we discuss ways of coping with the loss of people, roles, and self-image discussed in the 'Losing What's Important to You' section, earlier in this chapter.

Seeing the wide angle view of relationships

When grief is long-lasting or involves complex issues, people often focus on the details of their loss instead of trying to get the whole picture. In other cases, they latch onto some specific aspect of grief, such as the emptiness they feel. Having such a narrow focus can block your ability to work through the effects of your loss. It can also stop you facing up to difficult feelings and issues, meaning you then can't work through them.

We suggest broadening your field of vision to help you reconstruct all aspects of the lost relationship and what it meant to you. You need to take into account that a person generally has both positive and negative qualities. Ask yourself the following Grief Exploration Questions. You may want to write down your answers to these questions in a notebook.

- ✔ What was my life like with this person?
- ✔ What did I value in this person, and what did I struggle with?
- ✔ What did I learn from this person (both good and bad)?
- ✔ How has my life changed as a result of this loss?
- ✔ What feelings of resentment do I hold about this person?
- ✔ What things do I feel grateful for about my relationship?

Take your time answering these questions. They may need careful thought. They may also bring up unexpected pain. After working through this task you may want to discuss, and possibly compare, your feelings with those of someone you really trust, who also knew this person well.

After completing the Grief Exploration Questions, you may find it helps composing a letter to the person you lost. It can help understand and come to terms with the meaning of the relationship, and the nature of your loss.

When you avoid feelings, you keep them trapped, churning round and round inside you. Expressing your feelings can help with healing.

Bruce's mother died when he was a child. Now, many years later, Bruce is a father. He finds himself having sad feelings. Bruce comes to the conclusion that he has unresolved grief. Bruce answers the Grief Exploration Questions, and then works through his grief in a letter to his mother (Figure 13-1).

Eileen left her husband two years ago. She experienced what seemed to be inexplicable sadness, guilt, and anger. Her therapist helped her connect unresolved feelings about her divorce as the cause of these emotions. Eileen first answers the Grief Exploration Questions we list earlier in this section. Then she writes the letter that you see in Figure 13-2.

After seeing the wide-angle view of the relationship, you're likely to be more prepared to deal with your next problem.

Dear Mum,

Guess what? My wife and I have a baby. A girl – we named her after you. I've got a job and a house. And I'm doing pretty well. But after the baby, I started having some really sad times. I did some reading and I think it's about never really dealing with your death. I know if happened a long time ago, but I guess I never got over it.

I was only 12 years old when you left me. I was outside playing and a police car drove up. I ran up to the porch. Dad was standing there, already crying. I never saw him cry before. Mum, things changed so much after you died. Dad never got over it; he was sad and started drinking too much. I started getting into more and more trouble. My life was pretty hard. I even spent some time in jail. I never talked about you to anyone. It hurt too much.

I knew I was sad, but I didn't realise until now how mad I am. I'm mad because I remember when you were home, you'd usually be in the bedroom. Somehow, I thought it was my fault you were always crying. I was lonely and scared. I'm angry and upset, Mum, because you were so depressed but you didn't get help. I'm furious because Dad didn't get you help. Mum, I sometimes think that if you cared about me, you wouldn't have killed yourself.

Now, I've said it. I feel really furious with YOU. But over the years I've learned that depression is an illness. And that you and Dad probably didn't realise that people could get help and get better. So, Mum, I forgive you for leaving me. And I promise I'll work on preventing my own sad feelings from hurting my own child.

Love,
Your son,
Bruce

Figure 13-1:
Bruce's
letter to his
mum.

When you're ready, ask yourself how you can begin moving on and replacing what you've lost with active alternatives, such as:

✔ **Going out with new people:** This can feel scary, but ultimately, though you may well doubt it, you can discover how to love again.

✔ **Grief support groups:** You may find comfort in sharing your experience, and being supported and understood by others who've gone through similar losses. You can find support groups for bereavement as well as for the loss of a relationship.

✔ **Leisure activities:** People who are grieving tend to drop many activities they used to do for fun, but don't restart them when their grief starts fading. Refer to Chapter 11 for information on rediscovering pleasure.

✔ **Religious and spiritual groups:** These groups can provide support, comfort, meaning, and connections, and can nourish your soul.

✔ **Voluntary work:** This can be a great way to re-establish connections and get a sense of renewed purpose.

Dear Henry,

Why did I leave you? I was afraid. Your rage was carefully hidden at times, but I never knew when it would surface. Henry, you never hit me, but the punishment was worse than being beaten. You tortured me with silence – silence that seemed to last forever. Silence for the holidays, on trips, for birthdays and graduations. Silence at the dinner table and after we made love.

We never played with ideas or worked on compromise. You were always right; you knew the truth. I feared expressing my thoughts, feelings, or emotions, because if they differed from what you wanted to hear, you were angry. When you got angry, I was punished. The more critical you were with me, the more I withdrew from you. I couldn't properly plant tomatoes or fold the laundry, After losing self-confidence, self-worth, and self-control, I got help. And I became more independent and more ambitious – so that I could stand alone, and so that I wouldn't need you.

I know you were deeply hurt as a child. I understand how my own overreactions to your criticism stemmed from my childhood issues. Now, from a distance, I remember the good times. You are a brilliant man and generous to a fault. You care about people. I hope you are happy.

Take care,
Eileen

Figure 13-2:
Eileen's letter to her ex-husband.

Rolling through roles

As we discuss in the 'Changing with the Times' section, earlier in this chapter, changes in your circumstances can mean you giving up one or more of your roles, such as that of parent, employee, student, or child. Because you might see these roles as marking your status and defining who you are, their loss can feel devastating. Experiencing job loss or re-deployment can be so painful that the experience has been dubbed 'industrial divorce'. All the hurt, loss, betrayal, and disappointed hopes for the future can apply as equally to the loss of a career as to the loss of a partner.

Society hasn't clearly defined transition as a type of loss. But the grief you feel can be as intense as the grief after a death or divorce. It can also leave you feeling bewildered and not knowing what to do next. If a role transition is causing you trouble, we recommend that you ask yourself Role Exploration Questions. Again, it's useful to write your answers down in a notebook.

- What did I enjoy about my old role?

- What did my old role allow me to do?

- What did I dislike about my old role?

- What freedoms and limitations did I feel in my old role?

- What were the negative and positive feelings I experienced when I gave up my old role?

- What did I resent about my old role?

- Do I feel grateful for having had my old role?

Your answers to the Role Exploration Questions can help you more fully appreciate and understand the nature of your loss. If you've been idealising your previous position, answering these questions can help you see your old role in a more realistic light. And when you review exactly what you feel was important in the loss, you can start searching for suitable alternatives. They may include finding a new role, looking for new ways to meet your needs, or exploring new interests and meaning to your life. See Chapter 19 for information on using developments from the field of positive psychology to help you in this exploration.

Mike retires from his position as a secondary school English teacher. For the last few years, he's been counting the days until his retirement. He plans to travel, read books he never had the time for, and go fishing. Four months into his retirement, he starts waking up at 4 a.m., unable to go back to sleep. He puts off his travel plans and fishing trips, and shelves his good intentions to read those books. Mike is having difficulty in adapting to his new role. His wife suggests that he answer the Role Exploration Questions. Here's what Mike comes up with:

- **What did I enjoy about my old role?** 'I liked the interaction with the kids. I loved getting through to an unmotivated student.'

- **What did my old role allow me to do?** 'I could make a real difference to some children's lives. That was fantastic.'

- **What did I dislike about my old role?** 'I hated all the endless paper-work, red tape, and evaluation. And those boring meetings just did my head in!'

- **What freedoms and limitations did I feel in my old role?** 'I loved the freedom of developing new ways of teaching. But as the years passed, there were more and more demands and red tape. We lost most of the freedom to choose materials.'

- **What were the negative and positive feelings I experienced when I gave up my old role?** 'I couldn't wait to start fishing! And seeing new places really excited me. I felt such relief being free from the day-to-day grind. And I was just so happy. Later, I felt a deep sense of loss. I miss working with the kids. And I miss thinking of myself as a teacher.'

- **What did I resent about my old role?** 'The salary, of course. I also resented the increasing pressure from management to pass students who really were way below standard. I also hated not being allowed to give out top marks, as we weren't supposed to use that grade – 'So why have it in the first place?' I'd ask myself! And I resented the lack of respect from some parents, which only seemed to worsen over the years.'

- **Do I feel grateful for having had my old role?** 'Not many people get a chance to make a difference in other people's lives. I know I did that. And despite the pretty poor salary, I feel quite grateful for the excellent retirement package and benefits.' The holidays were pretty good too.

After he reviews his answers, Mike more fully appreciates the sources of his grief. And he realises that he can replace some of what he's lost by doing voluntary work or taking up some part-time paid work at the local adult education centre. Literacy and maths coaching are in high demand. Working locally also means no more awful commuting like at the last job. He can use his skills as a teacher to make a huge difference in the lives of enthusiastic older students who really want to learn. And not worry about parental aggro!

Your depression may be stemming from experiencing significant changes in your life. Change has both positive and negative effects. Remember the pluses and the minuses of getting married, starting a new career, or having a baby? Remind yourself that all adjustments take time, energy, and planning.

Chapter 14

Revitalising Relationships

*D*epression can place a big strain on relationships, especially on a partner, and close friends or family. But all isn't lost! There's a great deal you can do to lessen the strain and lighten the burden, and improve the quality of your relationship when you're suffering from depression.

In this chapter, we discuss the ways that depression affects important relationships, and we offer effective techniques for improving your relationship skills. We particularly focus on techniques for improving intimate relationships, because experiencing a difficult relationship with a partner can sometimes be the cause of depression, or worsen an existing depression, making it more and more difficult to escape the vicious circle.

If you're in a problematic relationship, think about asking your partner or close friend to read this chapter as well.

Being in an abusive relationships can lead to depression. If you believe that your partner has been, or is being, emotionally or physically abusive, you may need to end the relationship. However, when you're depressed, making such a decision can be particularly difficult. Get professional guidance if you're having doubts.

Looking at the Depression–Rejection Vicious Circle

Depression makes you feel awful – you experience sadness, tiredness, pessimism, and feelings of worthlessness. These feelings can be difficult to deal with in their own right. But then, to add to your misery, depression can increase the likelihood of rejection. Rejection hurts, and such pain can further worsen your depression.

When a person gets depressed, partners, close friends, and family normally respond with sympathy and support. But after a while, and as much as they want to help, they can find themselves struggling to keep up their support. Spending long periods with someone who's clinically depressed is difficult – the depressed person seldom has the energy to respond positively to others, and retreats into themselves. Others may then begin to feel rejected themselves, withdrawing support and become less caring and distant.

Adding to the increased likelihood of facing rejection, a person with depression can often misinterpret what is being said to them, in three self-defeating ways:

- Magnifying the negative intentions of others.
- Looking for negative feedback even when it doesn't exist.
- Getting angry and defensive in response to legitimate criticism.

These tendencies then trigger still more interpersonal problems, and so the vicious cycle continues. The following sections look at each of the three reactions in turn.

Exaggerating the negative

When people suffering from depression receive negative feedback, they usually read more into it than is intended – they can greatly magnify what they perceive as rejection.

Keith's story illustrates how depression clouds vision. Keith is offered a place at a Scottish university. His first year begins unremarkably, but as autumn turns to winter and the days start to shorten, Keith's mood deteriorates (refer to Chapter 2 for information about seasonal affective disorder). He has trouble getting himself out of bed in the mornings and starts missing lectures. His roommate tries hard to help – offering to wake him up in time, suggesting he sees a counsellor, and inviting him to social events.

But Keith responds with grumpy withdrawal. One morning, feeling at his wits' end, his roommate snaps, 'That's it! I've had it! I've done all I can for you. Why don't you just quit feeling sorry for yourself and get out of bed, or at the very least, go and get help!'

Rather than understand his roommate's frustration, Keith concludes his roommate has had more than enough of him, and no longer wants his friendship. While it's true that his roommate's remark was mostly negative, it stemmed from concern and worry. But Keith magnifies and personalises the message into one of total rejection.

Go to Chapters 5, 6, and 7 for more information about how depression can distort your perspectives about events in your life.

Monochrome or technicolour? Seeing what you're feeling

Depressed people are often on the alert for disapproval and disparagement. Research shows that people suffering from depression actually seek negative feedback. And when that's what they get, they feel even worse.

Do these findings mean that depressed people actually *want to* feel rotten? We don't think so. There's a lot of evidence showing that most people are highly motivated to *self-verify;* they're actively seeking out information that confirms whatever it is that they believe about themselves, and rejecting alternative views. In the same way, people with positive self-beliefs work at maintaining their particular outlook, while people with negative self-views work just as hard at doing the opposite.

Sometimes, depressed people actually *seek positive* reassurance from their partners. But ironically, if they then receive such support, they find a reason to reject and deny it, given the powerful drive to self-verify. Unsurprisingly, the partner then feels rejected. And a rejected partner typically withdraws and provides less support. This pattern can turn into the vicious circle of rejection and worsening depression (along with a deteriorating relationship).

Bill has chronic, low-level depression known as dysthymia (refer to Chapter 2 for more information about dysthymia). He complains to his wife that he's a failure at work. He expects she'll agree, after telling her about all the mistakes (in reality, very few!) that he's been making. When his wife contradicts him and supportively says she believes he's actually very successful his depression causes him to reject her support, saying, 'You don't know what you're talking about.' His wife feels hurt. She withdraws. And their relationship slides further downhill.

Cancelling out constructive criticism

Although this may appear contradictory to what we've been saying about negative outlooks and depression, some people with depression occasionally *do* try to deal with criticism. However, they rarely succeed. Instead, the depressed mind goes for a defensive response, denying or counter-attacking any positive feedback. Again, a cycle of negativity and rejection follows.

Pursuing Positives

Depression encourages withdrawal, avoidance, and isolation. The depressed mind predisposes you not only to expect negative reactions, but also to go out of your way to find them. Your relationships can suffer as a result. Resisting the tendency of looking for negative feedback requires a lot of effort, not easy when you're depressed. But you can override what your mind's telling you to do and start reaching out to the ones you love, taking one step at a time.

If you've been depressed for quite a while, you've probably fallen into some pretty bad habits in your relationships. Even if you don't seek negative feedback, you probably don't feel like actually doing anything that is going to lead to positive interactions. And your depressed mind may be telling you that if you do get your act together and do something positive, others are most likely to reject you anyway – so what's the point?

Repeating the same old behaviours isn't going to improve your relationship. You have think about taking positive steps. What do you have to lose? Initiating a positive two-way relationship rarely causes trouble! If you don't get an overwhelmingly positive response from your partner first time round, keep at it. Persistence is the key to success.

Enjoying a two-way relationship is the glue binding a couple together. Everyone likes an occasional pat on the back, and when you include pats on the back in your relationship, your relationship inevitably improves. And improving your relationship helps lift your depression, The following sections give you ideas on how you can build 'pats' into your day-to-day relationships.

Giving compliments

Receiving appreciation, thanks, gratitude, and compliments feels good. Set yourself the goal of expressing one or more of these good feelings to your partner each day. Find a way to remind yourself to do so. Perhaps you can write a note in your daily planner or put a "post-it" note on your mirror. Don't forget that, when you're depressed, your memory (or the disturbance of it) can ambush your best intentions (refer to Chapter 8 for more information on depression and memory).

Keep these few things in mind when saying nice things and giving compliments:

- **Be specific.** Don't merely say, 'I appreciate you.' (Although that's fine occasionally.) Try to highlight specifics as to exactly what you appreciate, such as your partner's help with cooking, cleaning, shopping, or finances. Or compliment your partner about specific aspects of his or her appearance, problem-solving ability, or special talents.

- **Avoid 'buts'.** Stay clear of the temptation to give a compliment and then take it back. Don't tell your partner, 'I appreciate your attempt to balance our cheque-book, but did you know you've made a mistake?'

- **Be sincere.** Don't give false flattery. Only say things you really mean. Look really hard and you'll probably find something positive.If you can't, don't tell fibs! And if you really can't think of anything at all that's positive, your relationship could well benefit from expert help.

Adding a nice touch

Compliments can be very useful, but actions speak louder than words. Again, depression may make both thinking of and doing nice things difficult, so try this list to help you get started. It can spur you into action even when you're not feeling like it (Chapter 9 gives information on how taking action can make you feel more motivated). Circle the items you think your partner will like, and feel free to add some of your own. Make a goal of doing one positive action two to three times a week. We call this plan The Magic Touch.

- Bringing home flowers.
- Cooking a romantic meal.
- Expressing how much you care.
- Giving a hug.
- Holding hands.
- Making a quick phone call to show how much you care.
- Offering your partner a backrub.
- Preparing and serving breakfast in bed.
- Putting a loving note in your partner's lunch box.
- Running an errand.
- Sending a card.

> ✔ Taking over a task that's normally your partner's – like the ironing.
>
> ✔ Suggesting your partner takes a hot bath while you do the washing up.
>
> ✔ Cleaning your partner's car.

The Magic Touch isn't an instant remedy, so don't expect results straight-away, and don't keep score. Over a few weeks, The Magic Touch exercise is likely to bring warmer feelings into your relationship. If it doesn't, think about seeking relationship counselling.

Planning pleasurable times together

Many busy couples spend a lot of their time looking after others – playing chauffeur to their children, caring for their elderly parents, and additionally working long hours to impress management. The danger is that a couple can forget to give time to their own relationship. And if one partner is depressed and feeling neglected the relationship can rapidly go down hill.

You can improve your relationship by planning positive times together. These activities don't have to involve expensive holidays or overpriced seats at the opera. Simple pleasures can work wonders. The key is to sit down together to plan them, and then make sure you follow your plan. Be creative: choose an activity you both enjoy. Here are some suggestions to help you get started:

> ✔ Go out for a drink.
>
> ✔ Go dancing.
>
> ✔ Go out for afternoon tea.
>
> ✔ Sign up for an evening class together or join a society or club.
>
> ✔ Do the garden together.
>
> ✔ Go to the cinema and hold hands.
>
> ✔ Book a bargain-break.
>
> ✔ Buy a massage for two at a local spa.
>
> ✔ Take a walk together.

If you're feeling depressed, the thought of taking up a new interest or activity may well sound too much like hard work given how exhausted you're already feeling. However, do remember that when you're depressed, you probably aren't expecting much pleasure from any leisure pursuit. (Chapters 9 and 11 give information about overcoming tendencies to make negative predictions.

Including something enjoyable every day

A nice simple idea is for you and your partner to build time into your relationship for a daily 'catch-up' each evening. If you really don't have time every day, try to schedule catch-up time at least three times a week. We call this exercise The Daily News, believing that it can help you and your partner to get closer. Please note though that there are certain items you have to *include* in The Daily News and other items that you need to *leave out*.

- ✔ **Keeping clear of conflict:** Only discuss items that don't involve conflict between the two of you, and events that are outside your relationship.

- ✔ **Expressing empathy:** Tell your partner that you understand how he or she is feeling. Try to back up or accept your partner's emotions. You can say, 'Bet that would stress me out too!' or, 'I can see why it's so upsetting.' Stay focused on your partner's perspective; don't find fault. For example, if your partner is complaining about someone else's behaviour, it's not a good time to point out that the other person may be right – even though the reality points to this.

- ✔ **Practising active listening:** This means asking questions to find out more and for better understanding. Focus on your partner, and show interest through non-verbal and verbal cues such as head nods, light touches on the arm, and brief comments such as, 'I see,' 'Oh,' 'Uh huh,', 'Yeah' and 'Wow.' You can also show you are listening carefully by demonstrating affection and approval. For example, you can say, 'The way you've put that is spot on,' or offer a hug if you see distress.

- ✔ **Avoiding giving advice:** Don't give advice unless your partner specifically requests help with an issue. And even if your partner does ask, keep it brief, and offer it merely as one possible option to consider.

- ✔ **Talking one at a time:** Let your partner talk for 10 to 20 minutes, and then have a similar amount of time for your turn.

You may be surprised by how much The Daily News can improve your relationship – sometimes in just a few days.

Anna and Natasha have been together for eight years. Their relationship starts to suffer as a result of Anna's depression. Anna is trying to cope with the menopause, complicated by her prolonged depression. Natasha, her partner, is still some years away from menopause. Although she sympathises with Anna, Natasha's patience wears thin after months of withdrawal, moodiness, and irritability. The women, who were once almost inseparable, find themselves becoming more and more distant.

After Anna talks to a counsellor she realises that given her depression, it's to be expected that she's withdrawing from Natasha. The counsellor tells Anna about The Daily News technique – a tool she can use to fight her depression and hopefully improve her relationship. Anna values her relationship and is determined to make it even better. Despite feeling pretty unenthusiastic, she explains, 'Natasha, depression's threatening to come between us. I can't promise instant recovery, but some positive time together can help. Let's make a point of having a daily cup of tea and a chat together.'

Feeling relieved that her partner is making an effort, Natasha responds to Anna with renewed understanding and compassion. Their daily conversation becomes a habit bringing them back together – and remaining that way!

Defeating Defensiveness

When a relationship starts to fail, a person can easily get into the habit of assuming the worst about their partner. Potentially ambiguous or even caring statements are automatically interpreted as having malicious or hostile motives. Depression, with its inevitably gloomy outlook, can increase the frequency of assuming the worst.

And when you start assuming the worst, you then typically do something that's especially self-defeating – you get defensive in response to the perceived attack. This defensiveness inevitably makes the other party hostile, even if it wasn't their original intention!

Nigel notices that his wife, Shelagh, has been lethargic and depressed for the past few weeks. The bills that she normally has the responsibility for paying begin to pile up, and Shelagh, who is usually meticulous about her appearance, has stopped wearing make-up. Nigel cares deeply about her and is concerned that she may be ill. One Saturday morning, he approaches her and says, 'Sweetheart, I'm worried about you. You haven't been taking care of things as you always do. Are you feeling okay?'

Shelagh retorts sarcastically, 'Great! You think I'm not doing my bit. Thanks for being so supportive. Here I'm doing my best, working ridiculous hours; in fact, all I ever do is work. On top of it all, criticism's the last thing I need!'

'Hang on a sec, Shelagh, I'm not being critical. It's just that you've changed. You don't seem to be your old self. I'm not trying to start an argument, I just want to help,' Nigel pleads.

'If you really want to help, just leave me alone. Can't you see I'm pushed to the limit already? Of course some things aren't getting done! I'm not a robot, you know!' Shelagh stalks off in floods of tears.

So just what is a defensive response? Basically, anything you may say to get out of taking the blame or responsibility for a perceived criticism. Now you may well wonder what could possibly be wrong with that. You may indeed have done nothing wrong whatsoever. Well, defensiveness can be a problem for two reasons:

- ✔ Defensiveness assumes without question that your partner intended to be hostile in the first place.

- ✔ Defensiveness all too easily invites more more criticism and hostility.

So what can you do to keep from falling into a defensive, critical mode when you feel that your partner may have said something you found upsetting or disparaging? The following sections discuss two particularly useful strategies.

Checking it out

The best way to counteract malicious assumptions that lead to defensiveness is to use the Checking It Out technique. This two-step technique requires you to sit on your automatic assumptions while you quietly make a careful examination of your partner's meaning and intentions:

1. **Stifle your urge to get defensive or attack.**

2. **Make a gentle enquiry about your partner's meaning and intent.**

In the previous section, Nigel says to Shelagh, 'Sweetheart, I'm worried about you. You haven't been taking care of things as you always do. Are you feeling okay?' Shelagh interprets Nigel's comment as critical and malicious, and she retorts defensively and sarcastically. But it would have been better if Shelagh had checked out her assumption by saying, 'Nigel, are you upset that I'm not doing enough? If you are, let's talk about it.'

In this case, Nigel would probably have replied something like, 'No, it's not that at all. I've just been worried that you're looking a little run-down lately. Tell me – is anything wrong?'

If you take the time to check out the meaning of what you think is criticism, you may well find that the intention isn't nearly as nasty as you thought. Feeling a bit defensive when you believe that you're being criticised is perfectly natural. But take a deep breath, and then check out your assumption before acting as if your assumption is true.

Occasionally, you may find that your partner has a genuine complaint. If so, try to stay non-defensive. Keep asking questions and consider using the techniques that we discuss later in this chapter to make your message more palatable and to defuse the situation.

Don't attempt to use Checking It Out, or any of the other communication techniques we discuss later in this chapter, if you're feeling angry, aggressive and/ or significantly upset. If you rate your distress above 50 out of 100 the chances are seriously remote that you're thinking anything that's useful or productive. Take a break, and return to discuss the issue when you're feeling calmer – perhaps in half an hour, a few hours, or even in a day or two. But don't put off talking for much longer than that, because resentments may build up. Remember that taking time to get into a better frame of mind on your own isn't a licence for avoiding communicating altogether.

Not taking things personally

When you take things personally you assume that your partner's tantrums, tirades, and upset remarks are all your fault. For example, Patrick spills a glass of water on the computer keyboard, and his partner Bella explodes. Patrick, already deeply embarrassed by the accident, feels even worse about himself after listening to Bella's outburst. Understandably, he assumes that Bella's anger is wholly about him and his clumsiness. Not so. In reality, Bella comes from a highly abusive family in which minor accidents were treated as catastrophes. Shouting at Patrick (and others) is a habit she acquired long ago. Someone other than Patrick may have responded to Bella without seeing the problem as his, (not taking it personally) and even by showing concern.

Not taking things personally means figuring out when your partner's reactions have less to do with you and more to do with the other persons history and upbringing that formed core beliefs about the meaning of certain types of events.

Everyone has core beliefs, formed during childhood, that continue to exert a huge influence on how they perceive and feel about events. (Refer to Chapter 7 for more information about core beliefs and how they work.) Core beliefs lie behind your hopes, dreams, and fears – all the issues you have strong feelings about. And you don't have to be depressed for one or more of these core beliefs to stir up a lot of emotion. Table 14-1 shows a few of the common core beliefs, or hot buttons, that can interfere with relationships.

Table 14-1	Relationship Hot Buttons (Core Beliefs)	
Hot Button	*What It Means*	*Common Origins*
Vulnerability/ Pessimism	Expecting the worst and having serious concerns about issues such as health, money, or safety	An impoverished childhood, introverted parents, and traumatic events during childhood
Abandonment	Fearing that anyone close to you will eventually leave	A parent who was never there for you when needed, parents who divorced when you were young, and other serious losses of people close to you
Dependency	Thinking that you need more help than you really do	A parent who stepped in to help whenever things got frustrating, or critical parents who gave messages that you were incapable of doing anything for yourself
Perfectionism	A driving need to make everything you do perfect, or believing that something just isn't good enough	Highly critical parents, who drive their children hard to achieve, or force their children to be highly accomplished.

Stanley grew up in a very unstable family, where money was always tight. He developed a core belief of there being little chance of happiness in this life and that no one could be trusted. Noreen's father abandoned his family when she was 6 years old. Her mother then became seriously depressed and withdrew into herself. Noreen developed the core belief that anyone who loves her is eventually going to abandon her.

Stanley and Noreen are now married. Stanley arranges for them to have a joint credit card. He then discovers that Noreen spent slightly more money this month than their combined salaries can cover. He confronts her: 'Noreen, we can't afford to pay the credit card bill this month. We're getting deeper and deeper into debt. If you keep this up, we're going to end up being bankrupt! You've just got to stop this wild spending at once!' Noreen begins to cry and sobs, 'Fine, if you want a divorce, just do it now. I always knew this marriage wasn't going to work out anyway!'

Are Stanley and Noreen crazy, or just irrational? Neither. Stanley's exaggerated response stems from his childhood experiences, when his family often had to struggle to find enough money to feed themselves. His hot buttons now concern his insecurity and pessimism. And Noreen's abandonment hot button stems from the actual loss of her father and the emotional loss of her mother. Both reactions may be excessive, but they make sense if you understand their backgrounds.

If your partner gets easily upset, distraught, or passionate about an issue, the chances are that one or more core beliefs are the underlying cause. Checking it out can help you find out which core belief may be affecting your partner's perspective. You can start by determining your own core beliefs (see Table 14-1 and also go to Chapter 7). Strange as it may seem, one of *your* core beliefs may help explain why your partner's feelings appear excessive or irrational to you.

Once you figure out which hot buttons are yours and which belong to your partner, you may find that you still disagree with one another. However, you can now see that many of the highly charged feelings aren't really about you. Distance yourself from the hot buttons and don't take it personally. Realise that the conflict is basically linked to your own or your partner's early upbringing, rather than being about you personally.

Clarifying Communication

Poor communication can destroy your relationship, while effective communication can strengthen and deepen it. Having good communication matters most when talking through difficult issues and conflicts.

Communication techniques aren't that difficult to master, yet some people are reluctant to use these techniques because sharing concerns can be incredibly difficult. But the alternative of attempting to squash and conceal problems only leads to resentment and hostility.

The following sections outline techniques for improving communication, which are particularly helpful if you're suffering from depression. These techniques help you talk about difficult issues and cam prevent discussion deteriorating into conflict. Why not give them a try? They can improve your communication with friends, family, colleagues, and loved ones.

Taking ownership

When two people disagree, the language they use to express themselves can be violent and hostile. A simple technique called Taking Ownership can stop the disagreement from getting out of control. The idea is to disclose your own feelings, rather than accuse or criticise your partner. This technique is an alternative to using blaming messages. Table 14-2 shows some examples of blaming messages and their more productive Taking Ownership equivalents. Read the examples of both types of messages Then, when you feel tempted to blame your partner, try rephrasing what you are trying to say, and at the same taking ownership of your feelings.

Table 14-2	The Taking Ownership Technique
Blaming/'You' Messages	*Claiming/'Me' Messages*
You never show me any affection.	I wish you'd hug me more often.
You spend too much money.	I feel worried about our finances; can we talk about it?
You're so critical about everything I do.	I feel like I'm not pleasing you.
You make me so furious.	I'm feeling angry.
You never do the things you say you're going to do.	I feel unhappy when you forget to follow through on something you promised me.

Making the message palatable

Removing the unpleasant taste gives you a way to sweeten any distasteful messages. Making the Message Palatable involves finding ways to soften any criticism you want to get across. You add a phrase to acknowledge the possibility that your position may not be wholly correct. After all, how often can anyone ever truly be 100 per cent certain that they are right about the detail of a particular event? Pretty seldom, you'll doubtless agree.

This technique offers the opportunity to discuss your concerns and opens the door to compromise. The following list provides some useful phrases:

- 'It's possible that I'm wrong here, but I'm worried that . . .'
- 'I may be making too much out of this, but . . .'
- 'Please correct me if I've got the wrong end of the stick, but I feel a little upset that . . .'
- 'Help me see this from your perspective.'

If you use more palatable phrases before talking about your concern or criticism, your partner is going to be less likely to go into a defensive or attacking mode. The technique increases the likelihood that you're going to be heard rather than dismissed.

Defusing situations versus being defensive

Applying Defusing helps prevent a criticism from escalating into a full-scale argument. This technique helps you deal with criticism (instead of being on the defensive or attacking the criticism). The Defusing technique is in effect the opposite of Making the Message Palatable (see the previous section). With the Defusing technique, you find *something* about the criticism that you can agree with. Apologising and acknowledging any truths in the disagreement doesn't hurt, either. Here are some examples of responses you can use to help defuse an argument:

- ✔ 'I'm sorry. I guess you may have a point there.'
- ✔ 'I admit that sometimes what you say probably is true.'
- ✔ 'I can see why you think that.'
- ✔ 'I can agree with part of what you're saying.'

Making excuses tells your partner that you care more about saving face than you do about your partner's concerns. When you provide a partial agreement and make a sincere apology (Defusing), you show that you're keen to heal your partner's hurt feelings. When you make excuses, you demonstrate that you're more interested in repairing your own ego.

When you're depressed and your self-esteem is low, you may feel like making excuses to stop your self-esteem from falling any further. If you work hard to avoid that temptation, you're more than likely to be rewarded in the long-run.

Putting it all into practice

Now that you know about the three techniques of Taking Ownership, Making the Message Palatable, and Defusing, you may want to see them in action. You can then fully appreciate the value of these communication strategies.

But first, we show you how difficult communication can be *without* using the three techniques. **Ruth** and **Dennis** are having a disagreement about house-work. Here's how their conversation goes:

> **Ruth:** You never help me with any of the housework. I'm getting absolutely sick and tired of it.

> **Dennis:** Yes I do. I mowed the lawn last week. Just what do you want out of me?

Ruth: The lawn's your job, not mine. I'm talking about the laundry, the cooking, the household shopping, and the washing up. You don't do any of these. My list's twice as long as yours. Face it, if it wasn't for me, this place would look even more like a pigsty than it already does.

Dennis: Look, I earn more money than you. I'm shattered when I get home. When we got married, you said if I was the main bread winner, you'd take care of the house. This just isn't fair!

Ruth: Fair? What are you talking about? I'm also working, you know. Why can't you can't even talk about a simple thing like housework without shouting!

Not a very productive discussion, is it? Both Dennis and Ruth resort to criticism, defensiveness, and anger. Nothing is solved, and the bad feelings worsen. Now we're going to take the same conversation and insert the Taking Ownership, Making the Message Palatable, and Defusing techniques.

Ruth: Help me see your take on this. (Making the Message Palatable). I feel a little overwhelmed with the housework (Taking Ownership), and it kind of seems like you're not doing as much as I'd like.

Dennis: Well, I agree that you do more of the housework (Defusing). I'm sorry that I've made you feel so overwhelmed. I guess I come home so tired that I often don't think about housework, but maybe I should (Taking Ownership). What do you need most?

Ruth: Sometimes I feel like I do everything (Taking Ownership). But maybe I'm overreacting (Making the Message Palatable). If you could help with the dishes after dinner, that would feel ever so much better.

Dennis: (Defusing) I can see why you'd like that. Let's face it, we're a big family which means a whole lot of dishes (Defusing). I'm just shattered after dinner (Taking Ownership). How about I do the washing at the weekend instead? And perhaps we start getting the kids' help with the dishes. They're old enough now.

Ruth: Well, that's a reasonable compromise, I suppose. Thanks for listening and hearing my concern.

That turned out a little better, didn't it? When you use the Defusing technique, you focus more on finding something to agree with (or even apologise for some aspect of the complaint), and you pay less attention to conjuring up defensive excuses. Making the Message Palatable allows you to express concerns in a gentle, non-confrontational manner. Taking Ownership keeps the focus on your concerns and stops you from blaming your partner. You can apply all three techniques to communicating with your partner as well as in other important relationships.

After reading the conversations between Ruth and Dennis, think about writing down a conversation that you've had with someone that didn't go too well. Then rewrite the conversation inserting as many Defusing, Making the Message Palatable, and Taking Ownership messages as possible. Putting the three techniques into practice means that your communication skills are just going to get better and better.

Part V
Full-Bodied Assault: Biological Therapies to Fight the Physical Foe

'So following the therapists advice, we sent off for a pet to help Geoffrey over his depression.'

In this part . . .

*E*very year, new treatments for depression are trumpeted. Evaluating all your options can be overwhelming. We bring you the latest information about medication for treating depression. More importantly, we help you make a decision as to whether medication is the right choice for you.

Other alternatives for treating depression also exist. In the following pages, you can read about natural alternatives such as herbs or light therapy. And finally, we discuss electric shock treatment and other biologically based treatments for treating difficult cases of depression.

Chapter 15

Maximising Medication Benefits

Many people used to believe that depression was triggered by a character flaw or weakness. Because of that belief, those suffering from depression often didn't seek treatment. Feeling embarrassed, guilty, and worthless, they went on suffering in horrible silence. Or worse, ended their pain with suicide. But the antidepressant medication that's available nowadays is easing suffering for millions. Research is showing that there are biological factors underpinning your mood.

In this chapter, we help you decide your best treatment option(s) – psychological help, medication, or a combination of both. We tell you about where to get help, how long you may have to take medication, and when combining psychological therapy with medication may be your best choice, helping you get better faster than just following one treatment on its own. Finally, we give you information about the most common prescription drugs.

Barry is reluctantly seeing his GP, having tried in vain for several months to 'just snap out of it' 'I'm sorry if I'm wasting your time. I'm a bit of a fraud in a way, but I haven't the foggiest idea what's wrong with me. I just feel absolutely awful, from the moment I wake up to when I finally fall asleep. Every night it takes ages to drop off, but then I'm wide awake by 4 a.m. and can't get back to sleep. I'm restless all the time, and everyone and everything irritates me. My whole body feels painful, but it's like it's all over, not anywhere in particular. Do you think it's a brain tumour?'

After a complete check up and some further discussion, the doctor decides that Barry is suffering from severe depression. She explains to Barry that he has a 'chemical imbalance', and she prescribes antidepressants. Slightly puzzled as to how his brain chemicals have got out of synch but willing to give the drugs a go, Barry takes the prescription to his local chemist.

The pharmacist encourages Barry to read the information leaflet on the commonly-used antidepressant his doctor prescribed. But the more Barry reads about possible side effects, the more he worries. Headaches, dry mouth, dizziness, stomach upsets, and – oh no! – sexual dysfunction. Barry wonders whether to just forget the whole idea and wait for things to improve by themselves. But after some thought, he decides to give the medication a try because his depression's making him feel so awful. Besides, Barry works out that if he experiences bad side effects, his GP may be able to suggest an alternative that won't affect him in that way. Barry makes the right decision. To his enormous relief; his depression starts lifting within a couple of weeks.

Depression is an illness that affects both body and mind. Left untreated, it can banish happiness, and also take a physical toll. (For more detail on these aspects of depression, refer to Chapter 1.) Do get help if you're feeling depressed. Trying to ignore depression and hoping it's going to go away all by itself just isn't the answer.

Selecting the Best Weapons to Fight Depression

The greater part of this book provides techniques you can use to improve your mood and defeat depression. Most of these are from the fields of cognitive behavioural therapy (a combination of cognitive therapy reviewed in Part II and behaviour therapy discussed in Part IV). We want to encourage you to adopt healthy thinking and behaviour as your first line of defence in your battle against the blues. But no way is psychological therapy the only tool!

There's a huge body of studies available comparing prescribed medication with psychological therapy, mainly cognitive behavioural therapy (CBT), for the treatment of depression. Most studies agree that both types of therapy are equally effective for the treatment of depression. And several studies suggest that a combination of the two brings even better results.

Combining medication with therapy appears to give a slight edge over using only the one form of treatment, allowing a person taking antidepressant medication to make better use of psychological therapy.

Ultimately, it's your decision whether to take medication for your depression. If you choose to stick to self-help using psychological therapy, you need to work conscientiously through the exercises provided in this self-help book, and/or work with a therapist. Don't expect to get better without a lot of effort. With work, you can expect that the skills you develop are likely to help you against any future struggles with depression. But for many people, medication is one important part of the solution – and for good reason.

Whatever path you choose, don't forget that depression is an illness that can be treated successfully. If the initial solution you've gone for doesn't work, don't give up hope. Be patient, get help, and try something different.

Exploring the Medication Option

Given all the evidence that psychological therapy works, why do people choose to take medication? Well, there are a range of views, with some studies suggesting that for about 90 per cent of depressed people, a single medication or a combination of medicines can lessen symptoms or completely cure depression. Other studies suggest that medication is only effective in around one third of cases, and partially effective in another third, with the final third getting very limited or no benefit at all. With such differing opinions, making a decision is even more difficult, especially as a depressed person is often troubled by uncertainty and doubt!

The following sections sum up common reasons why people take medication, or choose not to.

Awarding drugs the thumbs up

Doctors agree that the medication route is best when:

- **You have serious suicidal thoughts or plans.** In this case, you need help now. First, see a mental health professional to decide on the best treatment for you. Sometimes antidepressant medication can start to have an effect faster than cognitive behavioural therapy and other psychological therapies.

- **You have bipolar disorder or depression with psychotic features.** Medication is a particularly important element of treatment those with bipolar disorder or people whose depression is so severe that they are hearing voices or seeing things that aren't really there (refer to Chapter 2). However, the addition of psychological therapy often helps to stabilise mood even further, encouraging people to continue taking their medication and so preventing relapses.

✔ **You've given cognitive behavioural therapy (CBT) or interpersonal therapy (IPT) a good try and your depression keeps recurring.** Evidence shows that untreated depression becomes more severe, frequent, and resistant to treatment. If your depression keeps recurring, consider including long-term medication along with other treatment. (See Chapter 4 'What Works? The effective therapies', for more information on CBT and IPT)

✔ **Your symptoms of depression are mostly physiological.** For example, you have problems with your appetite or sleep, or you feel overwhelming fatigue, forgetfulness, and poor concentration. *Caution:* Not everyone with the physical symptoms of depression responds better to medication, and some of those with physical symptoms may be trying to avoid examining their feelings and thoughts. So, if medication doesn't work, seeing a therapist may be a very good idea.

✔ **Depression takes control of your life.** If severe symptoms cause you to neglect the important tasks of everyday living, you may need medication to get you going again. But, after you're feeling a bit better, consider self-help or cognitive behavioural therapy to keep up your improvement.

✔ **Medical conditions cause your depression.** Sometimes people with other illnesses become depressed. (Refer to Chapter 2 for more on causes of depression). Different physical conditions may lead to depression in a number of different ways, sometimes by affecting the brain directly. Medication may be the quickest way to overcome this type of depression.

✔ **Panic or anxiety accompanies depression.** You may have too much on your plate to wait for the benefits of psychological therapy. Again, when the medication starts taking effect, you may have more mental energy available to tackle anxiety and depression in therapy or with the aid of of self-help books like this one or another of our titles, *Overcoming Anxiety For Dummies* by Elaine Iljon-Foreman, Laura Smith, and Charles Elliott (Wiley).

✔ **Psychological therapy doesn't work.** A few people just don't seem to benefit from psychological therapy, or they may have complicated issues that need a very long period of therapy. In this case, medication may be a good choice.

✔ **Your depression has lasted most of your life.** Some evidence suggests that chronic depression (such as dysthymia; refer to Chapter 2) may benefit a great deal from medication plus psychological therapy.

✔ **You don't have time for psychological therapy.** For some people, such therapy is too time consuming. If your schedule is already overfull, we hope you at least put some time aside within your busy day to read through this book.

> ✔ **You are having difficulty accessing psychological therapy on the NHS, and can't afford to pay for private therapy.** Your local communality mental health team may not offer a service to people with your problem or level of depression, and there can be a lengthy wait to receive psychological therapy through your GP practice, assuming it does provide this service. You can try a combination of self-help, along with medication to support you.

Many people even today feel guilty about taking medication for depression, telling themselves it's the 'easy way out'. Be honest. If you're diabetic, do you think you ought to feel bad about taking insulin? And if you have an infection, don't you take antibiotics? And have you never, ever, taken pain relief for a headache? So what's so special and different about taking antidepressant medication?

Giving medication the thumbs down

If taking medication works, then where's the problem? Why doesn't everyone try it? Here are some common reasons why people may choose not to take prescription medications for depression:

> ✔ **Getting scared by bad press:** Some of the earlier antidepressant drugs had a bad image. This is summed up in lyrics like the Rolling Stones' 'No more running for the shelter of a mother's little helper. They just helped you on your way, through your busy dying day.' But a great deal has changed since those days, both in respect of the chemical formulae of many drugs, as well as doctors' knowledge and prescribing practices.

> ✔ **Being put off by side effects:** More than a third of people prescribed antidepressant medication stop taking it, mainly because of the side effects, which can include nausea, headaches, insomnia, dry mouth, weight gain, feelings of apathy, and sexual dysfunction.

> ✔ **Avoiding drugs while pregnant or breastfeeding:** Research about the effects of antidepressant medication on the foetus or infant comes from animal studies or case examples, so ithere's not enough information available to judge the safety of most antidepressant medications. Talk to your doctor if you're planning on getting pregnant, might be pregnant, or are breastfeeding. In most of these cases, psychological therapy is a better choice than medication.

Depression after the birth of a baby is a common problem that can become serious if left untreated, and can have lasting effects on your baby's emotional development. Please get help if you experience more than a couple of days of baby blues (Refer to Chapter 2 for more on postnatal depression).

✔ **Worrying about long-term effects:** If you have more than one major depressive episode, if depression was severe or long-lasting, if you have bipolar disorder (refer to Chapter 2), or your depression has never completely lifted, your doctor may recommend long-term medication to prevent recurrence. Although long-term use of antidepressant medication appears to have little risk, some research highlights concerns about the lack of evidence proving the safety of taking antidepressants long-term.

✔ **Just saying no:** Some people don't want to take medication, for a variety of reasons, including religious and philosophical ones. If that's you, please get help for your depression through cognitive behavioural or interpersonal therapy techniques. Depression does require treatment. If your mood doesn't improve within a few months of self-help or if your depression is severe, do go to a mental health professional for assistance (refer to Chapter 4 for information on finding professional help).

Seeing What Suits: Working with Your Doctor to Find the Correct Medication

A positive, two-way relationship with your GP or psychiatrist (refer to Chapter 4) may be the most important ingredient for successful treatment of depression. You and your doctor need to discuss openly your particular symptoms of depression, your response to the medication, and any side effects you may experience.

Unfortunately, it's unclear which particular antidepressant medication is the most likely to work for any one individual. Research studies show that people opt for taking medication to help them in different areas of their lives and go for psychological therapy in other areas. However, there's no general agreement on how effective this approach is to treating depression. Some people respond to the first drug prescribed; others may need to try several different ones. The drug your doctor chooses depends on a number of factors:

✔ **Specific depressive symptoms:** Your doctor needs to know about all your symptoms before choosing a medication. The doctor may ask the following: Do you sleep too much, or too little? Have you gained or lost weight? Do you have aches and pains? Do you feel anxious as well as depressed? Do you have difficulty concentrating?

✔ **Side effects:** For most people, the first choice in medication is the one with the least side effects. But side effects of a drug can sometimes be employed to advantage. For example, people with sleep problems may do better with a medication that has a side effect of sedation. Again, no one can predict the precise degree to which any side effects are going to affect you. Sometimes a change in medication, or a change in the dose, or even the addition of another drug is used to manage side effects.

✔ **History of depression:** If you have had previous depressive episodes and been successfully treated with a particular antidepressant, the same one is likely to be the first choice. This time round, though, your doctor may well decide to continue the medication for a much longer period.

✔ **Family response to antidepressant medication:** Although there is limited evidence showing that genetics affect how different antidepressant medications work, if a member of your family had a favourable response to a specific antidepressant medication, let your doctor know. Depending on many other factors, that antidepressant may be the best first choice.

You need to be able to talk freely with your doctor, so that he or she knows how best to help you. Tell your doctor:

✔ **About any other physical conditions you have:** Discuss all your current health concerns with your doctor, especially liver disease, hepatitis, diabetes, high blood pressure, or kidney disease.

✔ **If you think you may be pregnant, are trying to get pregnant, or are breastfeeding:** Certain medication may not be safe.

✔ **If you want to drink alcohol while on the medication:** Generally, you should avoid alcohol when you take antidepressants. Alcohol may interact with some antidepressants, increasing the alcohol's effect, increasing fatigue, or even blocking the drug's effects. Drinking too much regularly can also cause depressed mood, and this improves when the drinking stops. However, an occasional drink is probably harmless, depending on which medication you are on, so do discuss this with your doctor.

✔ **About any other medication you're taking:** Antidepressants may interfere with other medications, or vice versa. Be sure to also mention any non-prescription medications in your discussion.

✔ **About any herbal treatments, alternative treatments or supplements you take:** Again, there may be interactions with antidepressants. For more about herbs and supplements, see Chapter 16.

✔ **About any and all side effects:** Although many troublesome side effects cease within a couple of weeks, don't suffer in silence. Your doctor may be able to help you manage the side effects by changing your prescription or dosage, or by combining it with another drug. Don't be embarrassed by the nature of the problems – side effects like decreased sexual pleasure, loss of libido, or inability to achieve orgasm aren't rare and treatment is available.

Hang on in there. Antidepressant medication usually takes at least two weeks to begin working and may take up to six weeks for maximum benefit to occur, although many people start to respond more quickly. Sometimes the people around you will notice an improvement before you do. You may well not respond to the first drug. Give your doctor a chance to help you. You may have to go through months of trying different medication to find the one, or combination, that suits. The good news is that after you find which works, it is likely to continue to be effective in easing your depression.

Research suggests that less than a quarter of people treated with medication for depression get adequate treatment, meaning receiving a reasonable number of psychotherapy sessions with treatments found to be effective for depression (refer to Chapter 4 for an overview of those treatments) or take an adequate dose of medications for a long enough period. About 10 per cent of people with prescriptions for antidepressants start the medication, but then discontinue it within a week! Many more stop the minute they feel a little better. Unfortunately they then quickly slip back to how they felt before the medication started. If you choose to be treated for depression with medication, complete the prescribed course. Otherwise, your risk of relapse increases.

Understanding How Antidepressants Work: Revising Biology

Scientists continue to study the relationship between depression and biology. They've found some differences when comparing people with and without depression (refer to Chapter 1). However, we also know that the biological aspect of depression isn't a simple, easily measured and counterbalanced chemical deficiency. If that were the case, an intravenous infusion (directly into the vein) of the precise quantity of a specific antidepressant would be the instant solution. No such luck, unfortunately!

To understand how antidepressant medication works, you need to know some basic information about your brain and body. We're going to keep this simple, and don't worry, there's no final exam. Promise!

The brain is made up of nerve cells called *neurons.* Neurons take in information about the state of the world both outside and inside the body and react to these internal and external happenings. Basically, neurons are the backbone of the *nervous system*, which controls all actions, thoughts, and emotions (see the nearby 'Knowing the nervous system' sidebar). Neurons allow you to walk, talk, and smell the roses, and they give you the ability to love, to remember, to acquire knowledge, and to feel. But to do this, neurons have to communicate between one other. Depression can disrupt neural communication.

TIP

Knowing the nervous system

The human nervous system senses activity in your body and outside of it. The brain takes in the sensory information and plans a response. The nervous system then responds with action. For example, when you touch a hot cooker with your hand, pain messages surge to your brain. Your brain reacts almost instantly with the information that touching something hot caused the pain. Your brain sends a message to your hand to quickly pull away. Hopefully, your brain will remember the experience so that next time you won't touch the cooker when it's hot.

The nervous system is made up of the central nervous system (CNS) and the peripheral nervous system (PNS). The CNS includes the brain and the spinal cord. The CNS takes in information and using this, then tells the rest of the body what to do. The PNS contains nerves that carry information to and from the CNS. The PNS acts as the go-between with the CNS and skeletal muscles, sense receptors, smooth muscles, cardiac muscles, and glands. Antidepressants primarily affect the CNS.

So how do the 100 billion or so neurons in your brain talk to each other? They communicate by sending chemical messengers back and forth. Scientists estimate about 100 trillion different lines of communication exist between all those neurons. But to save time, let's look at just one such neuronal conversation . . .

Pretend that Nick and Nina are neighbouring neurons (see Figure 15-1). Nina Neuron has an important message to tell Nick, so she sends a jolt of energy down a long tube called an *axon*. When this burst of energy reaches the end of Nina's axon, chemical messengers, or *neurotransmitters*, are released into a tiny space, called a *synapse*, between Nina and Nick, the two next door neurons.

The neurotransmitters hang around outside both 'front doors', that is in the synapse. But then Nina becomes anxious (as all good neurons do) that she's released so many chemicals, so she starts up a pump that sucks some neurons back in from the synapse. But in the meanwhile, Nick the neighbour welcomes some of the chemical messengers with open arms called *dendrites*. After they're inside, these neurotransmitters talk to Nick and may even start telling him what to do. So, the upshot is that some of the neurotransmitters enter the neighbouring neuron and some return to the original cell.

When depression occurs, the chemical conversations between neurons break down. When neurons can't communicate well, the mind is unable to use all its resources to deal with events such as stress. This depleted state leads to a communication breakdown, taking the form of depression.

Competing theories

Why does antidepressant medication take so long to work? One theory is that when the neurotransmitters are too few, or low in strength, the receiving cells enhance the sensitivity of their receptors. After the antidepressants have increased the number of available neurotransmitters, then the receptors return to their normal level of sensitivity. This process takes about the same amount of time that it takes for a person to feel the beneficial effects of the medication.

Another theory relates to what kinds of messages the neurotransmitter gives to the receiving cell. Some scientists hold the theory that, despite normal amounts of chemical messengers, the communication between cells and their responses have somehow become defective. With new research, scientists hope to find better ways to predict responses to medication, and find faster routes and drugs with fewer side effects. Watch this space!

Some experts believe that depression results when there aren't enough neurotransmitters to get the message out. Others think that depression may stem from neurotransmitter systems that aren't working properly. Different drugs act on different neurotransmitters in different ways. The bottom line is that no one is entirely certain exactly why antidepressant medications work, other than the fact that they do seem to improve communication among neurons (see the nearby 'Competing theories' sidebar).

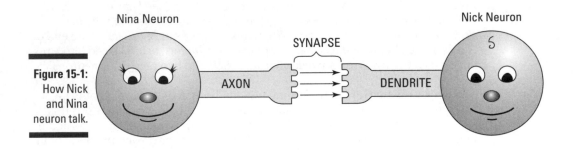

Figure 15-1: How Nick and Nina neuron talk.

Exploring Medication

Although pharmaceutical companies spend billions of pounds searching for ever improved treatments for depression, there's still no overall consensus as to how antidepressant medication works. Most experts believe antidepressant medications somehow increase one or more of the neurotransmitters in the brain and that doing so improves communication among neurons and ultimately reduces depression (see 'Revising Biology', earlier in this chapter).

The relationship between the various neurotransmitters and depression isn't yet completely understood. But the three neurotransmitters that most anti-depressants target appear to relate to different symptoms:

✔ **Serotonin:** Problems with serotonin are associated with depressed mood, anxiety, insomnia, obsessive compulsive disorder, seasonal affective disorder, and even violence.

✔ **Dopamine:** Disruptions in dopamine seem to relate to problems with attention, motivation, alertness, increased apathy, and difficulty in experiencing pleasure.

✔ **Norepinephrine:** Disorders in norepinephrine match lack of energy, decreased alertness, and lethargy.

Your particular symptoms help point your doctor towards what's likely to be the best first choice of antidepressant for you. However, scientists haven't yet developed a completely accurate way of predicting which symptoms are best targeted by which medications.

Antidepressant drugs are classified by how they affect one or more of these neurochemicals. In the following sections, we examine the most commonly prescribed antidepressants and explain their actions, common uses, problems, and side effects. The following discussion can give you practical information about each class of antidepressant drug. And remember that new antidepressants are constantly being developed.

We believe that knowledge helps you get the best medical care for your depression. The information we give you below is going to help you communicate with your health care provider. Working together, you can find the right medication for you.

Selecting SSRIs

Ever since Prozac came on the market in the late 1980s, *selective serotonin reuptake inhibitors* (SSRIs) have been the most popular antidepressants. One reason for their popularity is that their side effects are less severe than older antidepressants and the consequences of overdose are also less dangerous.

An SSRI is often the first choice of antidepressant medication. These drugs are used for the treatment of major depressive disorder, dysthymia, and seasonal affective disorder. (For more about these disorders, go to Chapter 2.) SSRIs are commonly used when depression and anxiety are mixed. (They are also used for treating anxiety-related disorders that aren't accompanied by depression, such as obsessive-compulsive disorder, panic disorder, generalised anxiety disorders, premenstrual syndrome, eating disorders, and some types of chronic pain.)

SSRIs combat depression by increasing the available levels of serotonin. Remember Nina the neuron from the 'Revising Biology' section, earlier in this chapter? Imagine that Nina sends out a burst of serotonin into her synapse. Normally, some of the serotonin she releases is taken in by Nick, the neighbouring neuron, while Nina pumps some of the serotonin back into her cell. An SSRI antidepressant works by clogging Nina's pump so that she can't reabsorb her serotonin. There's therefore more serotonin sitting in the synapse outside Nick's door, for Nick to invite in!

SSRIs usually take about one to four weeks to become effective. However, many people notice a slight improvement after a few days, and some people will not experience the full benefit for six weeks or even longer. Side effects may include increased anxiety, fatigue, upset stomach, insomnia, apathy, lack of sexual interest, or inability to obtain orgasm. You might also experience dizziness, sweating, tremors, dry mouth, headache, and weight loss or gain. Side effects are most severe for the first few weeks, and then tend to lessen..

SSRIs may bring additional complications and problems. Bear in mind:

- ✔ If you have bipolar disorder, SSRIs may be dangerous. Occasionally, these drugs induce a manic state, which can involve dangerous or risky behaviours (refer to Chapter 2 for more information about bipolar disorder).

- ✔ Abruptly stopping SSRIs (or for that matter, any antidepressant medication) can produce anxiety or flu-like symptoms such as nausea, headache, sweating, fever, and chills. Sudden withdrawal can also cause vivid dreams and problems with sleep. Talk to your doctor if you decide to stop taking SSRIs for advice on how to do so safely.

- ✔ The UK Committee on Safety of Medicines banned the treatment of childhood depression (suffered by children under 18) with any SSRI except Prozac in 2003, because evidence exists to suggest a small raised risk of suicide or suicidal thoughts in children taking these drugs

- ✔ Taking SSRIs with other classes of antidepressants, especially, but not only, MAO inhibititors (see the later section in this chapter) can cause a life-threatening reaction. Other drugs may also interact negatively. Tell your doctor about all of the medications you are taking.

Table 15-1 shows you the six SSRIs currently available on the market. We've put typical dosage ranges for treatment of depression in the community. Higher doses may be permitted for inpatients or in the treatment of other conditions that may also be present (e.g. OCD/panic/anxiety disorders). However, your doctor will work with you in deciding what's appropriate for you.

Table 15-1	Selective Serotonin Reuptake Inhibitors (SSRIs)		
Brand Name	**Generic Name**	**Usual Dosage (In Milligrams)**	**Comments**
Cipralex	Escitalopram	10–20	A chemical cousin of Celexa, which may work faster.
Cipramil	Citalopram	10–60	May have fewer interactions with other drugs. Not particularly stimulating or sedating.
Faverin	Fluvoxamine	50–300	Generally more sedating than the others. The first to be approved for obsessive–compulsive disorder.
Lustral	Sertraline	50–200	Not as stimulating or sedating as some of the others.
Prozac	Fluoxetine	10–60	Stimulating, may cause insomnia if taken late in the day. Causes increased anxiety in some people. Clears out of body very slowly and therefore has the least withdrawal symptoms if abruptly stopped.
Seroxat	Paroxetine	20.0–50.0	Somewhat sedating. May be associated with more weight gain and more pronounced withdrawal symptoms.

Untreated depression often lessens sexual interest. SSRIs can also interfere with sexual arousal and pleasure. If you're in a relationship in which sexual intimacy has already been disrupted, speak to your doctor about your concerns.

Getting more for your money

Antidepressant medication probably works by increasing the amount of certain neurotransmitters in the brain. SSRIs target serotonin, but some antidepressants increase more than one such chemical messenger or act on the neuron and its neurotransmitters in more than one way.

In the following list, we take a look at these medications, noting which neurotransmitter system the medication affects and how it acts on them. You don't need to know the complicated terminology represented by the initials, but we include it in case you come across the terms elsewhere. See Table 15-2 for more information on the following drugs:

- **SNRIs (Serotonin/Norepinephrine Reuptake Inhibitor):** Boosts both serotonin and norepinephrine

- **NDRIs (Norepinephrine/Dopamine Reuptake Inhibitor):** Boosts both norepinephrine and dopamine

- **NRIs (Norepinephrine Reuptake Inhibitor):** Selectively boosts norepinephrine

- **NaSSAs (Noradrenergic/Specific Serotonergic Antidepressants):** Enhances the release of norepinephrine and serotonin while blocking certain serotonin receptors

- **SARIs (Serotonin-2 Antagonists Reuptake Inhibitors):** Blocks the reuptake of serotonin while also blocking one specific type of serotonin receptor

Other older antidepressants also targeted multiple neurochemicals (see the section 'Taking tricyclics', later in this chapter). However, these newer versions appear to have fewer side effects and are more specific in their actions on the neurotransmitters than the older tricyclics.

Table 15-2		More Antidepressant Choices	
Brand Name	Generic Name	Usual Dosage (In Milligrams)	Classification/Comments
Cymbalta	Duloxetine	60	SNRI
Edronax	Reboxetine	2–8	NRI. Can improve attention and increase energy. May also increase anxiety.
Effexor	Venlafaxine	75–375	SNRI. May be effective where other antidepressants have not worked. May be more effective for severe depression. Fewer drug interactions than most antidepressant medications. Can elevate blood pressure in higher doses. Generally only used if other antidepressants have not worked.
Effexor XR		75–375	

Brand Name	Generic Name	Usual Dosage (In Milligrams)	Classification/Comments
Molipaxin	Trazadone	150–300	SARI. Sedating side effects. Used mostly when insomnia or agitation is a problem.
Zispin	Mitrazepine	15–45	NaSSA. Helps when insomnia is a problem. It may also cause weight gain.

Taking tricyclics

This class of antidepressant medication was the most widely used for many years. _Tricyclic_ medications are thought to have more general effects on neurotransmitters than the newer, more targeted medications (the ones we cover in the 'Selecting SSRIs' and 'Getting more for your money' sections, earlier in the chapter). The name is based on their chemical structure rather than the way they exert their effects, which can vary from one type of tricyclic medication to another.

The main reason that tricyclics are now less popular is that an overdose can be fatal. The newer antidepressants are generally much safer. Tricyclics are also associated with a host of side effects. These medications can cause dizziness from _orthostatic hypotension_, a sudden drop in blood pressure upon standing. Therefore, tricyclics are usually not prescribed for people at risk of falling, such as the elderly. Other side effects include weight gain, dry mouth, blurred vision, constipation, sweating, and sexual dysfunction.

Nevertheless, tricyclics may be more effective in severe depression than other antidepressants, and doctors often prescribe tricyclics when other medications haven't worked or when anxiety is mixed with depression. Lower doses are used when the patients is elderly. See Table 15-3 for more information.

Table 15-3	Tricyclic Antidepressants	
Brand Name	**Generic Name**	**Usual Dosage (In Milligrams)**
Allegron	Nortriptyline	50–150
Anafranil	Clomipramine	10– 250
Lomont	Lofepramine	140-210
Prothiaden	Dosulepin/dothiepin	50-150
Sinepin	Doxepin	30–300

(continued)

Table 15-3 (continued)

Brand Name	Generic Name	Usual Dosage (In Milligrams)
Surmontil	Trimipramine	75–300
Tofranil	Imipramine	75–300
Triptafen	Amitriptyline	75–200

Understanding MAO inhibitors

The first drug to treat depression was discovered in 1952, totally by accident. Scientists were experimenting with a new treatment for tuberculosis. Unfortunately, while the drug had no effect on TB, surprisingly, the patients taking the drug reported that their low mood lifted. Thus, the first antidepressant was born – a *monoamine oxidase inhibitor* (MAO inhibitor).

MAO inhibitors work by targeting a substance that destroys neurotransmitters. Because fewer neurotransmitters are destroyed, this then increases levels of serotonin, norepinephrine, and dopamine. MAO inhibitors are prescribed less often because of potentially serious side effects when combined with certain common foods or medications (although newer types of MAO inhibitors that may not have the same dangerous interactions are under development). Side effects can include dangerous spikes in blood pressure that can result in strokes or death.

People taking MAO inhibitors should avoid food containing *tyramine* (a natural substance found in the body that also forms as proteins breakdown as they age) such as sausages, beer, red wine, avocados, aged cheese, and smoked fish. Drug combinations to avoid include any other antidepressant medication, most drugs for colds and asthma, drugs for the treatment of diabetes, for high blood pressure, and some painkillers.

Despite all of the problems with MAO inhibitors, doctors still use them to treat some forms of resistant depression. When safer medications haven't helped, these drugs can be effective. They're especially useful for the treatment of atypical depression, which often involves overeating, sleeping too much, and irritability. Table 15-4 provides more information.

Table 15-4		MAO Inhibitors
Brand Name	**Generic Name**	**Usual Dosage (In Milligrams)**
Marplan	Isocarboxazid	10–40
Nardil	Phenelzine	45–90
Parnate	Tranylcypromine	30–60

Looking Beyond Antidepressants

For most people with depression, an antidepressant medication helps ease symptoms. You may have to go through a trial period, but usually one or more of the drugs we discuss in the 'Exploring Medication' section, earlier in the chapter eventually works. However, when several different classes of antidepressant medication haven't worked, your doctor (usually a psychiatrist) may try other types of drugs.

Depression is a serious problem. If the first tablet prescribed doesn't work, hang on in there. Your doctor is highly likely to suggest an alternative drug, or combination, that is more than likely to help Upping the downs: Smoothing out moods.

A group of drugs called mood stabilisers don't directly impact on serotonin, dopamine, or norepinephrine – the neurotransmitters that antidepressant medications target (see the 'Exploring Medication' section, earlier in the chapter). Mood stabilisers have multiple and complex effects on neurons. Many of these drugs seem to mainly affect two other neurotransmitters, glutamate and gamma-aminobutyric acid (GABA). Mood stabilizers, usually the first choice in treating bipolar disorder (refer to Chapter 2), are also used in combinations with antidepressants for treating resistant depression.

When taking some mood stabilisers, you're going to need to have periodic blood tests to find out the concentration of the medication in your system. These drugs can have serious side effects when levels get too high. Toxic levels can be fatal, so follow your doctor's instructions.

Some of the drugs described in Table 15-5 haven't yet been officially approved for the treatment of depressive disorders. However, specialists have safely and successfully used many of them in their practices.

Table 15-5		Mood Stabilisers
Brand Name	*Generic Name*	*Comments*
Depakote	Valporic Acid	An anticonvulsant, may be useful for treating persons with mood swings or mixed states. Toxicity or overdose are less common than with lithium.
Lamictal	Lamotrigine	Found to be useful for some with bipolar disorder. There are worries about skin reactions that can potentially be fatal.

(continued)

Table 15-5 (continued)

Brand Name	Generic Name	Comments
Neurontin	Gabapentin	Fewer side effects, less toxic. Generally ineffective by itself for mania. Used for anxiety and peripheral nerve pain. Needs more study.
Priadel Liskonum or others	Lithium	Used primarily for bipolar disorder but can be added in small doses to antidepressants to enhance treatment. Side effects can include weight gain and tremor. Increased tremor, disorientation, and slurred speech may indicate dangerously high levels of the drug that can result in seizures or death.
Tegretol Carbagen	Carbamazepine	Also an anticonvulsant and used to treat those with mood swings. Can be fatal in overdose. Interferes with the effectiveness of contraceptive pills.
Topamax	Topiramate	Has been used both as an anticonvulsant and mood stabiliser. Unlike many other choices, this drug is associated with weight loss.

Getting extra help for severe depression

For people with severe symptoms, a new class of medication, called atypical antipsychotics may help. They are also sometimes given to those people who get insufficient benefit from the other antidepressants that we discuss in this chapter. Antipsychotics may help when individuals suffer from psychosis, paranoia, or delusional thinking (refer to Chapter 2 for more information about these severe depressive symptoms). These drugs may also be used when people with depression have problems controlling their temper, over-reacting to small frustrations, or swinging back and forth from depression to mania.

Antipsychotic medication may have disturbing side effects. The newer atypical antipsychotic medications have a significantly decreased risk of a long-term side effect known as *tardive dyskinesia*, which involves involuntary movements, often in the face. When tardive dyskinesia appears, it usually does so after long-term use of the medication. Other serious side effects may include an intense feeling of agitation or restlessness, muscle spasms, muscle stiffness, shuffling gait, sedation, dry mouth, blurred vision, and hypotension. Weight gain is also particularly common and problematic.

Table 15-6 gives you more information about antipsychotic drugs.

Table 15-6	Atypical Antipsychotics	
Brand Name	**Generic Name**	**Comments**
Abilify	Aripiprazole	Has minimal tendency to cause sedation, weight gain, or movement disorders.
Risperdal	Risperidone	Helps decrease agitation and behavioral disturbances, can cause movement disorders in higher doses.
Seroquel	Quetiapine	Low risk of movement disorders, can cause weight gain and sedation.
Zyprexa	Olanzapine	Improves mood in bipolar disorder. Causes weight gain.

And there's more!

Your doctor may prescribe other drugs for the treatment of depression, or to combat the side effects of antidepressant drugs. Here are a few examples:

✔ **Stimulant medications:** These medications can be used to decrease fatigue, increase your sex drive, and improve attention.

✔ **Hormones:** Sometimes doctors advise hormone therapy because of abnormalities or as an augmenting agent. Augmentation is adding a second drug to increase the effectiveness of the first one.

✔ **Sedating medications:** These drugs can help calm agitation or help with sleep.

Chapter 16

Help and Hope: Exploring Complementary Therapies for Depression

*W*hen the darkness of depression closes in, cheerfulness fades into dark desperation, and hope sinks into despair. Depression is painful, and recovery seems almost impossible at times. Then you read an article offering a supplement, another pill, a completely new therapy or medical procedure, a change in diet, or a special light bulb to help banish your depression. With renewed hope comes a lightening of mood, a little relief, and a ray of optimism. Hope itself can be a powerful tonic for depression.

Wanting to see the light at the end of the tunnel and start leading a normal life again is a powerful incentive for searching for the most effective therapy to put you back on an even keel. But putting your faith into treatments that haven't yet been proved to be effective, is unwise and even dangerous. Following a certain course of treatment may lead to some improvement, purely because of your belief that it is going to be helpful. There's nothing wrong with that – if the treatment is indeed harmless. But, at the same time, we want you to be careful not to be taken in by false promises. That's our purpose in writing this chapter.

In this chapter, we give you information about complementary therapies, helping you to decide whether the treatments are suitable for you. We think of treatments as *complementary* (or alternative) if they're not widely accepted as being effective by conventional mental health and medical professionals, or if the professionals don't use that treatment as their first choice when treating major depression.

How popular are complementary therapies?

A study published in 2008 in *Current Opinion in Psychiatry* looked at complementary therapies in the treatment of anxiety and depression. The study highlighted differences between the use of complementary therapies to treat anxiety and depression in the US compared with other countries.

In the US, people with anxiety and severe depression often use complementary therapies. In fact, more than half of those suffering from severe depression said they'd tried complementary therapies in the year before the survey. But people who were suffering from severe depression said that they were also using conventional mental health or medical treatments for their depression. That's pretty sensible, because the conventional medicine approach has the support of a large body of research.

Surveys carried out in Europe and Australia also reveal positive public attitudes towards the use of complementary therapies. However, the UK lags behind: only 14 to 30 per cent of people in the UK use complementary therapies.

Doctors today are increasingly advising the use of complementary treatments for easing depression.But it's vitally important that you discuss with your doctor any alternative therapies that you're thinking of tryingt Your doctor can give advice on whether a particular therapy is known to work, or whether the therapy might interact harmfully with medication you're already taking.

If you or someone you love suffers from severe depression or has thoughts of suicide, you need to get professional help, at once. Remember, it's extremely rare for staff of health food shops to be qualified mental health professionals.

Sampling Supplements and Herbs

A lot of people suffering from depression head for the health food shop seeking what they hope is a 'natural solution' to their problems. Many have researched complementary therapy options on the Internet first, others just ask the sales staff for advice. The Internet can disgorge a variable feast of choices, with page upon page, product upon product of herbs, supplements, and vitamins promising relief from your depression. Some therapies may indeed be helpful, while others may not. And beware, *some* of the advertised therapies are potentially harmful.

You may believe that taking herbs and supplements for depression is a relatively harmless, natural alternative. However, it's very important that you only take these powerful substances under medical supervision. Some substances can significantly interact with other medication you're taking and prove harmful. So, if you're considering trying any complementary therapies, including the ones we discuss in this section, please consult your doctor first.

St John's wort

Hypericum perforatum, better known as St John's wort, is a small woody perennial used since the time of ancient Greece for a variety of medicinal purposes, from curing stomach problems to healing wounds. In recent years, people have been using St John's wort extensively as a treatment for depression. St. John's wort is thought to work by increasing chemicals in the brain – such as serotonin, norepinephrine, and dopamine – that affect mood. (Refer to Chapter 15 for more information about how these brain chemicals work.)

St John's wort has been widely studied throughout Europe and in the US. Some studies show that St John's wort is as effective as certain antidepressant medication, while other studies show it to be about as effective as a placebo (see the nearby sidebar 'The placebo effect').

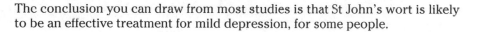

The conclusion you can draw from most studies is that St John's wort is likely to be an effective treatment for mild depression, for some people.

If you decide to take St John's wort, buy it from a reputable company. Make sure that it has at least 5 per cent hyperforin, which researchers believe is the active ingredient in St John's wort. Watch out for side effects, including gastrointestinal upset, over-sensitivity to sunlight, and agitation.

SAM-e

S-adenosylmethionine, or SAM-e (a compound found in human cells), is a more recent dietary supplement that appears to have a variety of positive effects on the body (from treating liver disease, to combating memory loss, and for arthritis).

A growing body of research supports the usefulness of SAM-e for treating mild depression. SAM-e is thought to boost mood and even improve the effectiveness of medication when given with other antidepressants. Because SAM-e is associated with fewer side effects than prescribed antidepressants, it has also become a popular complementary treatment for depression. Nevertheless, more research is needed to find out how exactly how effective SAM-e is in the treatment of depression.

And SAM-e does have its drawbacks:

- It's not available on the NHS, so it can be quite expensive.

- People with bipolar disorder should never use it because it may trigger an episode of mania (refer to Chapter 2 for more information about bipolar disorder and mania).

- It can cause heart palpitations, gastrointestinal upset, and headaches.

Tryptophan and 5 HTP

Tryptophan is an amino acid found in many common foods such as milk, potatoes, turkey, sunflower seeds, and chicken. The body converts tryptophan into *5 HTP* (another type of amino acid), which it can then convert into *serotonin,* a chemical messenger that seems to have a positive effect on mood.

Tryptophan as a dietary supplement was banned in the US after a contaminated batch caused severe illness and death. Thirty-seven people died and about 1,500 people were permanently disabled after taking tryptophan in the late 1980s. They contracted the disease EMS, or eosinophilia myalgia syndrome, which resulted in paralysis, neurological problems, fatigue, and heart problems. Almost all the people who were affected had taken a supplement from one Japanese company that was believed to have supplied a contaminated batch of the supplement.

However, 5-HTP is still available in the US as a dietary supplement for the treatment of depression. Because many antidepressants increase levels of serotonin, it is believed that 5-HTP can be an effective antidepressant.

The most recent comprehensive review in the UK in 2002 concluded that tryptophan and 5-HTP are better than placebo in easing depression. However, they suggest that further studies are needed to evaluate the efficacy and safety of 5-HTP and tryptophan before their widespread use can be recommended.

Because the safety of 5-HTP hasn't been firmly established, getting your serotonin boost from foods such as turkey or sunflower seeds is probably a better bet at this time. Organic produce is always safer, because it is less likely to contain pesticides. As with all supplements and complementary therapies, make sure that you first seek advice from your doctor.

Omega-3 fatty acids

Omega-3 fatty acids play a role in the function of dopamine and serotonin – critical neurotransmitters affecting mood (refer to Chapter 15 for more information about neurotransmitters). You find omega-3 fatty acids in flax seed, soya beans, avocados, tofu, and fish, or you can buy it as a supplement.

Research shows that increased levels of omega-3 may help lessen depression, and for manic depressives it may cut the chance of relapse. Also, studies clearly show that increasing your intake of omega-3 helps reduce the risk of cardiovascular problems and may even help lower cholesterol levels. So make sure that you include foods that are rich in omega-3 in your diet, or think about taking a supplement. Once again, do first discuss it with your doctor.

Multivitamins

If you're suffering from moderate to severe depression, taking extra vitamins and minerals isn't likely to cure you. But a lack of certain vitamins and minerals does seem to be related to depression and memory problems. The research clearly shows that when people have a deficiency of vitamin B (especially B6, B12, and folic acid) they are also often depressed. These critical vitamins help keep neurotransmitters working properly, (see Chapter 15 for more on neurotransmitters).

Deficiencies in calcium, magnesium, potassium, iron, selenium, zinc, and sodium also seem to be associated with depression. However, research shows that most people suffering from depression haven't any marked deficiencies in these vitamins or minerals.

Try taking a complete multivitamin and multmineral supplement. Be sure that the vitamin contains the recommended daily values of the B vitamins. Increasing your intake of folic acid may also help improve the effectiveness of some antidepressant medication. Between 400 to 800 milligrams of folic acid is recommended daily.

You don't need to take mega quantities of vitamins and minerals, and doing so isn't likely to help your depression. Too much of certain vitamins can actually be downright dangerous, so stick to the recommended daily doses. Remember, rather than lifting your mood, too many supplements can have the effect of raising your credit card bill instead.

Hyped-up herbs?

Visit any health food shop or Internet herbal website and you'll find masses of herbs claiming they contain properties that can lessen depression. Some of the herbal remedies listed include:

- Basil
- Black hellebore
- Clove
- Ginger
- Oat straw
- Rosemary
- Sage
- Thyme

Before rushing out and spending your hard earned cash on herbs be aware that the actual research showing that these and many other herbs and tonics are effective for treating depression still remains scarce – although you may still be able to cook up some interesting and tasty dishes. Tell yourself that sometimes it's more beneficial to stick with what's known to work.

Food for Thought

Depression can cause a loss of appetite and lead to weight loss. Depression can also give rise to cravings, which means you start putting on weight. Eating too little food or too much unhealthy food leads to poor nutrition, the body is deprived of the nutrients your brain needs for proper functioning. And when the brain doesn't function well, the intensity of depression increases. When you're depressed, maintaining a healthy diet is especially important.

We recommend that you:

- Eat sensible, well-balanced meals.
- Don't skip meals.
- Drink alcohol only in moderation, or not at all.
- Don't beat yourself up if you occasionally indulge in 'naughty food' such as sweets and chocolate.

Also look at your carbohydrate intake. Put simply, carbohydrates boost mood. Have you ever craved something sweet when you felt sad or upset? Just think of the yummy smell of freshly baked chocolate chip cookies. A craving for sweets may be your body's way of telling you that it needs a car-bohydrate fix. The body breaks down carbohydrates and converts them to *glucose* (sugar), which is the fuel that keeps you going.

There are two different kinds of carbohydrates: simple and complex. The body quickly converts simple carbohydrates (such as white rice, bread, cakes, crackers, beer, wine, and most pastas) into sugar. The spike in your blood sugar level after eating simple carbohydrates may temporarily lift your spirits.

The problem with simple carbohydrates is that the quick conversion into sugar also tells your body to produce extra insulin. The insulin then causes your blood sugar level to fall. For many, the drop in blood sugar then leads to a lowered mood, irritability, and more craving for sugar. Doctors believe that these rapid peaks and troughs in insulin levels aren't good for you for many reasons, but there is a real possibility that they may contribute to the devel-opment of diabetes and heart disease.

Eating complex carbohydrates is a good way of improving your mood. You find complex carbohydrates in whole grains, beans, vegetables, roots, and fresh fruits. They break down into sugar more slowly, allowing your insulin levels to stay more stable. They don't increase cravings or lower moods. Some nutritionists argue that complex carbohydrates also raise serotonin levels. So eating complex carbohydrates may be helpful in improving your mood with-out the peaks and troughs that occur with simple carbohydrates.

Lighting Up the Darkness: Light Therapy

If you're continually feeling sad and blue in winter (assuming you're wearing suf-ficient warm clothing!) then you may be suffering from *seasonal affective disorder*, or SAD (refer to Chapter 2 for more information on SAD). Winter is a time when many people feel a little down, the sun rising late and setting early day after day, and heavy clouds blotting out the sun. However, people with SAD feel more than just a bit low – experiencing symptoms of a major depressive disorder (refer to Chapter 2), such as loss of pleasure and interest, and having very little energy.

In the UK, researchers believe that SAD affects at least 1 in 50 people, and many more, up to 1 in 8, get *the winter blues* – a less severe form of the condi-tion. SAD is less common in people who live in countries near to the equator where the hours of sunlight are more constant and it's brighter throughout the year. In Europe people usually first develop SAD in their twenties, It can happen at any age, and is four times more common in women than men.

You can treat SAD with all the usual treatments for depression that we dis-cuss in this self-help book. Light therapy is becoming a highly popular treat-ment. With *light therapy*, a light box exposes you to bright light that is 10 to 100 times more powerful than a standard 100-watt light bulb. You use it for between 30 minutes to two hours a day.

The effectiveness of light therapy is disputable. Some studies suggest that two out of three people respond well to this therapy, but a few studies show no more improvements than those obtained with a placebo (see the earlier sidebar 'The placebo effect'). Light therapy for SAD isn't available on the NHS, although some private medical insurance policies may cover the equipment. But you can buy your own light box for around £50 to £300, and some companies allow you to 'try before you buy'.

Some advantages of light therapy are:

- ✔ It often works quite rapidly (sometimes within three to four days).
- ✔ It has fewer side effects than most medication.
- ✔ After the initial purchase of the equipment, it's inexpensive to run.

However, light therapy does have a few, usually mild, side effects. These include headaches, nausea, eye strain, jumpiness, sleep disturbance, and agitation. Studies show that patients who use light therapy for many years don't suffer from eye problems. However, the long-term effects of light therapy aren't yet known. If you do suffer from any eye problems, check with an ophthalmologist before trying light therapy.

To help drive away SAD many doctors recommend a daily walk outside during the brightest part of the day as an alternative to light therapy.

Treating Severe Depression

Unfortunately, some cases of depression are particularly difficult to treat, and both medication and psychological therapy can fail to ease the pain and suffering. The following complementary treatments are used specifically for what is termed *treatment-resistant depression*. We include these treatments in this chapter on alternative therapies because they're not now regularly used as a treatment for depression.

Electrifying results

In April 1938, Italian doctors gave a severely psychotic man an electric shock, after which the man apparently lived a normal life. Thus, *electroconvulsive therapy* (ECT), popularly known as *electric shock therapy*, was born. Interest in ECT for the treatment of depression steadily grew through the 1950s, but then the emergence of antidepressant medication heralded a decrease in the popularity of ECT. However, ECT is still in use, particularly for cases of severe, treatment-resistant depression.

Thanks to old black and white horror films ECT conjures up images of patients strapped onto a table and thrashing wildly with electrodes attached to their scalps. But the reality of modern-day ECT contrasts sharply with that image.

Eddie suffers from major depressive disorder. Severe depression runs through both sides of his family, and his eldest brother and two uncles committed suicide. Eddie is on several different antidepressant medications and has tried a variety of psychological therapies over a number of years. Yet, after a particularly stressful month, his medication seems to be ineffective and he's tormented with suicidal thoughts. Eddie's psychiatrist suggests ECT as an alternative. Desperate for help, Eddie agrees.

Eddie's psychiatrist carries out several tests, checks his heart, and declares him fit for the procedure. The doctor then administers general anesthesia and muscle relaxants. Eddie isn't going to feel a thing. The doctors attach monitors and put electrodes on the right side of his head. The treatment lasts for about 30 seconds. Eddie's big toe wiggles a bit. He wakes up confused, muttering, 'Where am I? What's going on?'

Eddie doesn't remember anything about the procedure, but as he leaves the hospital, his mood already starts brightening. Eddie remarks to his wife that the procedure was so much easier than he'd feared.

If your doctor recommends ECT, your experience is probably going to be similar to Eddie's. However, be aware that some patients complain about a variety of memory problems, and others have headaches. Generally, these side effects are mild and short-term, but they can be more serious.

Most ECT treatments take place within a series of sessions, such as two to three times a week for a month. Patients typically respond to ECT soon after receiving treatment.

Overall, ECT appears to be more effective in the short-term than drug therapy, especially for difficult, severe cases of depression. In that sense, ECT can be considered a mainstream treatment for depression. However, we're including ECT in this chapter on alternative treatments because doctors use ECT much less frequently than medication and psychological therapy for depression, with the important exception of especially severe cases.

Unfortunately, relapse rates are high following ECT, probably because of the severity of the depression in the people who undergo the treatment (see Chapter 17 for more information about relapse). But the relapse may be due to something about the ECT itself. Patients often need antidepressants, psychological therapy, or extra ECT to stay depression-free. And like drug therapy, the effects of receiving ECT over many years are not known, because long-term studies of patients having ECT haven't yet been carried out.

Stimulating nerves

Scientists are constantly searching for new treatments for depression. One of the newest currently under investigation is *vagus nerve stimulation* (VNS). It was first found to be effective in preventing seizures during the 1980s. More recently doctors have used VNS for serious, treatment-resistant depression.

The *vagus nerve* is one of the 12 nerves running through the head, controlling your heart rate, vocal cords, bronchial constriction, and movements within the digestive tract. A study reported in the *Journal of Psychosomatic Medicine* shows that VNS can interfere with memory of negative information, thus acting as an effective antidepressant.

The procedure involves implanting a device, which intermittently sends out a mild electrical impulse to electrodes woven around the vagus nerve, in the upper part of the chest. Patients who undergo this procedure report mild side effects, including:

- ✔ Facial muscle weakness
- ✔ Hoarseness or cough
- ✔ Mild sore throat
- ✔ Shortness of breath

These side effects are worse while the stimulation is being applied, but they usually decrease over time. Stimulation is typically applied for about a half minute every three to five minutes, 24 hours a day. Patients are given ways to shut down the device if they find it too uncomfortable.

Early evidence suggests that VNS can bring a great improvement for a significant number of patients. The vast majority of those who improve don't experience early relapse. The treatment takes quite a while to work, but it may also improve in effectiveness the longer it continues.

VNS treatment is currently not available on the NHS and it's expensive: costs are difficult to establish in the UK, but in the US vagus nerve stimulation costs as much as $25,000. Also, the evidence for its effectiveness is at a very early stage and the treatment is still considered experimental. Only consider this therapy if you're experiencing seriously treatment-resistant depression.

Magnetising depression

Since the close of the 20th century, a body of research has emerged on a new treatment for depression known as *transcranial magnetic stimulation* (TMS). It involves putting an electrical coil, which produces a strong magnetic field, on the scalp. The magnetic field is aimed, at varying frequencies, at certain areas of the brain. This treatment is showing promise as an alternative to ECT (see the earlier section 'Electrifying results') for treating stubborn, treatment-resistant depression.

TMS has two different approaches: one of which involves inducing a seizure (like ECT), It's unclear which strategy works best. However, TMS's real advantage is that it doesn't seem to cause short- or long-term cognitive impairments. Patients also say they tolerate the procedure quite well.

However, there isn't enough evidence currently for recommending TMS as a replacement for ECT. Some research has been promising. For example, in 2007 the *Journal of Biological Psychiatry* reported a study in which people responded significantly better to TMS than to placebo (see the earlier section 'The placebo effect'). Some other studies are less positive about TMS results.

Perhaps in a few years, more data will be available to help your doctor determine whether this may be the best procedure for you. In the meantime, TMS must be considered rather experimental in nature.

Searching Further

There is a vast amount of literature on complementary therapies which include treatments for depression. We assure you, no way are you going to want to know everything anyone's ever written or said about the subject – but here are just a few other intriguing possibilities.

New complementary treatments, as well as new medication and refinements in psychological therapy techniques, are continually being explored for the treatment of depression. We urge you not to give up hope. We know many people who didn't show much improvement following a range of medication and therapies, but then eventually discovered the formula that is now working for them.

Air ionisation

You can purchase devices that have been designed to increase the negative ion concentration in the air. Manufacturers suggest using these devices for treating SAD (refer to Chapter 2), because negative ions appear to increase serotonin levels (see Chapter 15 for more info about serotonin), which decrease in autumn and winter. And according to two controlled studies, this type of device may actually help ease the symptoms of SAD.

Much more research is needed about these machines before we can strongly recommend them Up to now, the only type of depression they've been tried for is SAD. However, they have shown potential, and they may actually have little or no side effects.

Massage

Massage therapy, delivered by a trained therapist, involves the manipulation of the body's soft tissues. Most people agree that a massage feels good, but can it improve depression? Two controlled studies have actually suggested that repeated massages may help treat depression. However, these studies didn't assess the long-term outcomes of massage therapy. Again, more research is clearly needed. However, massage probably won't hurt you, and it may have both short, and even long-term, benefits.

Relaxation

Various techniques exist for teaching people how to relax their muscles. We discuss several of these in detail n *Overcoming Anxiety For Dummies* by Elaine Iljon Foreman, Laura Smith, and Charles Elliott (Wiley).

Around half a dozen small, controlled studies suggest that relaxation may be effective for treating depression. Once again, more research is called for – studies haven't yet shown if relaxation training reduces depression in the long run.

Although relaxation training as a possible treatment for depression has fallen out of fashion, the early results appeared to show some worthwhile benefits. Relaxation has very few negative side effects, and it may indeed help ease depression.

Part VI
Life After Depression

'Feeling better, Mr Toggthwaite?'

In this part . . .

Read these chapters only when you've largely overcome your depression. While depression frequently
recurs, the good news is that you can take action to
reduce the chances of that happening. And if depression
should return, we give you other ideas on how to overcome it yet again. But good isn't good enough! We want
you to feel better than good. Positive Psychology offers
ideas for finding true, authentic happiness. We draw on
Positive Psychology for suggestions enabling you to find
renewed purpose and meaning in your life.

Chapter 17

Reducing the Risk of Relapse

In This Chapter

▶ Understanding the nature and risks of relapse

▶ Protecting yourself against relapse

▶ Managing relapse

After successfully getting to grips with your depression, it's very important to keep up your new found improvement. Most of this book suggests many techniques for helping you conquer your depression and maintaining your wellbeing. However, if after putting in a lot of personal effort your depression still hasn't improved much, seek professional help. Or, if you're worried that your improvement is slipping and that you're in danger of falling into a relapse – keep on reading this chapter.

Pippa took a new post as headteacher of a secondary school last year. But somehow she just hasn't felt like her normal self for the past six months. Pippa usually tackles problems head-on, so she makes an appointment with her GP, who prescribes antidepressants (refer to Chapter 15 for information on antidepressant medications). After just six weeks of regularly taking her prescribed medication, Pippa feels back up to scratch. She has no remaining symptoms of depression. Although her doctor recommends continuing the medication for at least a further six months, Pippa chooses to ignore her doctor's advice and stops. Pippa 'knows' that she's going to be alright; after all, she hasn't felt this good in years. Besides, she slowly tails off her medication dosage, so that she can avoid the withdrawal effects that her doctor warned her about. Five weeks later, Pippa suffers a relapse and, with her low mood worsened by disappointment, ends up feeling even more depressed than she did before she started on the medication.

In this chapter, we discuss relapse and depression. *Relapse* refers to a recurrence of depression that occurs after apparently overcoming and recovering from depression. We explain how relapse occurs, give you advice on reducing the risk of relapse, and ideas for dealing with relapse, if you're unlucky enough to be experiencing it.

Facing Up to the Potential of Relapse

This book talks about the reality of depression. Our approach to cognitive therapy (see Part II) recommends that you use objective, evidence-based thinking rather than delude yourself with simplistic, positive self-affirmations as a cure-all for your depression. We want you to see yourself and the world as they are, not as a fairy tale or fantasy. Denial only makes things worse. Remember the lines from the song 'Just call me Cleopatra – I'm Queen of De Nile!'

So when it comes to the treatment of depression, we give you the good news and the bad. The good news is that, with the wide array of both tried and tested and new therapies, and the range of medication currently available, the vast majority of people with depression can be successfully treated. By successful treatment, we mean that many of your depressive symptoms can be reduced and possibly got rid of for at least six months or more. The bad news is that the risk of relapse is distressingly high.

Fortunately, we have more good news – you can do quite a bit to reduce the risk of relapse, and if you do suffer a relapse, you've got a good chance of overcoming your depression once again.

Reaching your verdict: Relapse versus low mood

In Chapter 3, we explain that recovering from depression isn't usually a smooth process, it's uneven, having many ups and downs. In fact, not one of us has worked with anyone who's never experienced a setback. Everyone has a low mood, or a lousy day from time to time. So how can you tell if what you're experiencing really *is* a relapse?

When you're experiencing a full-blown relapse, you have clear signs of one of the types of depression we discuss in detail in Chapter 2, seemingly coming from nowhere after a period of six or more depression-free months. Your symptoms may be mild, and not meet the criteria we described in Chapter 2. If so, then see this as an early warning sign – something to be taken seriously, but not an actual relapse. The suggestions we offer in the 'Creating a Prevention Plan' section, later in this chapter, can be helpful in dealing with these early warning signs. If you *are* actually experiencing a relapse, read the later 'Reining in Relapse When It Recurs' section later in this chapter.

Getting the low-down on relapse rates

So, just how high is the risk of your relapsing? Well, research shows that up to 50 per cent of people who have recovered from one episode of depression find themselves experiencing another bout within the next year or two, and if you've had more than two episodes, there's an 80 per cent chance you're going to have another. In part, your likelihood of relapse depends on whether your depression was treated with medication or psychological therapy.

If you stop medication not long after your depression improves, then the chances of a relapse are more than 50 per cent over the next year or two. Your odds are a bit better if you received cognitive therapy on its own, with, or following antidepressant medication. Interpersonal therapy (we discuss elements of this therapy in Chapters 13 and 14) also shows some promise in reducing relapse. Your odds of reducing the risk of relapse further improve if you also have behaviour therapy, such as problem solving (go to Chapter 12 for more) or one of the newer developments of cognitive behaviour therapy called 'Mindfulness' (see Chapter 18).

Combining medication with the therapies we talk about in this book is a very effective way of reducing your risk of relapse.

Although there are many treatments available to help reduce the likelihood of relapse, your risk of relapse is much greater if you stop treatment before your symptoms of depression disappear. Don't stop your treatment until you have six months or more of normal energy, appetite, sleep, and you're back enjoying your interests and activities.

Rating your risk

As well as the reasons for relapse occurring that we outline in the previous section, one other intriguing, possible reason is emerging. New evidence suggests there's a surprising problem that may increase the likelihood of a recurrence of your depression.

Try doing the Relapse Quiz in Table 17-1 to get an idea of whether this particular relapse risk factor applies to you. Rate how much you agree with each statement, on a scale of 1 to 7. Use 1 if you *completely disagree,* 2 if you largely disagree, 3 if you disagree a little, 4 if you don't agree or disagree, 5 if you agree a little, 6 if you generally agree, and 7 if you *totally agree* with the question.

Table 17-1	Relapse Quiz		
Question		**Disagree**	**Agree**
I'll sacrifice my own needs in order to please other people		1 2 3 4 5 6 7	
I feel I must have the approval of others if I'm going to be happy		1 2 3 4 5 6 7	
I know I can control depression if it returns		1 2 3 4 5 6 7	
There's nothing I can do to deal with depression		1 2 3 4 5 6 7	
When I feel sad, I'm sure that my view of life is realistic		1 2 3 4 5 6 7	
When I'm depressed, I absolutely know that my thoughts and emotions don't accurately reflect what's going on		1 2 3 4 5 6 7	
I'm the cause of my own depression		1 2 3 4 5 6 7	
I get depressed when I make a mess of things		1 2 3 4 5 6 7	

You score this quiz a little differently to most self-tests. You don't add or subtract any of the scores. Rather, the more items you *totally agree* or *completely disagree* with, as indicated by a rating of 1 or 7, the higher your chance of relapse.

We know that it sounds strange to hear that your relapse risk rises if you *completely agree* with items such as:

✔ I know I can control depression if it returns.

✔ When I'm depressed, I absolutely know that my thoughts and emotions don't accurately reflect what's going on.

And we also know that having an increased risk of relapse sounds strange if you *completely disagree* with the statements:

✔ I feel I must have the approval of others if I'm going to be happy.

✔ When I feel sad, I'm sure that my view of life is realistic.

You may be wondering why we don't want you to totally believe that you can control your depression when it recurs. And also why, if you're sad, don't we want you to completely believe that you're viewing life and events unrealistically? Well, we do, sort of, but just hang on a moment.

In Part II, we describe how cognitive therapy can help you view yourself and the world *realistically*. If you've experienced a bout of serious depression, absolutely and completely controlling your depression if it recurs probably doesn't sound all that realistic. It may be more reasonable to say that you have *some* confidence in your ability to manage your emotions, but not total confidence. You may even be able to say that you have *quite a lot* of confidence, but not *complete* confidence. Stating that you don't believe you need other people's approval to be happy may also be realistic. But isn't it likely that you may just have some doubt?

Idealistic, overly optimistic thinking just may set you up for relapse. In Chapter 7, we explain that viewing yourself as superior to other people can increase your risk of experiencing disappointment and depression. Similarly, unrealistic, over-optimistic thinking can do the same.

Our Relapse Quiz isn't a scientific test, so don't get depressed if you score quite a few 1's or 7's. Research by Dr John Teasdale and colleagues suggests that it's important to reframe any thoughts that you're having that are fixed or extreme. Do be aware that if you've never suffered from depression, this quiz is unlikely to predict if you're likely to develop depression in the future. Because you've never been through the darkness of depression, it's probably more reasonable for you to have greater confidence in the views you hold about yourself and the world.

Equipping Yourself to Prevent Relapse

If you completely ignore the real possibility of your depression returning, relapse may very well lurk just around the corner, ready to jump out and pounce on you. But you can do a lot to minimise the danger. We're now going to look at strategies for preventing relapse.

Sustaining success

When depression finally goes away, most people feel like stopping treatment. And we don't blame them for feeling that way. All treatments for depression (including self-help) require time, energy, and at least some money.

Given the demands made by treatment, why work harder and longer than you have to – especially when you're feeling good again? The reason is that the risk of relapse is much higher if you stop your treatment too soon, especially when you consider the debilitating nature of depression.

Most professionals believe in treating depression until the symptoms completely subside, not just until they're partially resolved. Also, therapists typically recommend continuing treatment for at least a few months after being free of depression – and a return to normal energy, concentration, appetite, sleep, and enjoyment of life's activities.

The suggestion to continue treatment is based on the idea that adopting new skills, behaviours, and ways of thinking is the best approach. These newly acquired, fledgling skills won't survive in the face of the inevitable adversities of life. You need to repeatedly practise the skills you acquire.

Continue practising the strategies that first helped you to ease your depression until you feel you've completely mastered them. Also, you may want to try something different (such as behaviour therapy or relationship therapy) and rehearse those new skills. If you haven't yet tackled cognitive therapy, we strongly urge you to do so because cognitive therapy not only defeats depression, it also helps prevent relapse.

The more skills you acquire and master for handling depression, the less likely you're going to experience relapse in the future. Continuing with psychological therapy or self-help for some months after your depression has gone away helps prevent relapse.

If you choose to treat your depression by using medication alone,, we suggest that you continue taking the medication for at least 6 to 12 months after overcoming your depression. Doing so helps to reduce your chances of relapse, although we highly recommend trying psychological therapy, such as cognitive therapy (see Part II), as well as medication. Alternatively, some people with a history of recurrent depression find that continuing with lifetime antidepressant medication provides them with reasonable protection against relapse (Refer to Chapter 15 for more information about medication).

Monitoring the signs

In Chapter 2, we review the many ways that depression affects your thoughts, behaviour, body, and relationships. If you've challenged and fought your depression, you no doubt know in what ways depression affects you. We suggest that you keep track of how you're feeling by checking out the symptoms we discuss in the following exercise.

Carry out a weekly Depression Review. Choose a convenient time to schedule this activity into your calendar. We recommend continuing doing this review for at least a year after the depression lifts. In your Depression Review, rate yourself on the Happiness Depression scale (see the Introduction for a copy of this) and then ask yourself the following questions:

- Have I been having negative or unhappy thoughts?
- Have I started avoiding people or situations that make me feel uncomfortable?
- What is my mood on a 1 to 100 point scale (extremely depressed to completely happy)? Has my mood dropped from its usual rating by more than 10 points and stayed lower for more than a day or two?
- Am I having any noticeable problems with my appetite, sleep, or energy?
- Have I been unusually hard on myself?

✔ Have I been more irritable than usual?

✔ Have I been having more guilty feelings?

✔ Am I having problems with concentration?

If you answer yes to one or more of the questions above, beware! This list contains the early warning signs of possible depression. Of course, anyone can experience a few low thoughts, a little guilt, and difficulty concentrating but still not go on to develop full-blown depression. And we certainly don't expect you to feel 100 per cent fulfilled every week of your life. But, if you're having a lot of negative thoughts they can be warning signs of depression. Pay the signs serious attention, and start some form of treatment, including self-help, if your symptoms are mild, or life feels unsatisfacory.

Preparing a Prevention Plan

No one knows when or where a fire is going to break out. That's why the law requires public buildings such as hospitals, shops, offices, schools to have a regular programme of fire safety drills. Having a fire prevention plan in place makes sure that you're ready and know what to do in the event of fire. The result? Effective damage limitation.

A Prevention Plan for limiting the effects of depression does the same thing. In your Prevention Plan you vividly imagine potentially challenging times and events, and then explore how you *could* cope with them. Finally, you imagine yourself *actually coping*, and doing so in a productive manner.

None of us can predict what the future holds, which is perhaps a good thing, on the whole! However, you probably know what types of events have been difficult for you to handle in the past, and also have an inkling about what you fear about the future. Rather than pretend that your life is going to be a bed of roses, we suggest that you make a list of potentially distressing events that could happen to you at any time and that you fear could overwhelm your capacity for coping.

Here are a few possibilities:

✔ Humiliation

✔ Failing to meet a deadline

✔ Financial reversals

✔ Illness

✔ Injury

✔ Losing a loved one

✔ Rejection

Next, choose just one item from your list. Imagine that event happening and finding a way of coping. When you make your Prevention Plan, use the questions in this list to help you come up with ideas on how you're going to cope:

 ✔ How would someone else handle this situation?

 ✔ Have I dealt with something like this in the past? How did I do it?

 ✔ How much effect is this event going to have on my life a year from now?

 ✔ Is this event as awful as I'm making it out to be?

 ✔ What creative ways can I find to deal with this challenge?

People often dread the future, because they assume they're not going to be able to cope with what life throws at them. However, when you face your fears head-on you find that you can cut them down to size. That's why we recommend that you develop a Prevention Plan that addresses the items on your list of worrying possibilities.

Robert recovered from his bout of depression about a month ago. He feels much better than he did, but he realises that he needs to take the problem of relapse seriously. He therefore monitors his early warning signs of depression (see the preceding 'Monitoring the signs' section) and realises that he's starting to avoid certain people and situations. He knows that, in the past, he's been over-sensitive about potential embarrassment and rejection.

So Robert decides to make a Prevention Plan. In his mind's eye he imagines himself asking Brenda, whom he finds very attractive, to go out on a date. He then imagines her refusing, in no uncertain, even downright hurtful terms. Here's how Robert answers his coping questions:

 ✔ **How would someone else handle this situation?** 'Actually, I bet this happens to people all the time. I guess the key is to accept the rejection, ask myself if there's anything I can take away from the event, and move on. It's not like the rejection is going to be plastered all over my forehead for everyone to see.'

 ✔ **Have I ever dealt with something like this in the past? How did I do it?** 'I've been turned down before, and I did get through it. Though I didn't like it, I argued with myself and decided that it was really her loss, not mine.'

 ✔ **How much effect is this event going to have on my life a year from now?** 'Well, putting it that way, and given how many fish there are in the sea, I guess the answer has to be not much at all.'

 ✔ **Is this event as awful as I'm making it out to be?** 'No. I guess I've been telling myself that it's awful, and that it means I'm a total reject. But let's face it: just having those thoughts doesn't make them true.'

✔ **What creative ways can I find to deal with this challenge?** 'Maybe I could try out that new speed-dating service where you meet something like 20 people in an hour. I may meet somebody interesting, and even if I don't, maybe I can find a way of dealing with rejection by getting loads of practice.' Robert's Prevention Plan helps him to realise that his ability to cope with feared situations is greater than he's led himself believe. He then imagines getting turned down and dealing with the rejection many times. After realising that he can deal with this problem, he asks Brenda out.

Prevention Plans are most effective if you first read about cognitive therapy, in Part II. Cognitive therapy helps you understand how to tackle difficult events using logical, reasoned ways of thinking. Working out your Prevention Plan provides extra practice in using this type of thinking.

All too often, people suffering from depression also struggle with exaggerated feelings of anxiety and worry about future events. Anxiety can be lurking in the background of your depression. If you suffer from both anxiety and depression, we recommend that you read *Overcoming Anxiety For Dummies* by Elaine Iljon Foreman, Laura Smith, and Charles Elliott (Wiley). Dealing with your anxiety, helps you to make a much more effective Prevention Plan to ward off a relapse.

Achieving wellbeing: More than simply defeating depression

If you work hard on overcoming depression and seriously search for solutions, you're likely to be successful. But given that you also stand a good chance of defeating your depression, why stop there?

You may no longer be feeling depressed, but are you achieving a solid sense of wellbeing? If not, Dr Giovanni Fava at the University of Bologna has been investigating strategies for preventing relapse and encouraging wellbeing and feelings of satisfaction in your daily life. We review three of his techniques.

Chapters 18 and 19 give you lots more information for increasing your overall sense of wellbeing. Reading these chapters can help you enhance your resilience and ability to prevent relapse.

Monitoring your wellbeing

Some people say they hardly ever experience real feelings of satisfaction or wellbeing, even when they have never suffered from depression. However, when asked to monitor their wellbeing, they usually discover that certain types of situations and events give them greater satisfaction than others. This discovery often inspires them to get much more involved in doing things that are satisfying and enjoyable.

Find the time to think about the activities that feel satisfying to you. Write them down in a notebook. Then record the thoughts you have in response to those events, as well as how much satisfaction they give you. Rate the intensity of your satisfaction on a scale of 0 to 100. You can use the Satisfaction Tracker to help you identify which activities improve your sense of wellbeing (see Table 17-2 for an example). Then you can use that information to increase those activities, thereby increasing your overall satisfaction.

Alan no longer feels depressed, but he doesn't feel he's actually enjoying many things either. His therapist suggests that he use a Satisfaction Tracker to get a better idea of what kinds of situations increase his sense of wellbeing. Table 17-2 shows what Alan discovers when he records the level of the satisfaction he experiences when he takes part in specific events.

Table 17-2	Alan's Satisfaction Tracker	
Situation	*Satisfying Thoughts*	*Satisfaction Level (0 = none; 100 = total)*
Taking the dog to the park.	I love watching my dog run!	60
Going to a party.	I like talking with some of my friends.	40
Showing off my new car to Linda.	I think she might like me.	35
Washing and polishing my new car.	I feel great when I take good care of things.	65
Clearing out the shed.	It feels good to do things I've been putting off.	65

Alan discovers that there are quite a few more activities than he originally thought that give him satisfaction. He sees that taking the dog out and doing particular chores are surprisingly gratifying. He also likes catching up with Ken. He decides to make a point of scheduling in one satisfying chore, going out to lunch with a friend, and taking his dog to the park each week. But Alan notes that his satisfaction isn't as high as he would have expected on two items – going to a party and showing off his new car. This discovery leads him to the next strategy for enhancing his wellbeing.

Interrupting the interrupters

If you start monitoring your satisfaction with different situations as Alan did in Table 17-2, you're likely to discover that some activities are less satisfying than others. Look closely at your thoughts about such events. First, consider any thoughts you have that involve feeling good about the event. Then ask yourself if you've noticed any thoughts that *interrupt* that sense of satisfaction. We call those thoughts 'interrupters' – these are any thoughts that lessen and take the shine off your enjoyment of a positive activity.

For example, in Table 17-3 Annette tracks her satisfying activities in the same way as Alan in Table 17-2. She then chooses a few activities that she didn't find as satisfying as she'd expected. Table 17-3 shows what her interrupters are:

Table 17-3	Annette's Interrupters	
Event	*Satisfying Thought*	*Interrupter*
Volunteering at the home-less shelter.	I like contributing something to society.	But then I thought that I really should be working on my school project: I'm never going to get it done.
Going to a party.	I think Kevin might like me.	Then I thought that he's prob-ably already got a girlfriend, and he's just being polite.

Can you how Annette's interrupting thoughts manage to lessen her sense of wellbeing and satisfaction? If you're not feeling as satisfied as you'd expect with events try tracking your interrupters as Annette did. Then ask yourself the following questions about those disruptive thoughts:

- ✔ What evidence do I have that supports or disproves these interrupting thoughts?

- ✔ If a friend of mine told me that she had this interrupting thought, would I agree it was reasonable, or see it as self-defeating?

- ✔ Do I have experiences in my life that may disprove this interrupting thought?

- ✔ Is this interrupting thought distorted in any way?

- ✔ Can I come up with an alternative to this interrupting thought that may be more accurate and help me feel better?

When Annette puts her interrupters to these questions, she finds she can think up more satisfying alternatives. You too are likely to discover that looking closely at your interrupters pays dividends. When you answer the preceding questions, you're going to call those interrupting thoughts into question and come up with more satisfying alternatives. You'll find it helpful to keep track of this information in your notebook.

The strategy of challenging interrupters may be familiar if you've read Part II, which discusses cognitive therapy. In Part II, you find many more strategies for tackling problematic thinking. The main difference here is that you track *satisfying* events rather than disturbing, depressing ones. You then record which thoughts *interfere* with that satisfaction.

Changing your lifestyle

A third useful strategy for increasing your overall sense of wellbeing and lessening the likelihood of relapse is by looking closely at your lifestyle. Ask yourself these Lifestyle Analysis questions:

- Am I spending my time doing things that make me feel good, or do I merely switch off and escape by doing things like watching too much TV or overdoing the alcohol?

- Am I working longer hours than necessary?

- Am I driving myself scatty with self-imposed standards of perfectionism that cause unnecessary pressure for me?

- Do I take reasonable holidays and breaks?

- Do I take part in a reasonable amount of recreation?

- Are there things I've always wanted to do that I haven't got round to doing? If so, what are they, and what's stopping me?

Take time out to examine your life. Think about the way you spend your time. Does it reflect your priorities? If not, think about using your time differently. If you feel trapped and unable to make these changes, read Chapter 12. Discover a creative way of sidestepping your mind's trap.

Reining in Relapse When It Recurs

Sometimes depression returns despite all your efforts to fend it off. What do you do in this case? First, you need to know what real relapse looks like. (To find out what's a genuine relapse see the 'Reaching your verdict: Relapse versus low mood' section, earlier in this chapter.) Then if you decide that you're experiencing a relapse, take steps to deal with it.

The very first step in dealing with relapse is to seek professional help. If you've never been to your GP, a psychological therapist, or psychiatrist before, make sure you go now, because self-help on its own isn't enough when dealing with recurrent depression.

If you've already seen a professional, don't decide that this relapse means all professional help is useless.

If therapy helped before, then more therapy is likely to prove beneficial. If you previously tried therapy and it didn't help, you need further treatment – perhaps with a different therapist (refer to Chapter 4 for info on finding the right therapist or type of therapy, and Chapter 16 for complementary therapy).

If you haven't tried medication, do consider it. If medication worked for you before and you stopped, you may want to restart medication or add psychological therapy to your storehouse of therapies. Recurrent depressions are an indication that long-term medication may be necessary. (We review medication in Chapter 15.)

The most unhelpful thing you can do if you experience a relapse is to see it as a catastrophe, and assume that it means you've failed or that no one can do anything to help you. You have to understand that depression is a formidable foe with a variety of causes, including genetics, trauma, and no doubt many still unknown reasons. Professionals don't believe that depression recurs because of personal weakness, a lack of moral fibre, or any such 'fault' of yours. Remind yourself that facing your enemy again may not be fun exactly,, but we believe, and research shows, that you can defeat depression if you try.

The majority of depression relapses can be treated successfully. You have at your disposal a host of treatments and avenues to explore in your quest.

Chapter 18

Overcoming Depression with Mindfulness

*B*eing aware of the present moment is the goal of mindfulness. In a mindful state, you're aware, engaged, connected, and non-judgemental. Mindfulness is a central aspect of Buddhist teachings, but you don't need to be a practising Buddhist to benefit from mindfulness.

'But where's the link between mindfulness and depression?' we hear you asking. Well, cross-cultural research is being carried out on the use of mindfulness for preventing relapse in depression. Researchers have discovered that a adding mindfulness to cognitive therapy (see Part II for information about cognitive therapy) cuts the relapse rate by almost half among those people who've had three or more episodes of depression. That's a pretty impressive finding! If you've been suffering from depression and are keen to increase your chances of living life to the full and minimising the chance of a relapse, mindfulness may be just what you're looking for.

In this chapter, we're going to help you become mindful. The first step on your path towards mindfulness is by showing you the difference between you and your mind. Then we spotlight clutter clogging up your mind and show you how to tidy up the disorderliness. Finally, you discover how to apply mindfulness to your day-to-day life. So, keep reading this chapter if you're still having some depressive symptoms, or if you want to keep depression at bay. Live well, even with depression. Understanding the Difference Between You and Your Mind

The human mind is a thinking machine. Your mind is continuously weighing up the evidence and using language topass judgements on your thinking. The power of language has been recognised for centuries: the Greek poet Euripides, who died in about 406 BC, said, 'The tongue is mightier than the blade.'

But there is a danger that your mind can take over your thinking completely by making too many judgements and evaluations and presenting what you're thinking as reality. And when the mind is depressed, these judgements can be overwhelmingly negative. Believing that you *are* the same thing as those negative opinions and thoughts becomes all too easy. Yes, your mind is very important but we want you to realise that *you* are something more than your mind.

Think back to when you were a child. What was your life like? What were you feeling? Doing? Liking and disliking? Where were you living?

Do you have a picture of yourself as a child? Can you see yourself? If so, you probably can't remember a lot about your thoughts back then. When a person recalls their childhood, they usually can only remember facts. The *you* in your memory is made up of what you were doing and how you were feeling – rather than the thoughts that were running through your mind.

Another way of seeing the difference between you and your mind is to try the following experiment: sit quietly for a few moments waiting, watching, and listening for a thought to come into your mind. Perhaps the thought comes instantly, or it may take a little while. When your mind brings the thought to life, pay attention to it. Become aware that *you* are the one who's listening to and paying attention to the thought – *you* aren't the same thing as your mind and your thoughts.

The you that isn't your mind is the part of you that observes, experiences, breathes, and lives without judgement and analysis. The term mindfulness describes this state of awareness of thoughts, judgements and experienceWe think that the term mindlessness is far more descriptive. But alas, we succumb to convention in this chapter and stick with the term mindfulness. This awareness allows you to choose how you want respond to any situation. You no longer have to just keep reacting in your usual way.

If You Don't Mind Your Mind, It Doesn't Matter

Do you sometimes feel as if your thoughts are torturing you ? The mind is seldom quiet. All day long it's busy weighing up and passing judgement on what you're thinking. Depending on what your mood is at the time, your thoughts can change from negative, through neutral, to positive. This mind chatter even steals into your dreams, giving you nightmares and causing you to feel defenceless, exposed, or humiliated.

Mindfulness is about seeing the difference between you and your mind. In this section, we show you how to stop viewing thoughts as facts and start seeing them merely as mind chatter. We give you tools to help you challenge the belief that your negative thoughts about yourself are true. And we also show you how the mind's chatter stops you from living in the present because of continually focusing on the past or worrying about the future.

Seeing that thoughts are just thoughts, not facts

Have you ever just had a brilliant idea and then just when you come to act on it – Oh no! It's gone! That's what happened to two of us one morning, when we sat down to write this chapter. We realised to our dismay that we'd both completely forgotten what the idea was all about. 'No problem – we'll just look through our notes and find it.' No such luck. Then hard on the heels of our brilliant idea came a whole host of negative thoughts (refer to Chapters 5 and 6 for more on negative thoughts):

- How could we forget such a brilliant idea as this?
- Are we getting early dementia?
- How could we be so stupid as to not make a note and file the idea?
- We're completely stuck and can't come up with another idea.

Did we sink into despondency? Guess what? We didn't! Instead, we took our dogs for a walk noticing what a wonderful day it was. We witnessed the unrestrained delight of our dogs as they sniffed every bush, barked at the birds, and watered a few choice bushes.

How did we stay in a good mood and enjoy the walk? Well, although it's taken us a while, we view our thoughts less seriously than we used to – we know that *thoughts are just thoughts, not facts*. By letting go and not dwelling on our negative thinking, we simply came up with another way of presenting our idea.

All too often, the human mind responds to thoughts as though they truly reflect reality. Think of your favourite food. Visualise the colour, feel the texture, breathe in the delicious smell, and bring it closer and closer to your mouth. Are you salivating yet? Very often the body reacts as if the image is the reality.

The same applies to your negative thoughts. If you see them as real and solid, then get ready to experience pain and anguish.

In Part II of this book, we discuss in detail how, when you're depressed, your thoughts often contain distortions. In this chapter, we ask you to take these ideas further and to view thoughts merely as thoughts. Psychologists call your mind's incessant stream of thoughts *mind chatter*. Your mind is good at producing negative chatter. But when you're depressed, you can easily fall into the trap of buying into it, telling yourself that's how you are and how you appear to the world.

You can *decide* to take this kind of jabbering seriously, or you can hear it as mindless drivel and dismiss it as being just that. You have the power to choose.

In the following sections, we give you lots of ideas to help you separate thoughts from facts. Just remember that mastering this new skill takes time, so be patient with yourself.

Succeeding through sarcasm

When you notice negative, self-critical thoughts running through your mind, it can help if you distance yourself from them by thanking your mind for developing such an interesting idea! Be sure to inject a healthy dose of sarcasm into your response to your mind. Remember, *you* are not your mind. Here's an example of the sarcastic approach:

> **Your mind's thought:** I'm such a twit!
>
> **You:** Gee! Thank you, mind, for that lovely thought!
>
> **Your mind's thought:** I'll never find someone to love.
>
> **You:** Excellent job, mind! Thanks a bunch!
>
> **Your mind's thought:** I'm hopeless.
>
> **You:** Well done! Great! How in the world do you come up with these ideas, mind?
>
> **Your mind's thought:** I can't stand this feeling!
>
> **You:** Thank you, mind. You sure know how to make my day that much more enjoyable!

If this exercise feels too harsh and abrasive, think about experimenting with irony. For example, Elaine, one of the authors of this book, was driving to the airport to take a group of people who were scared of flying on a return flight to Europe. Her mind conjured up an ironic image: a newspaper headline reading 'Fear of Flying Expert Dies in Plane Crash!'. Elaine, though rather taken aback, agreed with her mind that this would be a truly ironic ending. Having identified that this was an exceptionally ironic *thought*, she then went on to challenge the probability of it actually happening (Chapter 6 explains how to do this by 'Taking Your Thought to Task').

Getting playful

Another useful strategy for dealing with negative, self-critical c thinking is to treat it playfully. Yes, really. Play with it. Surprisingly, you can change the meaning of your thoughts and your response to them if you start getting playful.

Write down the negative thoughts that are running through your head. Sing those thoughts to yourself over and over again. Then use the negative thoughts as lyrics to a popular tune, or make up your own melody. You find your negative thoughts becoming trivial, even amusing when you give them a tune. Alternatively, experiment with saying them out loud, but in a highly distorted voice. Try a Donald Duck, or Inspector Clouseau voice, or any other exaggerated stereotype. Buying into negative chatter is a lot harder when you hear it coming from Donald Duck!

Arguing for, not against, your negative thoughts (yes really!)

If you have a partner you trust and feel comfortable with, you can try an exercise that two of us often use. One person says their negative thoughts out loud. The other, rather than arguing against the negativity, actually goes along with, and expands further on the negative chatter. The whole scenario is carried out in an extremely silly tone, and the content is super sarcastic. Here's a taster:

> **Dr Elliott:** What I wrote today felt like junk. Who on earth is ever going to want to read this stuff?

> **Dr Smith:** That's right! You never write anything interesting at all. You may as well quit right now!

> **Dr Elliott:** You're right. I think I'll quit! Maybe I'll do something different.

> **Dr Smith:** Now, that's a really good idea. But who's ever going to employ you?

Obviously, this dialogue is meant to be a good natured, lighthearted exercise. If you try it, and it doesn't feel that way, just leave it alone. This technique only works if you and your partner fully trust each other, and also completely understand the nature of mind chatter, as well as the value of approaching it as a bit of fun!

Talking rubbish

Here's an exercise for reminding yourself that thoughts are *just* thoughts, *not* facts attempting to control and influence your actions. This exercise is similar to an exercise we present in Chapter 10, but it's worth repeating in this section. (If someone's reading this book to you on your behalf think up an alternative scenario that likewise reaffirms your power to defeat your mind's chatter.)

1. **Say these words out loud: 'I can't read.'**

2. **Say it louder: 'I can't read!'**

3. **Now, shout: 'I really can't read!'**

4. **One more time, 'Honestly, there's absolutely no way that I can read.'** Now, realise that you've actually read each of these statements in order to say them.

Thoughts, like statements, have no power over you, other than the power *you* give to them. Are you getting the idea of how just saying something, or equally just thinking it, doesn't make it true?

Recognising automatic negativity

Are you struggling to view your mind's stream of incessant negative thoughts as mere chatter? Well, try looking around you. If you're outside, look at the sky and take in the whole landscape. Or, if you're indoors, take a close look at all that you see in the room. Now, look for things to criticise and dislike. Surprisingly easy isn't it?

The human mind is trained to weigh up whatever you're thinking. And it can pass negative judgements at the snap of a finger. But does that make the judgement correct? Of course not! Too often when passing judgement on your thoughts, your mind can easily slip into automatic negativity.

Letting negative thoughts go

And here's another suggestion for dealing with your negative thoughts. When you notice yourself having negative thoughts, try picturing them balancing on a giant leaf and see yourself watching the leaf gently float down stream. Practise playing with your negative thoughts as being something outside yourself. Observe them. Watch them float away into the distance. See how they swirl and dance as they go by. Visualising your negative thoughts being washed away is a form of meditation. Try it out for 10 to 20 minutes each day. Simply sit and relax. Watching each thought float away.

You may prefer to visualise your negative thoughts as a swirling mass of clouds. Watch the clouds drift past you in front of your eyes, seeing them gradually dissolving into nothingness. Or, if visualisation doesn't work for you, write your negative thoughts down on a piece of paper. Take the paper outside, put it in an incinerator, and set your negative thoughts alight. Watch them going up in smoke right in front of you. Try backing away and putting some distance between you and your negative thoughts. From a distance quietly observe your negative thoughts (although of course if your negative thought is signalling danger, you need to act there and then). At most, consider your thoughts as possibilities, rather than statements of fact.

Knowing that resistance is futile

Everyone wants to enjoy a sense of wellbeing, that's perfectly natural. You find quite a number of self-help books promising that by just grabbing happiness and never letting go, you're never going to feel bad again!

So what does the mind do when it confronts a negative experience or thought? It tells you that you absolutely *must not* feel bad. Avoid, deny, and suppress all negativity! Refuse to accept what is.

Unfortunately, denying negativity causes a problem: The harder you try not think or feel something, the more certain it is that you're going to (see the sidebar 'Polar bears and negative thoughts' in Chapter 5):

- ✔ If you're afraid of feeling anxious, inevitably you're going to start feeling anxious.

- ✔ If you can't cope with sad events, you may well try to suppress your feelings. They can then appear in the form of depression.

- ✔ If you keep on telling yourself you absolutely must not make a hash of that presentation, and it's vital that you succeed. This, in turn, disrupts your performance and means that you're more likely to mess it up.

There's nothing wrong with experiencing a few negative thoughts and predicting potentially worrying outcomes. It's often the struggle to suppress the thoughts that intensifies and magnifies them so that they become overwhelming. Psychologists have studied what happens when people with depression attempt to suppress all negative thoughts. You guessed it; they actually experience *more* negative thoughts.

Psychologist Steven Hayes suggests that trying to suppress your bad feelings can in the long run bring on depression. For example, if you're angry and you don't let it out, you direct your frustration inwards at yourself. He suggests that you make a spare room available for bad feelings; inviting the bad feelings to stay for a while.

Dr Hayes tells the story of a little boy who had troubling, recurrent nightmares about monsters. More than anything the little boy wanted to drive his nightmares away. Dr. Hayes said that instead of trying to rid himself of the monsters, why not place a small box under his bed where the monsters could stay for a while. He told the boy that the monsters had nowhere else to go and needed a little space of their own. Soon the monsters were no longer disturbing the boy's sleep.

Yesterday and tomorrow: Living any time but now

Only humans, as far as we know, have the ability of looking back to the past and visualising the future. Sometimes looking back and looking forward can be a pleasurable activity. But too often the mind puts your life 'on hold' keeping you bogged down in the mire of the past, and filling you with dread about the future. The result is that feelings of guilt, resentment, revenge, self-hate, and sadness can well up causing you fear and anxiety.

In this section, we show you how depression can try to fool your mind and manipulate your past to sabotage the present. When you see how living in the past and future distorts your perspective, you're going to fully appreciate the value of living in the present.

Waiting to be happy

How often have you thought '*I'll be happy when I . . .*'? Perhaps you're going to be happy when:

- You finish writing the book you've been working on.
- You can buy that dream home.
- You retire.
- You finish your degree.
- You finally meet that special someone.
- You afford that new car.

Looking for happiness can involve you in a never ending struggle to fulfil your desires. Perhaps the price you're paying for being in a highly-paid job means working excessively long hours. Then you give yourself a new goal of finding happiness by looking for a job with a lower salary but more freedom. Being repeatedly seduced by the promise of future happiness persistently prevents experiencing the pleasure of the here and now.

Predicting a miserable future

Your depressed mind enjoys playing yet another trick on you: predicting that your future looks grim and you're never going to be able to cope.

 Janet, a teacher, has battled mild with depression for over a year. She's studying part-time for her master's degree, and is nearly at the end. To complete her degree, Janet only needs to write her dissertation. Only? Writing a dissertation is a formidable task. Janet's mind focuses on pictures of herself being drowned in a flood of of work. These images cause a motivational meltdown. Janet has no idea how she's going to move forward.

Eventually, Janet buckles down and starts working on her dissertation. When she finally completes her task, Janet looks back and is stunned to find that writing up her dissertation was a totally absorbing and satisfying experience: she isn't able to recall one single moment of working on her dissertation that caused her stress or sorrow. No, not one!

Playing the victim role

Knowing the origins of your negative thinking can be of value to you. For example, you realise that your response to an event has more to do with your past experiences than with what's happening to you right now. Seeing the difference between the two can help you make sense of what is going on right now (flick to Chapters 3 and 7 for more information playing the role of the victim and overcoming distorted thinking).

Watch out that you don't allow your mind to become fixed on past difficulties and disasters and picturing the injustices you've experienced throughout your life. You can so easily start seeing yourself as a victim, resenting and blaming others for all that has happened to you. Chapter 3 discusses the seductiveness of victim thinking as well as exploring ways to get out of that mindset.

Imperfect Past Makes Future Tense!

Your mind has a clever way of leading you into passing judgements on yourself based on your past. Falling into this trap makes it likely you're going to come up with some pretty harsh verdicts. You may even feel overwhelmed by guilt and self-loathing. But to be honest, can you think of anyone who wouldn't jump at the chance of changing some things about their past?

Of course, looking back to the past, and knowing what you know today, you're likely to do many things differently. But let's face it, you didn't know then what you know now. And anyway, you can't change the past. The past is useful for acting as guide for turning negative experiences into positive actions, now and in the future. It's crucial that you seize the opportunity for making those changes *now*.

Take a leaf from a dog's book. Dogs don't live in the past, even though they can learn from what they've been doing (well eventually, anyway). Have you ever come home and found that your dog has been misbehaving? You scold him, and no dog could look guiltier or more apologetic. But how long does it take your mutt to bounce back from being sorry? Three minutes? Your dog may have been feeling genuinely sorry for behaving badly – or at least he simply hated you being cross with him. But what you can be sure of is that he's not going to spend the next few days beating himself up about his misdemeanor. No, more likely five minutes later he's going to to be running around happily, just as if nothing had happened.

The next time you make a mess of something, try feeling as guilty . . . as a dog. Allow yourself to feel bad for only a short time, then drop it. Beating yourself up is going to do absolutely nothing to improve your life. Avoid wreaking havoc on the here and now.

Living Mindfully

We hope after reading the previous sections of this chapter, you've got to grips with mindfulness and can now think about applying mindfulness to your daily life. Mindful living covers two main areas: acceptance and connecting with experience.

When life deals you a hand of cards, acceptance keeps you in the game. And once you discover acceptance, you don't judge yourself as being a good or bad player, you just play. You view the dealer (fate) as neutral, not good or bad.

Connecting with experience means staying in the game. You don't spend time grieving over previous hands or worrying about future ones. If your hand is good, you enjoy playing it. However, if you're dealt a poor hand, you do the best you can. You don't throw your cards down in disgust and walk away. Perhaps you'll have better cards next time; perhaps not. Either way, connecting with the experience makes you willingly accept whatever deal you get.

Acquiring acceptance

Acceptance is a willingness to cope with *whatever* comes your way. Acceptance is the opposite of rejection and resistance. To become accepting, you must give up passing judgements on yourself, others, and events. Criticising yourself and others can lead to rejection and unhappiness.

Perhaps you find acceptance a novel idea? Your mind probably has been long trained to fight and resist anything and everything that feels unpleasant. To do the opposite seems downright illogical, self-defeating, and dangerous. Practically unthinkable.

How can we possibly write an entire book about overcoming depression, and suggest you think seriously about *accepting* depression? Do we *want* you to be depressed? Are we suggesting you *resign* yourself to depression? Actually, quite the opposite.

Your mind may be telling you right now, 'That's a ridiculous idea! You can't possibly accept feeling depressed! Don't listen to this rubbish!' But just hang on for a second, and all is about to become clear . . .

Psychologists are discovering something that Buddhist monks have known for many centuries. Acceptance provides a key to peace and harmony. Accepting what is happening to you now, although it may seem quite the wrong thing to do, has great value:

- **Acceptance allows you to walk away from the struggle.** Imagine you're playing tug of war with your depression. You fight your depression with all your might and throw everything you have at it. But inexplicably, your depression only deepens. Yet, this tug of war is no game. Depression is like a 20 foot, two-ton monster. And between the two of you gapes a huge chasm, so deep you can't even see the bottom. Every time you pull harder on your end of the rope, your depression in the shape of the monster pulls harder still. You feel you're being pulled over the edge. Desperation sets in. Then you have a bright idea. Just let go, and drop your end of the rope! The monster topples over backwards. You calmly walk away.

  Acceptance involves walking away from the struggle. That's because, as we say in the earlier section 'Knowing that resistance is futile', the more tenacious you are about avoiding feeling anxiety or depressed, the more likely it is that you're going to end up experiencing full-blown depression.

- **Acceptance of where you are now often helps you discover a better route.** Imagine that you're out driving at night on a dark country road, and you hit a blizzard. You've only got ten miles to go when your car slides into a snow drift. You press the accelerator and the wheels start spinning. You accelerate more; they just spin faster. You're completely and totally stuck. You're afraid you may die if you're not rescued soon. And you're in a place where there's no mobile phone signal. Petrified, you accelerate even more.

  So you tell yourself to 'Stop it!'. You think things through – 'Here I am, stuck in a drift and panicking – how helpful is this?' Just sitting reflecting on your situation, you remember that the way out most certainly isn't by flooring the accelerator. So you gently accelerate and when the wheels begin to spin, you reduce the pressure a bit. The car rocks back a little, and then you apply a bit more pressure on the accelerator. You get into a rhythm. Slowly but surely the car makes bigger swings to and fro. Eventually, you move on.

  You got out of your predicament by *accepting* the idea of dealing with where you are for a little while (stuck), allowing yourself to rock backwards (not where you want to go), and only then gently moving forward a little at a time. Working on your depression is much like digging yourself out of a snow drift.

Now that you understand what acceptance is all about, here are a couple of strategies for introducing acceptance into your life.

Accept where you are. Developing the skills of acceptance takes time and hard work. *Any* gains you make can improve your quality of life. Acceptance isn't about assessing how accepting you're becoming. Don't be discouraged if you feel you're taking one step forward and two backwards. Acceptance doesn't see the difference between forwards and backwards.

Accepting without judging

Think about the value of accepting yourself as you are. If you must, try judging the consequences of your actions, rather than your 'self'. By the way, this is the same advice psychologists give to parents about bringing up their children: identify a child's behaviour as bad or undesirable, but don't label the child as 'bad'. If you're unhappy with something that *you* have done, tell yourself that you can always find new and better ways of behaving.

You're probably far harder on yourself than you are on others. You like your friends and acquaintances for who they are, warts and all. Try behaving towards yourself as if you were one of your best friends.

Living as if no one will know

Imagine no one ever knowing anything about you – what you've been doing with your life, your successes and your failures. No one is in a position to pass judgement on you. Now ask yourself what changes would you make in your life if no one knew anything about your successes and failures? Would you change the way you live your life, if it wasn't subject to the scrutiny of others? If so, you're making changes in response to the judgement of others. Try living for yourself. You do need to consider what others want, but without being dominated by them.

Addressing self-absorption

A number of psychologists have identified the role of *self-absorption* (preoccupation with yourself) in a range of emotional disorders, including depression. The more you focus on yourself, the stronger your negative feelings become. Focusing on your thoughts and feelings is understandable, as you try to gain some kind of 'insight'. This can cause more harm than good. Also, much of this self-focus involves judging and evaluating the self, often negatively. According to Professor Williams and colleagues, when we become preoccupied, we lose touch with the world, with those around us including those we most love, and who most love us. We deny ourselves the rich input of the whole experience of living. By practising mindfulness, and the cognitive therapy discussed in Part II, means you're less likely to be self-absorbed. Even though the exercises in this book do ask you to try looking at yourself from another angle, you're probably going to end up being far less preoccupied with self.

Connecting with experience: Life's no spectator sport

Do you know the saying 'the past is history, the future is a mystery, but the here and now is a gift, which is why we call it the present!' This saying nicely sums up what cognitive therapy and mindfulness are about.

Here's the story of two Buddhist monks on a journey. Reaching a stream, they see a small, frail woman. She asks to be carried across – the water's too wide and the current too strong for her. Despite the prohibition of touching a woman, the first monk picks her up, carries her across, and the two monks continue on their way. After two hour's silence, the second monk bursts out 'I can't get over it! You carried that woman! Across the river!' The second smilingly says 'Yes. But I put her down hours ago. You're still carrying her.'

As you bring acceptance into your life (see the earlier 'Acquiring acceptance' section) you're preparing to experience life grounded in the present. The idea of being connected with present-moment experience is rather strange for many people. Staying connected with 'now' takes practice. However, even small steps towards acceptance can lead to some respite and peace in your life.

Few people truly know how to mindfully accept what is. You are constantly being bombarded with countless pressures and distractions. With such competing stimuli, you need to give yourself time to acquire the skill of mindful acceptance. Be non-judgemental about your attempts. Your mind is going to go on throwing up disrupting thoughts as inevitably as the sun rises and sets each day. You can acquire the skill of acceptance slowly and surely, acknowledging your achievements even while still being attacked by negative thoughts. It's a dog's life!

Fortunately, few people experience really horrific events in their lives; for most people it's the small stuff that's upsetting. Thoughts can all too easily get in the way of what you're actually experiencing, encouraging you to invent and focus all sorts of horrors or unwanted feelings.

Imagine you have the opportunity like Charles, one of the authors of this book, to break up your writing day with a bit of exercise. You take the dogs out for a long walk three or four times each week. Given the unpredictability of the British weather, you're bound to get rained on sometimes.

While out with his dogs Charles curses his fate when it starts to drizzle, and returns home as quickly as possible. But quite often Charles gets a thorough soaking. Then Charles notices that the dogs never seem to mind the rain. They just shake off the excess water and go on enjoying the outing as much as ever. Charles wonders how his dogs can connect with their experience apparently undaunted and unfazed. Then it hit him. Dogs don't have any pre-conceived idea about how awful it is to get soaked; they merely connect with the joy of the experience.

Can you do the same? Try taking another view of the rain, reminding yourself that it really doesn't feel that different to your usual morning shower . . . but a bit cooler! Like Charles, ask yourself does getting soaked matter? The experience of being outdoors, regardless of the rain, can feel wonderful, if you let the thoughts go and simply 'be'.

Of course, you may say, 'But what about lightning? Isn't that dangerous and don't I need to shelter?' Well, you're right, taking positive action in response to a negative thought does have it's uses.

On the occasions when thoughts warn you of real danger, you do need to listen to them. However, all too often, negative thoughts send out false alarms that are best ignored.

Take the same approach as Charles and try connecting with your experiences. When your thoughts magnify the awfulness of what you're going through, try disengaging from them. Merely connect with the actual experience, not with what you're making the experience out to be in your mind.

When you find yourself dwelling on past regrets or future worries, try the Connecting with the Present exercise. This exercise shows you how to observe your thoughts *mindfully*. We suggest you practise 10 or 15 minutes each day, for a few weeks. Try not to let yourself get upset if troubling or distracting thoughts interfere while you're doing the exercise. Remember, that's just what the mind does. If such thoughts come into your mind, merely notice them, rather than judging whether you're doing the exercise correctly.

1. **Focus on each moment that you're experiencing. Notice all the sensations in your body, including touch, sights, sounds, smell, and taste.**

2. **You're probably finding thoughts coming into your mind. Pay attention to them. Make a note of whether they're about the future, or the past. Just notice them, then return your attention to your body's sensations.**

3. **Focus on your breathing, feeling the air as it goes in your nose, into your lungs, and out again. Notice the rhythm of your breathing.**

4. **More thoughts are going to start coming into your mind. Remember, *thoughts are just thoughts*.**

5. **Return to your breathing. Notice how good the air feels.**

6. **If you have sad or anxious feelings, notice *where* you're feeling them in your body. Is your chest tight, or your stomach churning? Stay with those sensations. Give your sensations your full attention.**

7. If you have thoughts about your feelings, notice how interesting it is that the mind is taking stock of everything that is going on. Watch those thoughts and let them drift past, like leaves floating down stream, and the clouds drifting across the sky. Return to the present moment and the sensations in your body.

8. If more thoughts come, notice the *you* observing those thoughts in the present moment. If dozens of thoughts flood your mind, try imagining them as a torrent, rushing down a waterfall, while you stand watching behind the waterfall.

9. Return to your breathing. Pay attention to how nice and rhythmic it feels.

10. If you hear sounds, try not to judge them. For example, if you hear loud music outside, just notice the sounds as sounds. Not good or bad. Pick out the rhythm or the notes and let yourself hear them. If the phone rings, be aware of the sound, but don't answer it right now.

11. Notice what you see at the back of your eyelids when you close your eyes. See the interesting patterns and forms that come and go.

12. Once again experience the sensation of your whole body breathing.

If you have trouble with this approach to dealing with your thoughts, you may want to read or re-read Part II, which helps you understand how habitual thoughts often don't reflect reality. The techniques of cognitive therapy in Part II help you to reorganise these thoughts in a useful way. You can also use the strategies in this chapter to help you improve the way you're connecting with your thoughts.

When you start viewing your negative thoughts as just something to be noticed, rather than as statements of fact you're likely going to discover that you've been taking your negative thoughts far too seriously. Do be careful not to engage in negative thoughts about your negative thoughts! Recognise that forming a new relationship with your thoughts takes time. Your goal is to begin to connect more directly with your *experience*, rather than getting lost in your thoughts.

Connecting mindfully with all things great and small

The mind has such an interesting way of turning everyday tasks into something you'd rather avoid. Imagine you're queuing at the supermarket checkout, where each cashier's queue is longer than the last. Do thoughts like these run through your mind?

✔ This is awful. I've got so much to do today.

✔ Why did I choose this time and this supermarket? It's totally packed. Am I an idiot, or what?

✔ Oh no, the blinking light is flashing. It takes ages for someone to come! Then they have to get whatever it is sorted – I'll *never* get out of here!

✔ My queue just has to have the slowest cashier in the whole wide world.

Sounds familiar? Your thoughts are fighting against what is inevitably going to happen. And guess what? The negative thoughts stir up tension, anxiety, and angst. That's pointless and futile, because what is, is. It really can be as simple as that.

As an alternative to resisting what is, think about Accepting What Is. The next time you're doing something that your mind tries to tell you is unacceptable just accept the inevitable. Standing in that long queue at the checkout is a great chance of practising Accepting What Is. Here's how . . .

1. **Notice your breathing.**

2. **Feel the air go in your nostrils, down into your lungs, and out again.**

3. **Notice the rhythm of your breathing.**

4. **Notice how your feet feel, as they make contact with the floor.**

5. **Notice the sounds around you. Try not to judge them. Rather, hear the loud, sharp noises, the soft sounds, the background hum, and the unexpected disruptions.**

6. **Notice the people around you without passing judgement on them. See what they look like. Notice what they do.**

7. **If thoughts start to enter your head about things you must do, notice how *interesting* they are, and let them drift by. Then return to the here and now.**

8. **Notice your breathing once more. Feel the air.**

9. **Notice any smells wafting by. Again, don't judge them as good or bad.**

10. **Don't suppress thoughts; just notice them, otherwise they may try to interfere with your attempts at experiencing and accepting what is.**

How many mundane chores and tasks do *you* resist? Doing the dishes (or emptying the dishwasher!), mowing the lawn, vacuuming, or doing the household shopping? Bet you've got a pretty impressive list of things you try to get out of doing.

The more you resist what is, the more you're going to build up negative feelings and tension.

Try approaching life's tasks mindfully. At first, dozens of thoughts concerning past regrets, present irritations, and future worries are going to interrupt and disrupt your attempts at connecting with what is. With practice, you're going to become aware of them, let them drift by, and recognise that they really are no more than just passing thoughts. After getting the hang of doing things mindfully you're going to find you're no longer as irritated by or keen to avoid so many everyday tasks. You can even apply this strategy to your home exercise programme for helping you ease depression. (Refer to Chapter 10).

Enhancing pleasure mindfully

When you're suffering from depression your mind can deny you small pleasures by focusing on the past or the future, and blocking out what is happening in the present. How many times have you eaten a meal and hardly tasted your food? That happens when negative thoughts are racing through your mind.

The next time you do something that should be pleasurable (almost any activity is going to do), try to approach it mindfully. For example, if you're sitting down to eat, try the Food for Thought strategy:

1. Notice the food on your plate; observe the shapes, colours, and smells.

2. Spear a bite-sized piece of food with your fork. Bring it near your nose.

3. Smell the food for a few moments.

4. Touch the food first with your lips, and then with your tongue.

5. Put the food in your mouth, but wait a moment before you chew.

6. Feel the texture of your food on your tongue.

7. Chew ever so slowly.

8. Notice how your food feels and tastes on different parts of your tongue.

9. Swallow your food. Focus on both the taste and texture as it slides down.

10. Continue eating, paying close attention to the whole experience of your meal.

Try getting into the habit of mindful eating. You're likely to get much more pleasure out of your meal if you do. If troubling thoughts start to interfere, deal with them using the strategies we suggest in this chapter – notice your thoughts, reminding yourself that these thoughts are just thoughts, and then simply carry on eating. You're likely to discover how relaxed you feel when eating. You may even lose a little weight! Eating slowly allows the brain to spot when you're feeling full – stopping you from over indulging.

Thoughts are just thoughts . . .

Chapter 19

Heading for Happiness through Positive Psychology

*I*n this chapter, we look at the key ideas from the field of positive psychology. Hopefully, you've reached the point where depression isn't dominating your life. But we want you to feel better than merely 'not being depressed'. And in discovering how to enhance your experience of authentic happiness, we hope and expect that your depression is going to be less likely to recur.

Donald took over his father's building firm when his dad retired after Donald's mother was recovering from cancer, and his parents deciding it was high time they retired and started enjoying some quality life together. His father, always a happy, contented man, found it really satisfying and gratifying to go that extra mile whatever the job, giving 'beyond the call of duty' service to friends and neighbours alike.

Donald always thought his father was out of touch with the times, and he was impatient to start expanding the business. In just ten years, Donald quadrupled the turnover by subcontracting much of the work. He became very wealthy.

However, Donald overextended, and when the property market slumped and the credit crunch bit in the late 2000s, he wasn't able to meet his outgoings. Donald was forced into bankruptcy. He then fell into a deep depression. Antidepressant medication (refer to Chapter 15 for more information) helped him through his depression, and a year later he set up a successful domestic cleaning business. Although he was no longer depressed, Donald's life felt empty and pointless. He began to feel that something was missing, but what could it be?

The answer to Donald's feelings of emptiness may well be found on a newly sprouting branch of the tree of psychology, which started growing in the late 20th century. Dr Martin Seligman and colleagues are central figures in shaping a new development called *positive psychology*. Dr Seligman's starting point is that for far too long psychology has been focusing on what's wrong in people's lives, and working out how to fix it, without taking into account the benefits of fostering and enhancing positive emotions and outcomes. In only a short time psychologists have discovered a lot about what you can do to achieve genuine, otherwise known as *authentic*, happiness.

You're going to get the greatest benefit from this chapter if you've already got over your depression. If you're still wrestling with a major depression many of the ideas in this chapter may not work for you just now. So, do consider reading other chapters (such as 5, 6, and 7) or seeking professional help to overcome your depression before moving onto the next stage of achieving authentic happiness.

Searching for Happiness

Everyone wants to be happy, right? Well, not exactly. Some people feel that they don't deserve happiness. Others see happiness as a frivolous pursuit and essentially a waste of time. And some people both desire and search for happiness, yet fail to find it. We now explain why, for many people, happiness is so difficult to find.

Making the case for being happy

Perhaps you feel that you don't deserve to be happy. If so, you're probably someone who often experiences guilt and self-blame. If that's you, read or reread Chapters 3, 5, 6, and 7 carefully. You may need to do further work on certain core change-blocking beliefs or habitual ways of thinking (go to Chapters 3 and 7) before starting down the path towards authentic happiness.

Perhaps you feel you deserve happiness as much as anyone else, but you think happiness is an overrated idea? This perspective can spring from the messages you got from your parents when you were a child. Some children are told that work is the one and only valuable activity in life, and that anything else is merely a diversion from what's really important.

A growing body of studies increasingly highlights and confirms the value of happiness. Today we now know that happy people:

- Live longer
- Are more creative

✔ Have lower blood pressure

✔ Have more active immune systems

✔ Have more empathy with others

✔ Are more successful financially

✔ Are more productive

So, if work is your main concern in life, it seems that happiness means you're going to work more efficiently and productively. Happiness is also good for your health and wellbeing, and it also means you're likely to live longer. Now those are pretty convincing arguments.

Chasing rainbows : Looking for happiness in all the wrong places

What do a lot of advertisers, booksellers, drug dealers, cult leaders, pornography peddlers, and lifestyle gurus have in common? One way and another, they promise short cuts and quick fixes to happiness and wellbeing. Many people are buying into the messages from these quick-fix happiness traffickers – just take a look at the sales of cars, clothing, lifestyle workshops, gizmos, and even drugs compared with 40 or 50 years ago.

We're certainly not saying that everything on offer is worthless, useless, a scam, and bad for you! But it's interesting to see that though many people are financially better off, with more possessions, surprisingly, the number who describe themselves as 'very happy' has *declined* over the last 40 years. (fAt the same time, the divorce rate has increased, both violent crime, and suicide among young people has also risen. Dr Martin Seligman estimates that among the affluent countries in the world, depression now occurs at levels that are ten times greater than they were in 1960. He also suggests that people in less developed countries aren't significantly unhappier than those in the developed world

Many studies show that for most people, once their basic needs are met (such as food, shelter, clothing, and having a safety net) improvements in their finances doesn't especially lead to feeling happier. You're as likely to be happy if you just have enough money to get by as you are if you have more money than you know what to do with.

So if no pot of gold lies at the end of the rainbow, what can you expect to find when you get there? Perhaps you see a link between the following and happiness:

✔ Education

✔ Good climate

✔ Good looks

✔ Health

✔ Power

✔ Youth

But guess what? Just like money, not one of above ideas has been found to be a particularly strong predictor of happiness and wellbeing. Yet strangely enough, many people devote much of their lives to the pursuit of these very things, convinced that, if successful, their quest is going to lead to happiness: not realising that they're simply chasing an illusion.

Studies also show that enjoying good health is no guarantee of happiness, and on the other side of the coin, poor health isn't necessarily a barrier to happiness either.

But if these things don't lead to happiness, what does? Though no one knows all the answers, the field of positive psychology is beginning to reveal some interesting possibilities. In the rest of this chapter we explore some things more likely to bring happiness, and invite you to look at each carefully.

Getting Started on the Road to Happiness

The long road to happiness has no short cuts. So you may well wonder why, in Chapter 11, we recommend indulging in short-lived pleasures like drinking tea or eating chocolates. The reasoning behind these suggestions is that people typically do very few enjoyable things when they become depressed. Fleeting sensory delights don't lead to genuine, long-lasting happiness; but they can kick-start your efforts to climb out of depression. In the following sections, we look beyond tea and chocolate to discover what leads to lasting well-being, and , authentic happiness – the real thing!

Appreciating the value of gratitude

Gratitude? Not perhaps what you'd put top of your list, if we asked you to suggest what constitutes the basis of happiness. By *gratitude* we mean appreciating or being thankful for the good things that have happened to you through circumstances, or through the actions of other people.

Most of the world's major religions, including Buddhism, Christianity, Judaism, and Islam, praise the values and virtues of gratitude. And within literature references abound pointing to gratitude increasing your sense of wellbeing, happiness, and contentment. Does consciously focusing on feeling grateful lead to happiness?

Understanding gratitude

Gratitude is a powerful, pleasant emotion that people feel frequently. In 2007 Alex Wood, Stephen Joseph and Alex Linley reviewed the research into this exciting, comparatively new field. Current research suggests gratitude acts as a 'moral barometer' It motivates many people, meaning they are then more likely to help one another and it makes the receiver more likely to provide help to others in the future. We don't yet fully understand how, when and why gratitude leads to helpful behaviour. Part of the confusion is because at times people feel under pressure, socially and psychologically, to express gratitude even if it is not really felt. While philosophers and theologians have written on the role of gratitude for centuries, more recent research is being undertaken across several fields: personality, cognition and emotion, clinical, health, coaching, and positive psychology.

Positive psychologists have been studying a range of people. The research shows that gratitude can be described as a 'personality trait' which some people feel much more strongly and often than others. People who feel more gratitude are much more likely to have higher levels of happiness, and lower levels of depression and stress. Many other personality traits besides gratitude also relate to levels of mental health.

Gratitude plays a key role in how we relate to one another. The example of Beth and Bill illustrates what's been found from research.

Research suggests that gratitude can help you deal with social problems, illness and health problems by improving your sense of quality of life and helping you to increase your level of happiness and well-being, and decrease depression. Increasing gratitude, by noticing and recording it, seems a uniquely beneficial approach. In a study by Martin Seligman, people recording gratitude found on average their happiness scores rose by 10 per cent, and their depression scores also fell significantly. The link between gratitude, social relationships, and success is probably an interactive upward spiral, where being grateful leads to greater success, which in turn leads to gratitude, perpetuating the cycle.

Studying the effects of gratitude, Dr Robert Emmons and Dr Michael McCullough carried out a series of studies suggesting that gratitude leads to an increased sense of wellbeing. In these studies, the groups taking part were asked to list items for which they feel grateful. These items, which could be large or small, included waking up this morning, performing an act of generosity, or even being able to listen to a favourite band or rock group. Other groups were asked to list negative happenings, ways in which they felt others were less fortunate than themselves, and the hassles they experienced during the day.

Overall, the results of the studies were striking and impressive. Dr Emmons and Dr McCullough found that asking participants to focus on events for which they felt grateful caused a number of interesting changes (when compared with the groups that were asked to track different types of happenings). The groups that focused on gratitude:

- Had more positive feelings
- Helped other people with their problems more frequently
- Had less negative feelings (in one study)
- Slept longer
- Had better quality sleep
- Felt more connected to people
- Were more optimistic
- Exercised more, even though no one had asked them to do so (in one study)
- Reported fewer health problems (in one study)

These results are particularly amazing because the groups focusing on gratitude weren't told to expect any particular benefits. Also, these groups 'counted their blessings' for a short period of time, ranging from a couple of weeks to a couple of months. As well, people who knew the participants in the gratitude groups reported that they were able to see that the participants felt better about their lives.

Putting gratitude to work for you

Think about tracking what makes you feel grateful, as a way of improving your sense of wellbeing. The Gratitude Tracking Inventory works like this: over the next month or two, try carrying out the following tasks daily:

1. **Write down five things that make you feel grateful. Look over your whole day, and think about small and large events.**

2. **Reflect a few moments on how appreciative you feel about each item on your list.**

And guess what? That's it! This exercise only needs about five minutes of your time each day, but really can rev up both your enjoyment and your quality of life. And after you've started down the track and you're counting your blessings as a regular part of your life, the benefits you discover may very well surprise you.

When you're feeling down, you may think there's nothing for you to feel grateful for. However, even during those negative times, just stop and think really hard. You probably can find just a few small things to feel grateful about. But if you're so depressed that you find this exercise impossible, please do more work on your depression, including considering getting professional help (refer to Chapter 4) before having another go at this exercise.

Having A Really Nice Day

When things feel all too much, common advice is to take one day at a time. The only problem with this is it's all too easy to overlook the good things. Here's a good way to learn from experience.

For the next fortnight, keep a daily record writing down the main things you did that day. Pay particular attention to times when you felt gratitude, or others were grateful to you. Each evening, rate give the day an overall rating of 'Niceness' from 1 to 10, where 10 represents a brilliant day, 5 is an average day, and 1 is one of the worst ever.

Do this for 2 weeks, then put some time aside to learn from your experience. From your record, looking at days when you scored 6 or higher, can you spot any particular activities that are related to the good days?

I get by with a little help from my friends . . .

Social relationships are an important factor in being well and happy. But did you know that one of the best ways to nurture such relationships is with gratitude?

Here's an example for you. Bob is a grateful bloke. He notices when someone helps him, and is happy to express his gratitude. Beth, on the other hand, doesn't get on with gratitude. She's pretty ungrateful, and she doesn't say a thing someone does her a favour. Who do you think is more likely to succumb to depression – Bob or Beth?

If you said Beth, you're spot on. Researchers have found that grateful people are more likely to reciprocate when someone helps them out. So when Bob's neighbour George lends him a lawnmower, Bob is grateful, and he goes on to give George's wife a hand fixing a puncture on her bike. Gratitude causes an upward spiral of helping and mutual support.

An ungrateful person is less likely to do the other person a good turn, putting their benefactor off helping them or anyone else. When Beth's brother Simon helps her move house, Beth orders him about all day and never bothers to thank him. Simon feels hurt and annoyed, and he stomps out saying, 'Why did I bother?' Simon feels less inclined to be a helpful chap, and Beth is left lonely and blue.

Thanks to his gratitude and helpful nature, Bob has better social relationships than Beth. So when he feels down, he has plenty of friends to turn to. Beth, however, is less successful at maintaining friendships, and when she feels depressed, she struggles to find support.

So working on your gratitude is just one positive way to keep yourself happy, well, and connected to people around you.

The secret of this exercise is that you then plan more of these into your next fortnight, and from the daily rating, see if they continue to correlate with good days.

Pleasure and enjoyment can be maximised in this way, and we hope you will agree with the old saying that '*Happiness* is not having what you want, but wanting what you have'.

You're likely to be very surprised at how good you're feeling after carrying out this exercise. Keep on bringing gratitude into your life. We think that feeling grateful just may help buffer you against future episodes of depression.

Helping others

We believe that a connection exists between *altruism* (unselfish concern for others) and the ability to feel gratitude. Support for this idea can be found in the study we discuss in the 'Studying the effects of gratitude' section, earlier in this chapter. An increase in gratitude led study participants to help others more often. We suspect that the opposite may hold as well – that an increase in altruism, or helping others, may lead to an increase in your own feelings of gratitude.

Look for ways of helping others. You may wonder where to start. Here are a few suggestions:

- Checking out your local Voluntary Service Bureau, or looking up available opportunities on the Internet. For example, searching for 'voluntary work London' on www.do-it.org came up with 2,039 opportunities, from a site that promises to search through over 1,000,000 choices! Another useful website is the National Council for Voluntary Organisations (NCVO) (www.ncvo-vol.org.uk). You're certainly going to be spoiled for choice!

- Offering to help an elderly neighbour with some chores, such as taking their rubbish out.

- Giving support to a friend or relative who's having a bit of a rough time – doing an activity with them, or just listening and talking.You're going to find that half the fun of performing this exercise is in coming up with your own ideas, so now it's over to you!

If you're a bit of a cynic, you may scoff and say, 'How can people really have unselfish concern for others because, ultimately, if they're acting altruistically, they expect to get benefits?' Well, where's the problem? We actually believe that benefits do indeed flow both ways. We're certainly not suggesting that you perform kind acts in anticipation of actual personal gain, because that's not in the spirit of this suggestion. But why not give altruism a go? We think that you're going to get more lasting pleasure from altruistic activities than from passing pleasures such as eating a nice meal or watching your favourite TV show.

Getting in the groove: Feeling the flow

Short-term pleasures aren't going to lead to long-term happiness. But somehow society more and more often suggests you try out any one of a squillion cheap, quick-fix approaches to finding happiness. Although such short-term lifts are unlikely to work out in the long run, we're not advising that you give up on all small pleasures.

Instead, search for absorbing challenges. Dr Mihaly Csikszentmihalyi (pronounced 'Chick sent me high') describes an absorbing challenge as something that gives you what he calls *flow*. When you're in a state of flow, you typically find yourself totally absorbed in the activity you're engaged in (so much so that you lose all sense of time). These activities are the ones you never want to stop doing. They engage you so powerfully that your involvement feels utterly effortless, even if the pursuit is physically strenuous.

You may well have to search to find activities that give you this sense of total engagement and flow, but you're likely to discover great value both in the search and most certainly in the discovery of such completely absorbing, captivating challenges. Look back on your life and try to think of a time you were in the flow. Remember when time just flew past and how amazed you were. If you can't recall any moments at all, think through possibilities of any hobbies you currently enjoy.

For some people, sports like running or tennis do the trick. For others, a particular hobby like painting, gourmet cooking, dancing, or reading a book presents new and stimulating ideas. Even work, including writing, can put you in a state of flow. If, like us, you're fortunate enough to work in an area that's totally fascinating then you really are on to a winner. (What? Going home time already? Can't be! Where's the day gone?)

Activities stimulating flow require a great deal of effort – much more than needed for idle pleasures such as watching TV, going to the cinema, or snacking on junk food. Unlike transient delights and amusements, activities that put you in a state of flow often mean you have to postpone gratification for a while, until you get the hang of the activity. But hang on in there and you're very likely to reap immeasurably rich rewards from making the effort.

Most fully engaging challenges can also result in experiencing failure, both before and after the challenge becomes deeply rewarding. In most cases, we believe you're going to take these passing failures in your stride. However, if you're experiencing a major depression, we don't recommend that you start trying to find flow experiences. Make sure you've overcome your depression, and then turn your attention to finding activities that get you into the groove, and producing flow.

Focusing on your strengths

We want you to feel better than 'just okay'. But to do that, you need to focus on your personal strengths, rather than beat yourself up over your weaker points. If you're feeling depressed, you're probably going to need to work through other parts of this book (especially Part II) to allow yourself to let go of your negative thoughts and outlook. But if you've come out of your depression, then here goes . . .

Knowing what strength is – and isn't

By strengths, we don't mean attributes that are largely inherited like appearance, athletic skill, physique, a beautiful singing voice – these are all features about yourself to appreciate and feel grateful for, but they're not what we want you to focus on.

Think about it. You may enjoy hearing a friend sing, but that lovely voice is probably not why you value that person as a friend. Similarly, you may enjoy watching your children develop as athletes, but we suspect that their athletic skill has little to do with why you love them. When you think about what you really value in another person, don't you think more about their fundamental human qualities?

Strengths are the virtues, attributes, and characteristics that you value in others. Strengths involve a person's core character. The following list gives examples of important strengths, some of which we're sure you already have.

Appreciation of beauty/aesthetics	Joy in learning
Compassion	Kindness
Curiosity	Loyalty
Dependability	Listening skills
Empathy	Loving nature
Generosity	Perseverance
Helpfulness	Sense of humour
Honesty	Trustworthiness

Exercising your strengths

Look through the list of 16 sample strengths and think about which of these strengths are yours. Realistically not all people are lucky enough to have all these positive attributes, but we do believe that practically no one has none at all.

By identifying, appreciating, and building on your strengths, you can find value in yourself and increase your sense of wellbeing. Start by observing your strengths. Identify three personal strengths that you value the most in the previous list. Perhaps you've thought of a few strengths we've missed out. Over the next few weeks, do the following Appreciating Your Strengths exercise. Get out a notebook and make notes on your strengths.

1. **Notice each time you use one of your personal strengths.**

2. **Notice the type of occasion that allows you to express your strength.**

3. **Become aware of how you feel when you employ that strength.**

4. **Appreciate how that strength enhances your life.**

5. **Mentally pat yourself on the back for having that strength.**

We hope that, as you try out Appreciating Your Strengths, you're going to start feeling a sense of gratitude for your strengths. Next, begin building on your strengths. Exercise them. Look for opportunities to use your strengths at work, home, and play.

Anna cleans houses for a living. She struggles to get through each day and views her work just as something she has do to survive, full stop. Though she's not depressed, her life feels dull and lacking in purpose.

By contrast, Carol also cleans houses, but she creates meaning from her work by focusing on ways to express her personal strengths of appreciating beauty, kindness, and helpfulness. Carol approaches her work from the standpoint of how she can 'beautify' the homes she works in, not just merely clean them. As well as dusting she carefully arranges items in aesthetically pleasing ways. She looks for any opportunity to make her clients' lives easier. Thus, she readily reorganises cupboards and occasionally runs errands without being asked. Her elderly clients view her as an absolute treasure – in fact, her visits are the highlight of the week for many of them. They even get dressed up, knowing she's going to notice what they're wearing, and how the colours are coordinated. They make sure there's always a special pastry in the house, and time to stop and have tea together as friends, something that's enjoyable for both Carol, and for them. Although cynics may think that Carol's taking her job too far, the truth is that she really does get pleasure from expressing her personal strengths through her work. At work, Carol frequently goes into a state of flow (see the section 'Focusing on your strengths'), and this experience, achieved through her work, enhances her sense of wellbeing.

Try choosing work that makes the most of your personal strengths. Remember the saying: 'Find a job you love, and you'll never have to work another day in your life!' However, no matter what type of work you do, you can find ways of expressing your strengths and build on them if you try hard enough. And remember that work is just one part of life. Take the opportunity to discover, apply, and build on your strengths in every aspect of your life.

Rejecting the quick fix

Self-restraint, self-discipline, moderation, self-denial, temperance, self-control – these terms don't exactly conjure up images of joy and happiness. In fact, they may even sound downright dreary. Yet the fact remains that self-control actually guides you towards happiness more reliably and faster than any of the quick-fix approaches.

We live in a world that is forever making easy promises for achieving instant happiness and personal fulfilment. Though there's clearly a role for medication when it comes to treating certain types of depression (refer to Chapter 15), some ads suggest that taking a certain tablet when you're feeling a bit down is going to cure all your ills. Other ads suggest that you're never going to be happy until you buy that dream car, or own the best sound system.

Also, there are a wealth of books, DVDs, and workshop gurus telling you that you must feel good about yourself, end of story. And if you don't, they suggest simplistic solutions – like repeating mindless self-affirmations over and over every day.

Guess what:

- Quick fixes don't work.
- No one is happy all the time.
- The more you expect instant gratification, the more disappointed and miserable you're likely to be.

Psychologists have found that the ability to exercise self-control and delay gratification is closely linked to your wellbeing and happiness from childhood right through to adulthood. Although it's much better for you to learn self-control very early on , the good news is that you can still learn self-control at any stage of your life.

Moderation and self-control are valuable because:

- Satisfying goals need a lot of patience and hard work in order to obtain them.

✔ Too much of a good thing ends up being less enjoyable When you indulge yourself, without working for the goal, the activity usually loses much of its appeal. Psychologists call this phenomena *satiation*.

✔ Allowing yourself to feel way superior and have an over-inflated view of yourself can bring problems, such as rejection. (We discuss this in Chapter 7.) Go for moderation as a realistic path toward sustainable happiness. Money, alcohol, drugs, and self-indulgence are actually seductive illusions. If you focus your efforts on quick fixes, you're going to find yourself disappointed time and time again.

Letting go and forgiving

Of all the paths towards happiness, figuring out how to forgive may be the most difficult. When someone wrongs you, it can be so tempting to hold a grudge and desperately desire revenge. And why not take revenge? After all, if you did nothing to deserve the injustice, don't you have every right to, at least have a *desire,* to give as good as you get? Absolutely. You're quite entitled to have those feelings, and in fact they're pretty normal!

But unfortunately, hanging onto those feelings is going to cost you. Quite a lot, actually. Nursing feelings of rage and revenge can make you feel like a victim. Chapter 3 discusses the harmful effects of taking on the role of the victim, and increasing anger and feelings of helplessness. We suggest that you read Chapter 3 to find ways of avoiding the role of the victim.

More importantly, working out a way to forgive is likely to enhance your sense of wellbeing. Several studies show that the more you cling to your resentments and grievances, the less happy and satisfied with life you're likely to be. But can you find forgiveness if you've been grievously wronged?

Horrible things can happen, such as sexual abuse or violence, that you may feel you just can't forgive. In such cases, it's probably more important to accept yourself and attempt to let go of any thoughts of revenge, rather than to actually attempt to find forgiveness, which you're possibly never going to manage to achieve.

Finding forgiveness is no easy task. Try this Revenge Reanalysis and Forgiveness Technique, and see how it works for you. The idea may seem pretty strange at first, but we believe that you're likely to discover surprising benefits after exploring the idea.

1. **Try remembering the wrong in calm, non-judgemental terms. Visualise the wrong happening in your mind, and see if there are any ways to minimise feelings of rage, revenge, or sorrow.**

   Play the tape of the event in your memory over and over until your powerful feelings begin to lessen, at least a bit.

2. **Try looking at the wrong from the wrongdoer's perspective.**

   This step may be particularly difficult. You may find it useful to realise that people typically hurt others when they feel threatened, frightened, or anxious. Sometimes they see a need to defend their honour or self-esteem, even though this perceptions may be misguided. Consider the possibility that many wrongdoers don't appreciate or understand the hurtfulness of their actions. Some may also feel the need to attack to enhance their self-image, which was destroyed by a traumatic childhood events.

3. **Form an image of yourself in your mind as someone who copes well, rather than as someone who's a victim. Think of yourself as someone with strength and fortitude who can rise above adversity and forgive.**

4. **If thoughts of revenge come into your mind, remind yourself that revenge is going to harm you at least as much as the wrongdoer, and probably even more so.**

   Thoughts and feelings of revenge can inflict damage on your emotional soul and hurt your body by releasing a load of stress hormones that raise blood pressure and may even, for some people, eventually damage the body.

5. **Dig down deep and forgive.**

   If you can tell the wrongdoer that you forgive them, then that's even better. Perhaps you may decide to write a letter of forgiveness. You certainly don't have to send it, but it can help to talk it through with others. Offer your forgiveness with as much altruism as you can.

The best things come to those who wait

Psychologist Walter Mischel and his colleagues carried out a fascinating study that was reported in the *Journal of Personality and Social Psychology*. They had a group of 4-year-olds come into a room one at a time. A single marshmallow was placed on one part of a table in the corner of the room, while two marshmallows were placed on another part of the table. The researchers told each child, 'If you wait until I come back, then you can have this one (pointing to two marshmallows). If you don't want to wait, ring this bell and bring me back. But if you ring the bell, you can only have one marshmallow.'

Some of the children couldn't wait, so they rang the bell. Others managed to delay their urges for instant gratification and hang in there for both marshmallows. The researchers followed the children for ten years. Interestingly, those who showed most self-control were better at getting along with other people, performed better academically, were better at coping with stress, and had fewer personal problems than those who showed less self-control, at the age of 4. They were also more self-reliant, skilful, trustworthy, and eager to discover new things.

Since this initial study, researchers have confirmed these findings with different types of self-control tasks and with many groups of children of varying ages and from various walks of life.

When memories of the wrongful act recur, go through the forgiveness process again. Don't expect saintly perfection from yourself. Every step you make in the direction of finding forgiveness really is going to end up helping you.

Finding meaning and purpose

There are many ways of finding meaning and purpose in your life. Generally this involves reaching out and relating to ideas that are bigger, long-lasting, and of greater significance than yourself. Of course, religion and spirituality are the most obvious ways of finding meaning, and are the routes chosen by the largest number of people.

If you're not very spiritually inclined, you can still find meaning in your life. Ask yourself what you want your life to be about. What do you want your legacy to be to the world? The following exercise, 'Singing your swansong', may just surprise you. Here's how it works:

1. **Sit back and relax for a few moments. Take a few slow, deep breaths.**

2. **Reflect on your life for a while, but don't dwell on past regrets.**

3. **Ask yourself what you want people to say and think about you at your funeral. How would you like to be remembered by friends, loved ones, and the world?**

4. **Think about what you can do with the rest of your life to fill it with meaning, and what you want to leave to the world.**

Very few people doing this exercise actually end up telling themselves how rich, handsome, powerful, and clever they are. Most people choose to emphasise their strengths of character (such as those listed earlier in this chapter, in the section 'Focusing on your strengths').

No matter what your age, you can devote at least a part of your life to the goal of enhancing its meaning – living each day as if it's going to be your last. Your purposes in life don't need to be over the top. Here are a few ideas:

- ✔ Being a kind person.
- ✔ Helping others.
- ✔ Advancing knowledge in some way.
- ✔ Doing something positive for the environment.
- ✔ Being kind to animals.
- ✔ Passing your skills and knowledge onto the younger generation.
- ✔ Forgiving yourself and others.
- ✔ Expressing gratitude.

You can fill your life with meaning in any number of ways. All you need to do is connect and give something (almost anything) that feels larger than your-self. Whether you have a day, a year, or decades left on this planet, you *can* make a difference.

Keep in mind the memorable words of the late comedian George Carlin, a counterculture hero famous for his routines about drugs, dirty words, and the demise of humanity: 'Life is not measured by the number of breaths we take, but by the moments that take our breath away.'

Part VII
The Part of Tens

'There, Mrs Nedthorpe, can't you just feel the yoga treatment easing away your depression?'

Part VI
The Part of Tens

In this part . . .

It wouldn't be a For Dummies book without the Part of Tens. Here's where you can find our depression-related top ten hits. We present ten quick ways of getting out of a low mood. And if you're reading this book because a child, friend, or significant other suffers from depression, we offer tips to help. Discover how to decrease the chance of depression in your children, as well as what to do if they should get depressed. Finally, you can see how to respond to a friend or loved one who is depressed.

Chapter 20

Ten Ways of Improving Your Mood

● ●

In This Chapter

▶ Chewing it over: Digesting your bad mood

▶ Using positive psychology

▶ Getting a breath of fresh air

● ●

Low mood or depression – what's the difference? Low moods are typically unpleasant but short-lived emotional states. Depression has a way of dragging on for weeks, or in some cases, far longer.

After overcoming your depression, you're still likely to come up against the occasional low mood. Nonetheless, recognising that your low moods are bearable and that you can do something to ease them is important. And to prevent your low mood from deepening and spiraling downwards into depression, this chapter gives you some tips on how to handle the blues.

Having a Little of What You Fancy

Various types of food reportedly affect mood. You're likely to turn to chocolate as often as to any other mood-altering food. Craving sugary food is thought by some experts to be a sign of stress and that the body needs calming down. Chocolate, contains sugar and caffeine, increasing levels of serotonin in the brain. As we explain in Chapter 15, serotonin is one of the powerful brain chemicals in antidepressants: making you feel happier for a short time. This may explain why almost everyone loves chocolate.

If you find that chocolate works for you, indulge in a little when you notice a low mood setting in. But remember: as with all things, moderation is the key.

WARNING!

If you feel that you're becoming addicted to chocolate, and you're extremely guilty when you indulge in it, then chocolate isn't the food for you when you're feeling low. Guilt just further depresses your low mood.

Being Nice to Others

Be inspired by the positive psychology we discuss in Chapter 19. Doing something nice for someone is one of the best ways of helping you lift your low mood. Doing a kind act helps you refocus your attention away from what put you into that low mood, and move it to other people, in a positive way. And your improved mood is likely to last a lot longer than it does when altered by other quick-fix pleasures like chocolate.

Getting Moving: Exercising to Raise Your Spirits

Exercise can lift the weight of your depression, raising you out of a low mood. Of course, when you're in a low mood, you probably don't *feel* like exercising. But just because you don't feel like it, doesn't mean you *can't*.

Knowing the difference between *can't* versus *won't/shan't/don't feel like it* makes a great start. Just start moving your limbs and you're away. Getting yourself moving is half the battle. When you get over that first hurdle, your momentum carries you forwards.

Go for a long walk, jog, lift weights, take up yoga using a video or DVD, or do any form of exercise that suits. Exercise releases endorphins, improves your health, and gives you a sense of wellbeing and achievement. For more information about the benefits of exercise, refer to Chapter 10.

Singing Your Own Special Song

If you enjoy singing, try it when you're feeling low. Belt out your favourite song at the top of your voice. Singing is uplifting – quite the opposite to feeling down. But do go for an upbeat tune, rather than the blues.

Putting your negative thoughts into a whimsical song is a clever way of raising your mood. (Refer to Chapters 5, 6, and 7 for more information about negative thinking). Use your negative thoughts as the lyrics to any popular song you know. Somehow your negative thinking loses its control over you when you sing out your thoughts in a silly song. Here's a fun example, jokingly described as the National Anthem of Siam: sing out loud 'Oh Wah Tah Nah, Siam!', three times through, to the tune of the first three lines of 'God Save The Queen'!

Reuniting: Calling to Reconnect

Try phoning a friend. If like a lot of people you've lost touch with old friends – just reconnect. Pick up your phone. Don't wait and talk yourself out of it. Just do it.

Research shows that social connections can help with all kinds of difficulties, including low moods. So, even if you can't trace any long-lost friends, phoning any friend at all helps. Remember it's good to talk – and reconnecting feels good.

Letting Music Move You

Do you like to dancing? If so, you just may be able to dance your way into a better mood. Dancing, like all forms of exercise, releases endorphins (refer to Chapter 10 for more info about endorphins). If you pick a melody with a strong, feelgood rhythm, the combination of music and movement can be a way of lifting your spirits and lightening your mood.

If you don't have a partner, you can just dance by yourself in the privacy of your home. There you can fling yourself around in wild abandon, getting the better of those pesky blues.

Washing Those Blues Away

Many people find that a long, hot bath helps soothe both mind and body. A hot shower can also do the trick. Often, when you're in a low mood, doing something soothing doesn't quite 'feel' right. Nonetheless, luxuriating in the feel of shower gel and steaming water cascading over your body is great for toning you up and giving you a lift. Trust us on this idea, and give it a try.

Getting a Pet

If you're in a low mood, try spending some time with your pet. Don't have one? Consider getting one. Seriously! Studies show that pets do help you feel better. A pet may even improve your health. Dogs love to jump and play. Just watching them is cheering: making you smile and even laugh.

Why does stroking a pet improve your health and mood? No one knows for sure. However, pets help stop you focusing on yourself and your problems – by demanding love and attention and giving you warmth and affection in return. Many studies show that being wrapped up in yourself deepens depression – shifting attention away from yourself is great for improving your state of mind.

Taking Time Out

Again, we can't exactly say why, but spending time outdoors seems to do a much better job of brightening moods than does staying in. In the winter, it may be the natural light that helps, because the sun gives out a far brighter light than you get inside a building. And bright light appears to ease seasonal affective disorder, or SAD (refer to Chapters 2 and 16 for more information).

However, being outdoors may lift your mood because it puts you in contact with nature. We don't know of specific studies suggesting that nature improves moods, but we do know that almost all our clients report feeling much better after spending time outdoors. When outside, try focusing on and absorbing what's going on around you.Rather than looking inwards – concentrate on looking outwards – leaving your worries and anxieties safely at home.

Mellowing Your Mood with Mindfulness

You may be able to get out of a low mood simply by accepting that it's an inevitable part of life. Sounds confusing? Actually, the idea isn't that complicated. Wringing your hands and wailing at your misfortune feeds and intensifies your low mood. But when you accept your low mood as unpleasant but unavoidable under the circumstances, it loses some of its power over you. If this idea still sounds confusing, read Chapter 18.

You may also want to think about living in the here and now. Try connecting with the present rather than dwelling on upsetting thoughts about the past or future. Ths exercise can help you refocus your thoughts, helping you to experience the here and now.

1. **Notice the rhythm of your breathing.**

2. **Feel the air as it passes through your nostrils and into your lungs.**

3. **Notice how good the air feels.**

4. **Notice how your body feels. Focus only on your bodily sensations.**

5. **Return to the rhythm of your breathing.**

6. **Feel where your body touches the surface on which you're sitting, standing, or lying.**

7. **Notice how nice the air feels as it flows through your body.**

8. **Imagine the oxygen being drawn into your lungs on the in-breath.**

9. **Now imagine as you breathe out that the oxygen is moving through your blood.**

10. **Feel the oxygen flowing down your arms and legs, and all the way to the tips of your fingers and toes.**

11. **Continue noticing these various sensations for five or ten minutes.**

When you connect with the present, you let go of negative thoughts about the future or past. The 'now' is usually far more tolerable, even pleasant, compared with your mind's worries about the future or its concerns about the past.

Chapter 21

Ten Ways of Helping a Child with Depression

In This Chapter

▶ Preventing depression in the first place
▶ Recognising depression in children
▶ Helping a depressed child

Depression in children is often called the 'tweenie blues', but children as young as 10 are being treated for depression. The Royal College of Psychiatrists says depression affects 1 in 200 children under the age of 12, and 2 to 3 per cent of teenagers. The increasing depression among children may relate to the pressure on them to grow up faster and to copy popular media idols. It may also link to more family breakdowns, and increased bullying in schools. (Refer to Chapter 1 for a more detailed discussion of the causes of depression.)

Stopping depression from occurring in the first place is of course the best solution. So, this chapter provides tips for reducing, minimising, and even preventing depression in children. We also discuss what to do if your child, or a child you care about, becomes depressed, because not all depression can be prevented, despite your best efforts.

Finding Fun

Children, like adults, thrive when they feel engaged, involved, and interested in what they're doing. Go looking for activities and hobbies that your child finds interesting and that he can enjoy. You may have to try many different activities, such as dance, drama, swimming, playing music, trampolining, tennis, computers, art, football, or cricket. Try to find a hobby that you know your child is likely to be reasonably good at and stands a chance of performing successfully.

Then make sure that your child has plenty of opportunities to take part in his chosen hobby or sport.

Helping your child to get involved in an absorbing activity can help in preventing depression. The hobby gives the child something to look forward to, and helps him develop social support networks and become more socially skilled. It can also be great fun, very satisfying, and strengthen the relationship between parent and child – what more can you ask?

Setting Boundaries

Many parents are reluctant to discipline their children. They're afraid that they're going to upset their children and make them feel bad, and that setting limits is going to drive their children away. They want to be 'best mates' with their children. But parenting isn't about being your child's best friend.

Care enough to discipline your child. Psychologists know that self-control and the ability to tolerate frustration are the two most important skills to pick up in childhood. Armed with these skills, children are more likely to be able to face whatever life throws at them. Children can't learn self-control unless their parents give them clear rules to follow and reasons for keeping them. following the rules provides an incentive for finding ways of coping.

Disciplining children can be hard work. Sometimes it may be *so* tempting to ignore unacceptable behaviour. But your children are counting on you. When your child misbehaves, use it as an opportunity to show your child an important lesson. Children who know how to control their feelings are far less likely to become depressed.

Giving Feedback

When your child behaves unacceptably, by all means point out the misdemeanor – criticise the *behaviour*, not the child. Calling a child 'stupid' or 'bad' paves the way for depression. You can label the behaviour 'bad' – for example, 'stealing is bad' or 'hitting your sister is wrong'. If you apply such labels to your child instead of the behaviour you risk laying the foundation of your child developing negative self-images and having fixed views (core beliefs and life-lenses) that are difficult to change. (Refer to Chapter 7 for more about core beliefs and life-lenses.)

Climbing Every Mountain

Try giving your child the opportunity to accomplish something difficult. Children learn self-confidence by mastering difficult, complex tasks. Help your child with creative play activities, or acquiring a skill such as riding a bike, playing a musical instrument (if you can!). During the learning process, your child is no doubt going to experience frustration and fatigue. Encourage perseverance.

Life isn't easy. Children who know about working hard carry that ability into adulthood. As a result, they're much more likely to be able to successfully and effectively tackle many of life's problems, including depression.

Reviewing Responsibilities

Many parents find it easier to do the household chores themselves rather than having to nag their children for help. That's a mistake. Children need to feel connected and useful. Participating in family responsibilities helps children develop into adults who share tasks and who have a sense of fairness and equality.

When you allow children to take without giving, they begin to feel special – perhaps too special. Laziness at home may be acceptable to some parents, but when children go out into the big wide world, others can regard that sense of being special and entitlement simply as proof that the child is spoiled rotten. The resulting rejection may be one of the triggers of depression. So don't be afraid to give responsibility, and help your children grow into happier adults.

Talking and Listening

No matter what, do make sure that your children are able to talk freely to you. What do we mean by 'talk freely'? First, listen without interrupting. Let your children tell their stories. Second, don't judge or criticise your children's feelings. The following example illustrates both the wrong way and the right way to listen:

Brenda sobs to her mother: 'No one likes me. Everyone thinks I'm stupid. I feel awful. I don't want to go to school any more.'

Her mother could respond with: 'Don't be ridiculous. There's no reason for you to feel awful. You've got loads of friends. And don't think for a second that you'll get away with not going to school!'

But a better response is: 'It sounds like you're feeling pretty miserable. What happened?'

The better response wasn't judgemental and encouraged more talking. Notice how the first response is likely to stop any conversation dead. Your child is only going to talk to you if she feels she is being listened to and understood. Even if you don't agree with what your child is saying, at least let your child come out with what's on her mind.

Recognising Depression

When children have depression, they experience similar symptoms to those that depressed eadults have. They feel sad, lose interest in things that they previously found interesting, have trouble concentrating, and have low self-esteem. (Refer to Chapter 2 for more on the signs and symptoms of depression.)

Children may differ from adults in that their moods can vary more over the course of a day. Depressed children are often irritable and moody. The early warning signs of depression in children include:

- ✔ Dropping out of school.
- ✔ Loss of interest in usual activities.
- ✔ Overreacting to criticism or rejection.
- ✔ Poorer marks at school.
- ✔ Risky behaviour, such as taking drugs or reckless driving.
- ✔ Vague physical complaints, such as headaches and tummy aches.
- ✔ Withdrawing from friends.

Don't ignore signs of depression in your children. Depression is a serious problem, and it isn't a normal part of childhood. Suicide rates have increased since the 1970s for males aged 15 to 19. Take changes in your child's mood seriously.

Looking Beneath the Surface

Depression stems from a variety of sources. If your child shows signs of depression, exploring all possible causes is very important. Although depression does have genetic and biological factors, outside stress often contributes to it.

Many parents blame themselves for their child's depression. But self-blame and guilt won't help your child. It's true that family life may play a role in depression. Do investigate the possibility, and get help if you find any indication that your family life is in some way affecting your child.

Children spend a lot of their lives outside the home. Possible causes of depression include:

- Bullying at school
- Emotional, physical, or sexual abuse (this may be unknown to the family)
- Social rejection
- Unidentified academic problems, such as learning disabilities
- Unidentified health problems

If your child is depressed, carefully explore all contributing factors. Trying to treat the depression without understanding the causes may sabotage the effectiveness of your child's treatment. For example, if your child is depressed because he's being bullied at school, although giving antidepressant medication may improve mood and concentration, it doesn't address the underlying problem.

Accessing Assistance

If you suspect that your child is depressed, do get help at once. Depression in children can be treated with many of the same tools that help adults, including psychological therapy and antidepressant medication. Be prepared to take an active part in your child's treatment.

Don't feel guilty or embarrassed about taking your child for help. If you get treatment early for your child's depression, you may prevent your child from experiencing repeated depressions later in life. Refer to Chapter 4 for advice on how to find the right help.

Loving Unconditionally

Part of growing up involves testing limits. Children play up, are disobedient, and wear weird clothes. But let's face it, what would adolescence be without a little rebellion? Some children do go to greater lengths, perhaps shocking their parents with body piercings or tattoos, or even shoplifting and using drugs.

Parents typically feel angry and outraged at such behaviour. However, you have to make an important distinction between reacting to unacceptable behaviour and bearing the consequences, versus the total rejection and rage. You need to let your children know that, no matter what, you love them. That doesn't mean that you can't express displeasure or disappointment. But do balance criticism with concern. Remember that care and love go hand in hand with discipline.

Chapter 22

Ten Ways of Helping a Friend or Partner with Depression

In This Chapter
▶ Being a friend – not a therapist
▶ Realising that your loved one's depression isn't personal
▶ Putting time on your side

*F*ew things are more distressing than seeing someone you love suffering from depression. You care, and you want to help. But most people don't know where to start. This chapter gives you ten ideas of how you can help someone you care about who's going through depression.

Recognising Depression

Recognising that your partner or friend is feeling depressed is the first and most important step in offering help. You can read the entire list of symptoms of depression in Chapter 2, but do remember that diagnosing depression is a job for the professionals.

However, perhaps you've noticed lately that your loved one is acting differently, showing such changes as:

✔ Losing her appetite or disturbed sleep pattern

✔ Belittling herself

✔ Losing interest in leisure activities

✔ Increasing irritability

✔ Feeling lethargic

✔ Lower mood than usual

✔ Problems concentrating or making decisions

If your partner has more than one or two of these symptoms, it is likely she is feeling depressed. It's unwise to make the diagnosis yourself, but what you can do is gently discuss the possibility of depression, and urge your partner to check this out with a psychological therapist or the family doctor (see the section 'Recommending Help').

Recommending Help

One of the most useful things you can do is to encourage your partner to get help. You can start by recommending *Overcoming Depression For Dummies* by Elaine Iljon-Foreman, Laura Smith, and Charles Elliott (Wiley) – just be sure you point out that you're not suggesting that your friend is thick! You can also suggest seeing the family doctor. If your partner agrees to see a therapist and doesn't get around to doing so, offer to help find one. Read Chapter 4 for ideas on how to go about finding a good therapist.

If seeing a professional feels too threatening for your partner, the Internet has lots of resources.

The Internet contains an incredible amount of useful information. However, this can't replace professional help. Be aware that although some Web sites are reliable, others are anything but! We give you the addresses of some helpful and trustworthy Web sites in the Appendix.

You can offer help to someone you know who's suffering from depression, but you really can't solve the problem for them. You can't be responsible for their depression, or even be responsible for making sure the person you care about gets help. Offering to help your partner to get the help they need is realistically as far as you can go.

Just Listening

More than anything else, be aware that it really isn't up to you to cure your loved one of depression. Even if you're a trained professional such as a counsellor, GP, or psychological therapist, it's almost impossible to treat someone you're emotionally involved with. Friends and relatives just can't stand back and don't have the necessary objectivity required for effective treatment. Your job is to be there to listen, not to treat, or solve, the problem.

Think of your role as that of a sounding board. Listen with empathy and concern. You may want to share similar feelings you've had in the past. As a listener you may find yourself being tempted to talk your loved one out of her depression. Don't give in to that temptation. You're most likely to come up against resistance, and even a possible worsening of the symptoms.

All your loved one needs from you is a sympathetic ear. Professionals are the only people who can actually intervene therapeutically.

Taking Care of Yourself

Helping someone you care about who's depressed can be draining. Listening to tales of woe and misery isn't always easy. We advise that you connect, listen, and empathise only as far as you can. While trying to help don't let yourself get dragged down into depression in the process.

Attending to your own needs is vital. Continue living your own life. Go out and enjoy yourself. Connect with friends and keep a balance in your life. If you put all that you have into helping your loved one, you can all too easily lose the capacity to help, even risk experiencing depression yourself.

Biting Back Criticism

If your loved one is depressed, the last thing he needs is you criticising him. Nonetheless, you may find yourself tempted to do so when you hear some of the things he's saying. For example, he may say something like, 'I'm no good to anyone any more.' Hearing something like that, you may find yourself sputtering 'That's ridiculous! How on earth can you say something so stupid?'

Try to use empathy instead. Perhaps say, 'I know you feel like that. I don't really agree with you, but it must feel pretty awful to think that.'

Also, your partner may make it seem as if he's goading you into criticising him. Given his increased irritability, he may then criticise you more than usual. You can then easily feel tempted to defend yourself. Try to resist biting back, recognising that his criticism probably springs from his depression, rather than anything else.

No Offence: Appreciating That It's Not Personal

When someone you love is depressed, it's pretty easy to think you've done something to cause it, so it's really all your fault. Do realise that depression has many causes, and can link to genetics, biological factors, disease, drugs, childhood events, cultural aspects, and many other reasons including no doubt some as yet unidentified. (Refer to Chapter 2 for more information.)

That's not to say that your relationship with your loved one has no bearing whatsoever on her depression. It may be very relevant, and even a strong factor. Be open to the idea of working on your relationship – perhaps through counselling, if that seems appropriate. And consider reading and putting the ideas we present in Chapter 14 into practice. But do remember that blaming yourself for your partner's depression won't help. And that anyway, in most cases, other things besides the relationship carry far greater weight.

Practising Patience

In the case of a major depression (refer to Chapter 2 for more information about the various types of depression), you need to understand that treatment takes time. Even antidepressant medication typically requires a few weeks to start working. Also, some depression takes considerable research to identify the right medication for the person, which can take several months.

Psychotherapy also takes time to work. On average, you can expect some improvement within two to three months, but many cases require a longer period of time. And as with medication, sometimes the first therapist doesn't work out, and your loved one may need to search for another mental health professional to receive the right type of help for her. (Refer to Chapter 4 for information about finding help for depression.)

Avoid falling into the trap of thinking that your loved one actually *wants* to feel depressed. We truly believe that no one wants to feel depressed. Sometimes a person with depression can act in ways that seem a bit irrational, or self-defeating, but that doesn't mean that the depression is actually desired.

Try to be patient. You may need to get the help of a therapist if the task of getting your loved one to see a therapist proves too difficult.

Showing That You Care

When people become depressed, they really do need the care and concern of loved ones more than ever. Unfortunately, people with depression sometimes push others away. Although it may seem as if your loved one actually prefers to be alone and isolated, don't you believe it.

Whether your efforts are appreciated or not, continue to do caring things for your partner. Send a card or flowers. In Chapter 14 we give you a whole host of nice things you can do for someone who's suffering from depression.

Providing Encouragement and Staying Hopeful

Feeling hopeless is one of the more common symptoms of depression. Yet, the vast majority of people with depression improve and eventually overcome depression.

If you listen too much to what someone with depression says, you may find yourself starting to buy into the hopelessness you're hearing. The fact is, many people with depression can present you with pretty convincing evidence about the awfulness and hopelessness of their lives. However, you need to understand that a depressed mind can generate thoughts that are nearly always greatly distorted. Thus, the 'evidence' your partner gives you probably isn't all that accurate. Refer to Chapters 5, 6, and 7 for more about how depression distorts thinking.

When you understand how a depressed mind can distort the hopelessness of a situation, it becomes easier to stay encouraging and supportive. Your loved one doesn't want you to give up, no matter what he says. So, do keep on staying hopeful. Your partner needs to hear your message saying 'I believe in you'.

Enabling Exercise

Earlier in this chapter, we stressed that if you're emotionally involved with the person suffering from depression it's impossible to be the therapist as well. That's not up for dispute. But there is one therapeutic activity you can encourage your partner to take up: try getting your loved one to do some form of regular exercise. Ideally, you can share the activity with your partner. Physical activity has a positive effect on depression. The more active you are, the better. Refer to Chapter 10 for more about the positive effects of exercise on depression.

Encouraging someone who's depressed to exercise is a good idea, but don't push too hard. Some people, especially those with severe depression, simply can't get themselves sufficiently energised to exercise. Pressurising someone into exercise isn't worth the possible damage it may cause to your relationship – especially if you find that you're hitting your head against a brick wall attempting to get your partner started. The saying 'You can lead a horse to water, but you can't make it drink' has some truth to it.

Appendix

Resources for You

· ·

*H*ere we provide some additional resources to help you find out more about depression and how to defeat it. In addition, we give you resources to help you deal with other emotional issues, such as anxiety and relationship problems, which sometimes contribute to depression. Many other excellent books and Web sites are available. In dealing with most emotional problems, reading more than one book is often a good idea.

Self-Help Books

A list of self-help books we recommend:

- ✔ *Authentic Happiness: Using the New Positive Psychology to Realize Your Potential for Lasting Fulfillment,* by Martin E. P. Seligman (Free Press)

- ✔ *Changing For Good: The Revolutionary Program that Explains the Six Stages of Change and Teaches You How to Free Yourself From Bad Habits,* by James O. Prochaska, John C. Norcross, and Carlo C. DiClemente (William Morrow & Co., Inc.)

- ✔ *Choosing to Live: How to Defeat Suicide Through Cognitive Therapy,* by Thomas E. Ellis and Cory F. Newman (New Harbinger Publications)

- ✔ *Cognitive Therapy of Depression,* by Aaron T. Beck, A. John Rush, Brian F. Shaw, and Gary Emery (Guilford Press)

- ✔ *Feeling Better, Getting Better, Staying Better: Profound Self-Help Therapy for Your Emotions,* by Albert Ellis (Impact Publishers, Inc.)

- ✔ *Full Catastrophe Living: Using the Wisdom of Your Body and Mind to Face Stress, Pain, and Illness,* by Jon Kabat-Zinn (Delta)

- ✔ *Interpersonal Psychotherapy of Depression,* by Gerald L. Klerman, Myrna M. Weissman, Bruce J. Rounsaville, and Eve S. Chevron (Basic Books)

- ✔ *Love is Never Enough: How Couples Can Overcome Misunderstandings, Resolve Conflicts, and Solve Relationship Problems Through Cognitive Therapy,* by Aaron T. Beck (HarperCollins)

- ✔ *Love, Medicine and Miracles* (Cancer self-help) by Bernie Siegel (Rider)

- ✔ *Mind Over Mood: Change How You Feel by Changing The Way You Think,* by Dennis Greenberger and Christine A. Padesky (Guildford Press)

- ✔ *Mindful Recovery: A Spiritual Path to Healing from Addiction,* by Thomas Bien and Beverly Bien (Wiley Publishing, Inc.)

- ✔ *Overcoming Anxiety for Dummies, by Elaine Iljon Foreman, Charles H. Elliott and Laura L. Smith (Wiley Publishing, Inc.)*

- ✔ *Overcoming Depression. Paul Gilbert* Constable And Robinson (United Kingdom), 2000 Paperback, 352 pages Size: 196x130 mm ISBN: 9781841191256 ISBN-10: 1841191256

- ✔ *Self-Coaching: How to Heal Anxiety and Depression,* by Joseph J. Luciani (Wiley Publishing, Inc.)

- ✔ *The Artists Way, Julia Cameron, 1994,* Pan Macmullan Ltd. - a 12 week course that helps you get beyone the critic in the mind & start being creative & self-directed

- ✔ *The Mindful Way Through – Depression: Freeing Yourself From Chronic Unhappiness* by Mark Williams, John Teasdale, Zindel Segal and Jon Kabat-Zinn. (Guilford Press)

- ✔ *The Feeling Good Handbook,* by David D. Burns (Plume)

- ✔ *The Four Agreements* by Don Miguel Ruiz (Amber-Allen Publishing)

- ✔ *The Guided Meditations for Busy People* by Bodhipaksa (available for Friends of the Western Buddhist Order stores) or from their Web site, www.wildmind.org)

- ✔ *The Noonday Demon: An Atlas of Depression,* by Andrew Solomon (Touchstone Books)

- ✔ *The Power of Now: A Guide to Spiritual Enlightenment,* by Eckhart Tolle (New World Library)

- ✔ *The Seven Principles for Making Marriage Work,* by John M. Gottman and Nan Silverman (Three Rivers Press)

- ✔ *Why Can't I Get What I Want? How to Stop Making the Same Old Mistakes and Start Living a Life You Can Love,* by Charles H. Elliott and Maureen Kirby Lassen (Davies-Black Publishing)

- ✔ *Your Perfect Right,* by Robert Alberti and Michael Emmons (Impact Publishers, Inc.)

Resources to Help Children

We recommend the following books for helping your child overcome depression:

- *Hollow Kids: Recapturing the Soul of a Generation Lost to the Self-Esteem Myth,* by Laura L. Smith and Charles H. Elliott (Prima Publishing)

- *Keys to Parenting Your Anxious Child,* by Katharina Manassis (Barrons Educational Series)

- *SOS Help for Parents,* by Lynn Clark (Parents Press)

- *The Optimistic Child: Proven Program to Safeguard Children from Depression and Build Lifelong Resistance,* by Martin E. P. Seligman (Perennial)

- *Why Can't I Be the Parent I Want to Be? End Old Patterns and Enjoy Your Children,* by Charles H. Elliott and Laura L. Smith (New Harbinger Publications, Inc.)

Helpful Web Sites and Electronic Resources

If you type the word *depression* into a search engine, you get access to an endless stream of possible resources. You need to beware, though, because the Internet is filled with clever advertisements and gimmicks. Be especially cautious about official sounding organizations that heavily promote expensive materials. And don't believe absurd promises of quick, instant cures for depression.

Many Web forums host chat rooms for people who have depression and other related emotional problems. Feel free to access them for support. At the same time, realize that you have no idea who you're talking to when you join a Web forum. The other people in the forum may be uneducated about depression or, even worse, trying to take advantage of a person in distress.

Here's a list of some legitimate Web sites that don't sell snake oil but do provide excellent information about depression and related emotional issues.

Good quality information is more likely to be found on websites provided by governmental, professional and charitable organisations.

A 2008 article looked at the variation in quality of information across a variety of websites. The conclusion reached is that good quality information is most likely to be found on websites provided by governmental, professional and charitable organisations. This is worth keeping in mind when surfing the Internet,

- ✔ **Electronic Quality Information for Patients** (`www.equip.nhs.uk`). An NHS Website with very helpful; information relating to quality health and social care information for UK patients, their families and carers. Also includes useful links to other websites

- ✔ **The British Psychological Society** (`www.bps.org.uk`). Provides information about the treatment of, as well as interesting facts about, depression and other emotional disorders.

- ✔ **Mindfulness Based Cognitive Therapy** (`www.mbct.co.uk`). This Web site provides additional information about Mindfulness-Based Cognitive Therapy.

- ✔ **National Institute of Clinical Excellence** (`www.nimh.nih.gov`). Reports on research about a wide variety of mental health issues. They also have an array of educational materials on depression. They provide resources for researchers and practitioners in the field.

- ✔ **BBC Health Conditions: Depression** (`www.bbc.co.uk/health/conditions/depression1`) Useful website with information and self-help tips.

- ✔ **The Centre for Mindfullness Research and Practice** (`www.bangor.ac.uk/mindfulness`) Offering an information resource on mindfulness-based approaches and a networking facility for professionals in the field in the UK and in Europe.

- ✔ **British Holistic Medical Association Self help tapes:** Each comes with an explanatory booklet and list of recommended reading, providing a programme especially designed to teach new self-help skills.

  - *Introducing Meditation*, by Dr Sarah Eagger

  - *Imagery for Relaxation*, by Dr Duncan Johnson

  - *Getting to Sleep*, by Dr Ashley Conway

  - *Coping with Persistent Pain*, by Dr James Hawkins

  - *Coping with Stress*, by Dr David Peters

  - *The Breath of Life*, by Dr Patrick Pietroni

Advice and Support

- **Depression Alliance:** Tel: 0845 123 2320; Web site: `www.depression alliance.org`. Depression Alliance is a UK charity for people with depression. Information and support services are provided to those who are affected by it via publications, supporter services and network of self-help groups for people affected by depression. A user-focused organisation, with offices in England and a sister charity in Scotland.

- **Fellowship of Depressives Anonymous:** Tel: 0870 774 4320; Web site: `www.depressionanon.co.uk`

- **Mind (National Association for Mental Health):** Web site: `Mind.org. uk` The National Association for Mental Health in the United Kingdom campaigns on behalf of those with mental illness. Very helpful factsheets and information.

- **SANE:** Web site: `sane.org.uk`. Mental Health Charity meeting the challenge of mental illness. Information on all aspects of mental illness including depression and manic depression.

Index

• *G* •

• *H* •

• *T* •

Notes

Notes

Notes

FOR DUMMIES®

Do Anything. Just Add Dummies

UK editions

BUSINESS

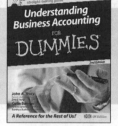

978-0-470-51806-9

978-0-470-99245-6

978-0-7645-7026-1

FINANCE

978-0-470-99280-7

978-0-470-99811-3

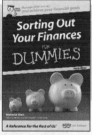

978-0-470-69515-9

PROPERTY

978-0-470-99448-1

978-0-470-51502-0

978-0-7645-7054-4

Body Language For Dummies
978-0-470-51291-3

Building Self-Confidence for
Dummies
978-0-470-01669-5

Children's Health For Dummies
978-0-470-02735-6

Cognitive Behavioural Coaching
For Dummies
978-0-470-71379-2

Counselling Skills For Dummies
978-0-470-51190-9

Digital Marketing For Dummies
978-0-470-05793-3

Divorce for Dummies
978-0-7645-7030-8

eBay.co.uk For Dummies, 2nd
Edition
978-0-470-51807-6

English Grammar For Dummies
978-0-470-05752-0

Fertility & Infertility For Dummies
978-0-470-05750-6

Genealogy Online For Dummies
978-0-7645-7061-2

Golf For Dummies
978-0-470-01811-8

Green Living For Dummies
978-0-470-06038-4

Hypnotherapy For Dummies
978-0-470-01930-6

12816

FOR DUMMIES

A world of resources to help you grow

UK editions

SELF-HELP

978-0-470-01838-5

978-0-7645-7028-5

978-0-470-75876-2

Cognitive Behavioural Therapy, Neuro-linguistic Programming, Emotional Freedom Technique For Dummies

HEALTH

Stop Smoking — 978-0-470-99456-6

IBS — 978-0-470-51737-6

Low-Cholesterol Cookbook — 978-0-470-71401-0

HISTORY

British History — 978-0-470-03536-8

Twentieth Century History — 978-0-470-51015-5

The Ancient Greeks — 978-0-470-98787-2

Inventing For Dummies
978-0-470-51996-7

Job Hunting and Career Change All-In-One For Dummies
978-0-470-51611-9

Motivation For Dummies
978-0-470-76035-2

Origami Kit For Dummies
978-0-470-75857-1

Patents, Registered Designs, Trade Marks and Copyright For Dummies
978-0-470-51997-4

Personal Development All-In-One For Dummies
978-0-470-51501-3

Psychometric Tests For Dummies
978-0-470-75366-8

Raising Happy Children For Dummies
978-0-470-05978-4

Starting and Running a Business All-in-One For Dummies
978-0-470-51648-5

Sudoku for Dummies
978-0-470-01892-7

The British Citizenship Test For Dummies, 2nd Edition
978-0-470-72339-5

Time Management For Dummies
978-0-470-77765-7

Wills, Probate, & Inheritance Tax For Dummies, 2nd Edition
978-0-470-75629-4

Winning on Betfair For Dummies, 2nd Edition
978-0-470-72336-4

FOR DUMMIES®

The easy way to get more done and have more fun

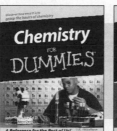

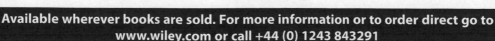

FOR DUMMIES®

Helping you expand your horizons and achieve your potential

COMPUTER BASICS

978-0-470-24055-7   978-0-470-13728-4   978-0-471-75421-3

DIGITAL LIFESTYLE

978-0-7645-9802-9   978-0-470-17474-6   978-0-470-17469-2

WEB & DESIGN

978-0-470-08030-6   978-0-470-11193-2   978-0-470-11490-2

12816_p4